The Passion of Teaching

Dispositions in the Schools

Edited by
Robert Lee Smith
Denise Skarbek
James Hurst

SCARECROWEDUCATION
Lanham, Maryland • Toronto • Oxford
2005

Published in the United States of America
by ScarecrowEducation
An imprint of The Rowman & Littlefield Publishing Group, Inc.
4501 Forbes Boulevard, Suite 200, Lanham, Maryland 20706
www.scarecroweducation.com

PO Box 317
Oxford
OX2 9RU, UK

British Library Cataloguing in Publication Information Available

Library of Congress Cataloging-in-Publication Data

The passion of teaching : dispositions in the schools / edited by Robert Lee Smith,
    Denise Skarbek, James Hurst.
      p. cm.
    Includes bibliographical references and index.
    ISBN 1-57886-203-5 (pbk. : alk. paper)
    1. Effective teaching. 2. Teachers—Training of. 3. Teacher effectiveness.
  I. Smith, Robert Lee, 1954– II. Skarbek, Denise, 1965– III. Hurst, James, 1960–
  LB1025.3.P27 2005
  371.1—dc22

SBENa6136225 10-28-2015   2004021533

∞™ The paper used in this publication meets the minimum requirements of
American National Standard for Information Sciences—Permanence of Paper
for Printed Library Materials, ANSI/NISO Z39.48-1992.

Contents

List of Tables and Figures

TABLES

FIGURES

1

A Brief Historical Context for Dispositions in Teacher Education

Tanice Y. Knopp and R. Lee Smith

The quest to identify effective teachers occurs in many arenas and across many mechanisms, for example, when a principal interviews a prospective faculty member and conducts faculty evaluations, when a parent chooses a teacher for his or her child, when a university student chooses a schedule. Parents, children, and students interested in effective learning seek the most effective teachers with the traits that each considers valuable. In education systems locally and nationally, there is an increased emphasis on accountability and the quest to identify teacher effectiveness, as the primary influence on student outcomes has intensified greatly. Today, despite years of extensive research into educational endeavors that utilize a variety of inquiry traditions, educators, researchers, policymakers, and politicians, indeed society as a whole, continue to struggle to answer the question: What makes a teacher *effective*?

Toward that end, researchers and policymakers in teaching and teacher education have recently appeared to agree upon a common set of concepts—*knowledge, skills,* and *dispositions*—to identify the primary constructs in effective teaching. Given that agreement, the questions may now be better framed: (1) What does an effective teacher need to know? (2) What teaching skills and performance abilities do they possess? and (3) Why do teachers who have been identified as effective choose to apply that knowledge and those skills while others with the same knowledge and skills do not? Perhaps, then, the key question is: Given the necessary knowledge and skills, what *disposes* a person to be an effective teacher?

The profession of teaching is one of the few that exist for which so many claim to have expertise. Most people have an opinion, usually based on their own lived schooling experiences, that they eagerly share about what makes a *good* (i.e., *effective*) teacher and what makes a *bad* teacher (i.e., *ineffec-tive*). One need only review the work of James Paul and Terry Smith (2000) to understand the profound effect of education on adult memories, some-times even a number of years after their experiences. In their research, Paul and Smith ask adults to recall the teacher they believed to be their *best* or *fa-vorite* teacher and to write a letter conveying their feelings about their learn-ing experiences with that teacher; then to do the same recalling their least fa-vorite teacher. Consistently, this exercise produces great emotion in the participants; many times eliciting tears of appreciation when describing ef-fective teachers and bitter tears when describing ineffective teachers.

The answer to the question, "Given the necessary knowledge and skills, what *disposes* a person to be an effective teacher?" lies in that singular con-cept adopted by professionals in teacher education—*dispositions*. The at-tention to dispositions is particularly evident in accreditation standards for the National Council for the Accreditation of Teacher Education, commonly called NCATE (2001) and the Interstate New Teacher Assessment and Sup-port Consortium (INTASC, 2001). The definitions of these professional and policy groups are located in Appendix A and Appendix B of this book.

For the past several decades, dispositions have been studied in many forms and across many constructs. In this chapter, a brief historical interpretation is presented in order to give a framework for the construct of dispositions.

OVERVIEW OF PAST RESEARCH

The sheer volume of research efforts toward identifying what causes or lies behind teachers' actions speaks to the importance placed on this quest by the field. For decades, researchers in teacher education and related fields have conducted numerous studies designed to answer the question posed above. In doing so, researchers have employed various terms. Sometimes the same or similar terminology was used differently from one study to an-other, sometimes interchangeably. This lack of cohesive and consist defini-tion has muddied the discourse and complicated the application of research findings. In Table 1.1, a few examples of the varying terms used in research conducted from the mid-1960s through the early 1990s are presented. Sev-eral researchers have comprehensively reviewed the research literature to elucidate the discourse. The works that have been selected in developing this chapter include Eisenhart, Shrum, Harding, and Cuthbert (1988); Fang (1996); Kagan (1992); Nespor (1985); Pajares (1992); Richardson (1996); and Tschannen-Moran and Hoy (2001). This research is representational of work in the field but is not intended to be a comprehensive review.

Teacher beliefs have been studied extensively and may add significantly to a professional understanding of the construct of dispositions. In their

Table 1.1.   A Few Examples of Various Research Terminologies Associated with Dispositions

Year	Researchers	Terminology
1963	Corrigan & Griswold	attitudes
1963	Getzels & Jackson	personality and characteristics
1963	*Stern	attitudes and values
1968	Harvey, Prather, White, & Hoffmeister	beliefs
1973	Peck & Tucker	personality factors and attitudes
1974	Brophy & Good	attitudes
1980	Copeland	affective dispositions
1981	Rose & Medway	beliefs
1981	Zeichner & Tabachnick	beliefs
1982	Guskey	expectations
1982	Munby	beliefs
1984	Gibson & Dembo	sense of efficacy
1984	Guskey	affective characteristics
1985	Katz & Raths	dispositions
1985	Nespor	beliefs
1986	Ashton & Webb	sense of efficacy
1986	Book & Freeman	characteristics
1986	Clark & Peterson	thought processes and beliefs
1988	Anning	theories
1988	Bousseau, Book, & Byers	beliefs
1988	*Eisenhart, Shrum, Harding, & Cuthbert	teacher beliefs
1988	Sparks	attitudes
1989	Feiman-Nemser, McDiarmid, Melnick, & Parker	conceptions
1989	Guskey	attitudes and perceptions
1989	Hollingsworth	beliefs
1989	Rogard & Pigge	attitudes
1990	Woolfolk & Hoy	efficacy and beliefs
1991	Calderhead & Robson	conceptions
1991	Richardson, Anders, Tidewell, & Lloyd	beliefs
1992	*Kagan	beliefs
1992	*Pajares	beliefs
1993	Avery & Walker	perceptions
1994	Tillema	beliefs
1995	Janney, Snell, Beers, & Raynes	beliefs and attitudes
1995	Mahlios & Maxson	beliefs

Sources: Knopp (2000); Pajares (1992); Renzaglia, Hutchins, & Lee (1997); Richardson (1996); Tschannen-Moran & Hoy (2001).
Note: *research summaries.

search for a working definition of teacher beliefs, Eisenhart et al. (1988) found *axioms, perspectives, rules of practice, practical principles,* and *constructs* offered among the varying definitions that abound in the educational research literature. Others summarizing and analyzing the literature have encountered the lack of definition to be a complicating factor. In his review and analysis of education research on teacher beliefs, Pajares (1992) encountered terms including *attitudes, values,* and *preconceptions,* thus calling for "cleaning up a messy construct" (p. 307). Through their examination of the literature on teacher efficacy measurement, Tschannan-Moran & Hoy (2001) sought to "capture an elusive construct" (p. 783). Virginia Richardson (1996) further elucidates concerns about the terminology and the associated confusion. In her extensive study of the research on teacher attitudes and beliefs, Richardson found that the terms attitudes, beliefs, knowledge, actions, conceptions, theories, understandings, practiced knowledge, and values were often used interchangeably.

Fang (1996) reviewed teacher beliefs and practices and determined that the growth of research into the causes of teachers' behaviors has been influenced by increased interest in the relationship of teacher cognition and pedagogical classroom practices. Fang maintains that this growth of interest "signals that research on teaching and learning has shifted from unidirectional emphasis on the correlates of observable teacher behavior with student achievement to the focus of teachers' thinking, beliefs, planning, and decision-making processes" (p. 47). This shift in focus to include teacher cognition is also evident in the work of Clark and Peterson (1986), who identified two major domains of the teaching process: (a) teacher cognition, which includes planning, thoughts and decisions, and beliefs and theories; and (b) teacher actions, which include student behavior and achievement as well as teacher behaviors. Furthermore, Shulman (1986) posits the "missing paradigm" in teaching research as the area of *how* teachers decide what to teach. Shulman elucidates his belief that the *how* question was largely ignored until the mid-1970s, with the prior focus on *what* teachers do (Fang, 1996). In the 1990s, although once again using different terminology to do so, Fang (1996), Pajares (1992), and Richardson (1996) all called for a clarification of terms. Perhaps the recent attention brought to the term *disposition* can lead to some clarity of concept, which is necessary to understand "teachers' thought processes, classroom practices, change, and learning to teach" (Richardson, 1996, p. 102).

With the construct of dispositions formally identified as a necessary and desirable component of teacher education programs used to measure teacher effectiveness and the effectiveness of teacher training programs, along with knowledge and skills, definitions of dispositions abound in teacher education research and teacher efficacy literature. Unfortunately, many of the attempts to clarify this construct propose definitions that employ the very terminology that has complicated the discourse up to now. Thus, these proposed definitions do little to clarify the muddied discourse.

DISPOSITIONS AND BELIEFS IN
TEACHING AND TEACHER EDUCATION

The proposal for attending to the construct of dispositions in teaching and teacher education is not new. In 1985 Katz and Raths put forth the argument that "the goals of teacher education programs should include a class of out comes [called] professional *dispositions*" (p. 301). They defined dispositions as "trends or summaries of frequencies of given categories of actions" (p. 307) and proposed that "because it is reasonable to assume that human behavior is stable, the summary of trends of a teacher's behavior, fundamentally descriptive, can also serve as a basis for predicting future trends in behavior (p. 302). Katz subsequently offered a more complete definition as follows: "a pattern of behavior exhibited frequently and in the absence of coercion, constituting a habit of mind under some conscious and voluntary control, intentional and oriented to broad goals" (see Katz, 1993, p. 16).

Katz and Raths use the term dispositions to indicate a descriptive construct rather than an explanatory construct. The working definition of dispositions proposed by Katz and Raths may be most effective in clarifying the dispositions discourse. However, given the focus on disposition related to teacher preparation programs, the discourse also must include attention to learning and changing of dispositions. That is, if those involved in the preparation, identification, and evaluation of effective teachers believe that dispositional behavior can be *learned* and *changed*, those involved in these efforts must look beyond the *what* and look at the *why* of effective teaching. Therefore, the study of teacher dispositions relative to identifying effective teaching cannot be conducted productively without also addressing teacher beliefs.

Katz and Raths again provide clarity to this discourse. Katz identifies beliefs as "pre-dispositions" (Katz & Raths, 1985; Raths, 2001)—the *why* or the explanatory construct of dispositions. The complexity of beliefs and beliefs change as related to teacher behaviors has been studied extensively.

But, once again, there are varied and conflicting definitions of beliefs that exist in the research literature (see Knopp, 2000). Dewey (1933) proposed *belief* as his third meaning of thought, to refer to "something beyond itself by which its value is tested; it makes an assertion about some matter of fact or some principle or law" (p. 6). Dewey emphasized:

> It is hardly necessary to lay stress upon the importance of belief. . . . It covers all matters of which we have no sure knowledge and yet which we are sufficiently confident of to act upon and also the matters that we now accept as

certainly true, as knowledge, but which nevertheless may be questioned in the future. (p. 6)

The extent to which the concepts of *attitudes*, *values*, and *knowledge* are considered interchangeable with or distinctly different from the concept of beliefs confounds much of the debate surrounding definition of beliefs and, thus, dispositions. However, despite the challenge of defining belief, some researchers concur as to the development and power of teacher beliefs. Pajares (1992) explains that development and establishment of beliefs is complex and circuitous. Once beliefs are formed, individuals have a tendency to build causal explanations surrounding the aspects of those beliefs, whether these explanations are accurate or mere invention. Finally, there is a self-fulfilling prophecy—beliefs influence perceptions that influence behaviors that are consistent with, and reinforce, the original beliefs (p. 317).

Beliefs drive action or behavior (Mahlios & Maxson, 1995; Pajares, 1992; Rokeach, 1972; Scheibe, 1970). The interpretation and structuring of experiences, which become one's beliefs, determine how people behave (Beck, 1985; Schutz & Luckmann, 1973). Therefore, it is reasonable to surmise that teachers' beliefs strongly influence the act of teaching.

No matter the extent of our education and training in our chosen vocation, not one of us has studied any area as thoroughly as we have studied the work of teaching. Almost every member of our society has spent time as a student and, during that time, made a careful study of the practice of teaching (Ashton, 1991; Lortie, 1975; Zeichner & Tabachnick, 1981). Our beliefs about teaching are embedded deeply from these years of study (Pajares, 1992). Teachers become, in essence, the creators and the products of their educational experiences (Bolster, 1983).

Studies reveal that teachers' beliefs are often the driving force behind strategy implementation (Ashton & Webb, 1986; Kagan, 1992; Munby, 1982, 1984; Nespor, 1985, 1987; Wilson & Silverman, 1991; Woolfolk, Rosoff, & Hoy, 1990). Even when considered by teachers, information from outside sources is filtered through and assimilated into their unique pedagogies (Kagan, 1992). Munby (1982) warned that the power of teachers' beliefs is such that the significance of beliefs to a teacher's decision-making process cannot be overemphasized. Although educational researchers fail to agree on a precise definition, most agree that beliefs have a powerful influence on teachers' behaviors and that beliefs are highly resistant to change.

The research literature extensively reports that professional development does not always change teacher practice (Guskey & Huberman, 1995). Some researchers assert that those who deliver professional development must pay close attention to teachers' knowledge and beliefs (see Borko & Putnam, 1995; Eraut, 1995; Fullan, 1995; Mevarech, 1995; Smylie, 1995) because "teacher's knowledge and beliefs are important resources and constraints on change; they serve as powerful filters through which learning takes place" (Borko & Putnam, 1995, p. 59). Mevarech (1995) further asserts that "professional growth in education is . . . a process of change in teacher's mental models, beliefs, and perceptions regarding children's needs and learning" (p. 52).

The complexity of beliefs, the role of beliefs, and beliefs development are perhaps surpassed only by the complexity of the role of belief in the behavior change process. In the early 1990s, several researchers substantiated significant implications of the role, function, and power of teacher beliefs for teacher education. Based on an exhaustive investigation as to the meaning and nature of beliefs structures to clarify a complex construct, Pajares (1992) maintained that teachers' beliefs influence their judgments and ultimately affect their classroom practices so much so that understanding those belief structures is essential to improving classroom practice. Given the effect of teacher beliefs on their classroom practice, Pajares (1992) verified a number of assumptions that can, and should, be made when studying teacher beliefs: (a) new phenomena are filtered through existing beliefs, which screen, redefine, or distort information processing; (b) the longer beliefs are held, the more resistant they become to change; and (c) rarely are beliefs changed in adults, so much so that some tend to hold beliefs based on incorrect information regardless of correct information. Smylie (1995) summarized:

> If schools are to improve, if instructional opportunities for students are to be markedly better, teachers must teach differently. In order to change practice in significant and worthwhile ways, teachers must not only learn new subject matter and instructional techniques; they must alter their beliefs and conceptions of practice, their theories of practice, and their "theories of action." In order to be successful, therefore, workplace reform should also proceed from our understanding of how teachers learn and change. (p. 95)

PROLOGUE

From the 1960s through the mid-1990s, researchers have paid considerable attention to the study of concepts or constructs that get at the *why* of effective teachers' behaviors as part of the question "What makes a teacher *effective?*" The work that has been done over the years to identify those traits, characteristics, attitudes, or beliefs that activate effective practice is the preface to the current construct and study of dispositions. The discourse about the dispositions as a construct, the research and findings, and the meaning of the research continue to be muddied by an interchangeable, overlapping, and incompatible use of terms.

Despite this lack of clarity and many noble efforts to clarify the construct, researchers and teacher educators are still infusing activities that teach and measure dispositions into the nation's teacher education programs. The question that began this chapter remains: Given the necessary knowledge and skills, what makes a person an effective teacher? The answer to that question is dispositions. This purpose of this book is to provide additional discourse to help define and interpret the construct of dispositions, to apply the construct to teacher education and related education professions, and to acknowledge the inherent complexity of the construct of dispositions, and predispositions, and the need for further study. In subsequent chapters, the numerous ways that the construct of dispositions weaves its way into the preparation of teachers are examined. The variety of topical approaches is evidence of the complexity of the tasks and related decisions and considerations the field of teacher education must address within the contemporary emphasis.

In Chapter 2, Karen Clark presents an overview and interpretation of more recent professional literature that has lead to the current state of the field in the study of dispositions in education. She discusses the connection between various educational issues and dispositions that were carefully examined in the 1990s, and she provides a conceptual framework for consideration.

Chapters 3 through 6 discuss some concepts and issues related to dispositions in education programs. In Chapter 3, R. Lee Smith discusses caring as an essential disposition in education. He presents the different definitions and conceptualizations of caring. A model is presented for consideration in using caring as a disposition in education and related professions. In Chapter 4, Kwadwo Okrah and Meryl Domina address multicultural issues in teaching dispositions. Today teachers are expected to work with an increasing number of diverse students who come from a variety of cultures. Okrah and Domina provide teacher educators with five keys to using multicultural education with this diversity through multicultural education and mention several dispositions necessary to successfully accomplish the task. In Chapter 5, Connie Deuschle discusses school counselor dispositions from theory to practice. She focuses on the affective and dispositional issues in school practices and offers strategies on how school counselors move from theory to the actual praxis of dispositional behaviors and attitudes. Using specific metaphors for dispositional aspects, she presents ideas that can help school counselors move from theory to practice. Jim Hurst focuses on dispositional aspects of clinical mental health professions in Chapter 6. He discusses the importance of dispositions to clinicians and presents a focus on the empathy as a necessary disposition.

Chapters 7 through 12 examine pragmatic issues, and cases are presented that demonstrate the infusion of dispositional education into teacher education programs. Judy Oates Lewandowski, in Chapter 7, presents an examination of teacher dispositions through the integration of technology. This chapter emphasizes the need for children to acquire the disposition to use technology in a productive, equitable, and ultimately ethical manner. She posits that cyber ethics must be taught at an early developmental level for children. This chapter aligns the need for relevant theories and proposes strategies for teaching age-appropriate cyber ethics. In Chapter 8, Dan T. Holm writes of exploring dispositions in teacher education through children's literature. He presents strategies for utilizing children's literature as a vehicle for discussing and teaching dispositions in elementary education. In Chapter 9, Gwynn Mettetal and Sara Sage discuss some of the aspects regarding the teaching and evaluation of dispositions in a preservice education course. They present a case that provides strategies and resources for teaching and measuring dispositional concepts in an undergraduate teacher education class. In Chapter 10, Linda J. Young and Diane C. Youngs present a case of how dispositions become evident in field experiences. They address students' and student teachers' abilities to demonstrate proficiency; and discuss how students are mentored during their teacher education preparation so that they reach the expected level of dispositional performance. E. Marcia Sheridan presents a graduate case study of teaching critical thinking skills and dispositions in Chapter 11. A teaching methodology used in a graduate course, with an emphasis on developing critical thinking skills, is discussed. In Chapter 12, the legal and policy issues in teacher education programs are discussed. David Freitas, Denise Skarbek, Ella Taylor, and Hilda Roselli examine education policy and the legal basis for professional judgment. Specific case law is mentioned along with practical considerations.

Chapters 13 and 14 examine some underlying philosophical issues of dispositions in teacher education programs from a faith-based perspective. Patricia A. Parrish and Denise Skarbek discuss teacher education in the Benedictine tradition in Chapter 13. The philosophical and dispositional bases are described with a focus on the Benedictine tradition and how that is presented in a teacher education program. This chapter also presents a brief overview of how certain dispositions interact with special education issues. Marsha Heck and Deborah Roose discuss dispositions from particular examples of Quaker and Native American traditions. The Educational Studies Program at Guilford College illustrates connections among Quaker education and the development and assessment of dispositions with future teachers. The term "habits of mind" is borrowed from Guilford's program and expanded as the conceptual framework for this chapter. The authors make recommendations about the principles that shape these approaches and ways in which they might be fitting to teacher education programs interested in developing disposition.

In the last chapter, R. Lee Smith, Tanice Knopp, Denise Skarbek, and Stephen Rushton present a model for classifying and researching disposition, beliefs, and traits in teacher education. The chapter presents a rationale and heuristic for more intensive and directed study of teacher dispositions, beliefs, and traits for the purpose of optimizing the identification, selection, and retention of teachers in an effort to ensure that effective educators are selected for and remain in our classrooms.

In summary, the concepts of disposition—such as *values, attitudes, traits,* and *beliefs*—were previously studied as constructs prevalent in psychology and teacher education literature. With the increasing national concern focusing on preparing and retaining quality professionals, dispositions of effective teachers will be at the fore of educators' interests. Therefore, it is paramount to understand and identify successful strategies for instilling a professional disposition as well as for promoting assessment practices of dispositions in a legal and ethical manner. As a profession, teacher education is charged with the responsibility to teach effective, ethical, and moral dispositions and to ensure that the nation's schools have teachers with the appropriate definitions.

REFERENCES

Anning, A. (1988). Teachers' theories about children's learning. In J. Calderhead (Ed.), *Teachers professional learning* (pp. 128–145). London: Falmer.

Ashton, P. T. (1991). A teacher education paradigm to empower teachers and students. In L. G. Katz & J. D. Raths (Eds.), *Advances in teacher education* (Vol. 4, pp. 82–104). Norwood, NJ: Ablex.

Ashton, P., & Webb, R. B. (1986). *Making a difference: Teachers' sense of efficacy and student achievement.* New York: Longman.

Avery, P., & Walker, C. (1993). Prospective teachers' perceptions of ethnic and gender differences in academic achievement. *Journal of Teacher Education, 44*(1), 27–37.

Beck, A. T. (1985). Cognitive therapy. In H. I. Kaplan & B. J. Sadock (Eds.), *Comprehensive textbook of psychiatry* (Vol. 4, pp. 1432–1438). Baltimore: Williams & Wilkins.

Bolster, A. S., Jr. (1983). Toward a more effective model of research on teaching. *Harvard Educational Review, 53,* 294–308.

Book, C., & Freeman, D. (1986). Differences in entry characteristics of elementary and secondary teacher candidates. *Journal of Teacher Education, 37*(2), 47–51.

Borko, H., & Putnam, R. T. (1995). Expanding a teachers' knowledge base: A cognitive psychological perspective on professional development. In T. R. Guskey & M. Huberman (Eds.), *Professional development in education: New paradigms and practices* (pp. 35–65). New York: Teachers College Press.

Bousseau, B., Book, C., & Byers, J. (1988). Teacher beliefs and the culture of teaching. *Journal of Teacher Education, 39*(6), 33–39.

Brophy, J., & Good, T. (1986). Teacher behavior and student achievement. In M. Wittrock (Ed.), *Handbook of research on teaching* (3rd ed., pp. 328–375). New York: Macmillan.

Calderhead, J., & Robson, M. (1991). Images of teaching: Student teachers' early conceptions of classroom practice. *Teaching and Teacher Education, 7*, 1–8.

Clark, C. M., & Peterson, P. L. (1986). Teachers thought processes. In M. C. Wittrock (Ed.), *Handbook on research in teaching* (pp. 255–296). New York: Macmillan.

Copeland, W. D. (1980). Affective dispositions of teachers in training toward examples of supervisory behavior. *Journal of Educational Research, 74*, 37–42.

Corrigan, D., & Griswold, K. (1963). Attitude changes of student teachers. *Journal of Educational Research, 57*, 93–95.

Dewey, J. (1933). *How we think*. Boston: D. C. Heath.

Eisenhart, M. A., Shrum, J. L., Harding, J. R., & Cuthbert, A. M. (1988). Teacher beliefs: Definitions, findings, and directions. *Educational Policy, 2*(1), 51–70.

Eraut, M. (1995). Developing professional knowledge within a client-centered orientation. In T. R. Guskey & M. Huberman (Eds.), *Professional development in education: New paradigms and practices* (pp. 227–252). New York: Teachers College Press.

Fang, Z. (1996). A review of research on teacher beliefs and practices. *Educational Research, 38*(1), 47–65.

Feiman-Nemser, S., McDiarmid, G., Melnick, S., & Parker, M. (1989). *Changing beginning teachers' conceptions: A description of an introductory teacher education course* (Research Report 89-1). East Lansing, MI: National Center for Research on Teacher Education, College of Education, Michigan State University.

Fullan, M. (1985). Change processes and strategies at the local level. *Elementary School Journal, 85*, 391–421.

Getzels, J., & Jackson, P. (1963). The teachers' personality and characteristics. In N. Gage (Ed.), *Handbook of research on teaching* (pp. 506–582). Chicago: Rand McNally.

Gibson, S., & Dembo, M. (1984). Teacher efficacy: A construct validation. *Journal of Educational Psychology, 76*, 569–582.

Guskey, T. R. (1982). The effects of change in instructional effectiveness on the relationship of teacher expectations and student achievement. *Journal of Educational Research, 75*(6), 345–349.

Guskey, T. R. (1984). The influences of change in instructional effectiveness upon the affective characteristics of teachers. *American Educational Research Journal, 21*, 245–259.

Guskey, T. R. (1989). Attitude and perceptual change in teachers. *International Journal of Educational Research, 13*, 439–453.

Guskey, T. R., & Huberman, M. (1995). Introduction. In T. R. Guskey & M. Huberman (Eds.), *Professional development in education: New paradigms and practices* (p. 1). New York: Teachers College Press.

Harvey, O., Prather, M., White, B., & Hoffmeister, J. (1968). Teachers' beliefs, classroom atmosphere and student behavior. *American Educational Research Journal, 5*, 151–165.

Hollingsworth, S. (1989). Prior beliefs and change in learning to teach. *American Educational Research Journal, 26*, 160–189.

Janney, R. E., Snell, M. E., Beers, M. K., & Raynes, M. (1995). Integrating students with moderate and severe disabilities: Classroom teachers' beliefs and attitudes about implementing an educational change. *Educational Administration Quarterly, 31*(1), 86–114.

Kagan, D. M. (1992). Implications of research on teacher beliefs. *Educational Psychologist, 27*, 65–90.

Katz, L. G. (1993). *Dispositions: Definitions and implications for early childhood practices.* Perspectives from ERIC/EECE: A Monograph Series, No. 4.

Katz, L. G., & Raths, J. D. (1985). Dispositions as goals for teacher education. *Teaching and Teacher Education, 1*(4), 301–307.

Knopp, T. Y. (2000). *The role of beliefs in effecting change in classroom practices: A case study of four teachers of students with serious emotional disturbance.* Unpublished doctoral dissertation, University of Florida, Gainesville.

Lortie, D. C. (1975). *School teacher: A sociological study.* Chicago: University of Chicago Press.

Mahlios, M., & Maxson, M. (1995). Capturing preservice teachers' beliefs about schooling, life, and childhood. *Journal of Teacher Education, 46*, 192–199.

Mevarech, Z. R. (1995). Teacher's paths on the way to and from the professional development forum. In T. R. Guskey & M. Huberman (Eds.), *Professional development in education: New paradigms and practices* (pp. 151–170). New York: Teachers College Press.

Munby, H. (1982). The place of teachers' beliefs in research on teacher thinking and decision making, and an alternative methodology. *Instructional Science, 11*, 201–225.

Munby, H. (1984). A qualitative approach to the study of a teacher's beliefs. *Journal of Research in Science Teaching, 21*(1), 27–38.

Nespor, J. (1985). *The role of beliefs in the practice of teaching: Final report of the teacher beliefs study.* Austin, TX: R&D Center for Teacher Education, University of Texas at Austin.

Nespor, J. (1987). The role of beliefs in the practice of teaching. *Journal of Curriculum Studies, 19*, 317–328.

Pajares, F. (1992). Teachers' beliefs and educational research: Cleaning up a messy construct. *Review of Educational Research, 62*, 307–332.

Paul, J. L., & Smith, T. J. (2000). *Stories out of school: Memories and reflections on care and cruelty in the classroom.* Stamford, CT: Ablex.

Peck, R. F., & Tucker, J. A. (1973). Research on teacher education. In R. M. Travers (Ed.), *Second handbook of research on teaching* (pp. 9410–9978). Chicago: Rand McNally.

Raths, J. (2001). Teachers' beliefs and teaching beliefs. *Journal on the Development, Care, and Education of Young Children, 3*(1), 1–10.

Renzaglia, A., Hutchins, M., & Lee, S. (1997). The impact of teacher education on the beliefs, attitudes, and dispositions of preservice special educators. *Teacher Education and Special Education, 20*(4), 360–377.

Richardson, V. (1996). The role of attitudes and beliefs in learning to teach. In J. Sikula, T. J. Buttery, & E. Guyton (Eds.), *Handbook of research in teacher education* (2nd ed., pp. 102–119). New York: Macmillan.

Richardson, V., Anders, P., Tidwell, D., & Lloyd, C. (1991). The relationship between teachers' beliefs and practices in reading comprehension instruction. *American Educational Research Journal, 28*(3), 559–586.

Rogard, M., & Pigge, F. L. (1989). The influence of preservice training and teacher experience upon attitudes and concerns about teaching. *Teaching and Teacher Education, 50*, 33–44.

Rokeach, M. (1972). *Beliefs, attitudes, and values: A theory of organization and change.* San Francisco: Jossey-Bass.

Rose, J. S., & Medway, F. J. (1981). Measurement of teachers' beliefs in their control over student outcome. *Journal of Educational Research, 74,* 185–190.

Scheibe, K. E. (1970). *Beliefs and values.* New York: Holt, Rinehart, & Winston.

Schutz, A., & Luckmann, T. (1973). *The structures of the life-world* (R. M. Zaner & H. T. Engelhardt, Jr., Trans.). Evanston, IL: Northwestern University Press.

Shulman, L. S. (1986). Those who understand: Knowledge growth in teaching. *Educational Researcher, 15,* 4–14.

Smylie, M. A. (1995). Teacher learning in the workplace: Implications for school reform. In T. R. Guskey & M. Huberman (Eds.), *Professional development in education: New paradigms and practices* (pp. 92–113). New York: Teachers College Press.

Sparks, G. (1988). Teachers' attitudes toward change and subsequent improvements in classroom teaching. *Journal of Educational Psychology, 80*(1), 111–117.

Stern, G. G. (1963). Measuring noncognitive variables in research on teaching. In N. Gage, (Ed.), *Handbook of research on teaching* (pp. 398–447). Chicago: Rand McNally.

Tillema, H. H. (1994). Training and professional expertise: Bridging the gap between new information and pre-existing beliefs of teachers. *Teaching and Teacher Education, 10,* 601–615.

Tschannen-Moran, M., & Hoy, A. W. (2001). Teacher efficacy: Capturing an elusive construct. *Teaching and Teacher Education, 17,* 783–805.

Wilson, A. J., & Silverman, H. (1991). Teachers' assumptions and beliefs about the delivery of services to exceptional children. *Teacher Education and Special Education, 14,* 198–206.

Woolfolk, A. E., & Hoy, W. K. (1990). Prospective teachers' sense of efficacy and beliefs about control. *Journal of Educational Psychology, 82,* 81–91.

Woolfolk, A. E., Rosoff, B., & Hoy, W. K. (1990). Teachers' sense of efficacy and their beliefs about managing students. *Teaching and Teacher Education, 6,* 137–148.

Zeichner, K. M., & Tabachnick, B. R. (1981). Are the effects of university teacher education washed out by school experience? *Journal of Teacher Education, 32*(3), 7–11.

2

A Contemporary Rationale for Dispositions in Education

Karen B. Clark

Throughout the 1990s, the quality of classroom teachers was questioned as was the quality of teacher education programs. As a result, educational leaders proposed new, more rigorous standards for licensing teachers. These standards were multidimensional and assessed knowledge, skills, and dispositions. Although many teacher education programs have always assessed what students knew and were able to do, assessing dispositions was a new aspect of teacher quality that had not been examined systematically.

Dispositions were included as part of the Interstate New Teacher Assessment and Support Consortium (INTASC) standards and integrated into other standards for teacher education programs. Several issues that emerged or gained momentum during the 1990s may be responsible for this relatively recent concern about teacher dispositions. Some of these issues include the standards movement, a moral view of teaching, a growing interest in an ethic of care, the recognition that schools and communities must form meaningful partnerships to address the increasingly diverse needs of students, and an increasing belief that teachers must engage in inquiry and exhibit a sense of curiosity.

The purpose of this chapter is to discuss the relationship between these areas and their impact on assessing teachers' dispositions. Other chapters in this book focus on dispositions and different educational trends that started earlier and also grew in the 1990s. After exploring the relationship between educational trends and dispositions, a review of the research on assessing dispositions will be presented.

THE STANDARDS MOVEMENT

During the past decade and a half, concern about the quality of classroom teachers has become a national focus. This concern actually emerged in the 1980s, when establishing standards for students and raising standards for teachers were emphasized (Wise, 1996). This movement was largely the result of scrutiny by three groups of professionals: the National Council for the Accreditation of Teacher Education (NCATE), the Council of Chief State School Officers (CCSSO), and the National Board for Professional Teaching Standards (NBPTS). Their efforts culminated in 1996, with the publication of the *National Commission on Teaching and America's Future*.

The National Commission was a 26-member panel that concluded that improving our nation's schools must include and is heavily dependent upon improving the quality of our teacher workforce. The commission set six clear goals in its report. The first one states, "All children will be taught by teachers who have the knowledge, skills, and commitment to teach children well" (Darling-Hammond, 1996, p. 196). This reference to commitment preceded the term dispositions.

The three professional groups that participated in the commission developed three sets of standards to guide teacher education programs: NBPTS, NCATE, and INTASC standards. INTASC standards, in particular, are divided into the categories of knowledge, skills, and dispositions. In addition, they stress the importance of performance-based assessments in evaluating teacher quality. In Darling-Hammond's summary of the commission's report, she writes:

> Children are compelled to attend school. Every state guarantees them equal protection under the law, and most promise them a sound education. In the face of these obligations, students have a right to competent, caring teachers who work in schools organized for success. (p. 194)

After the commission's report, the book *A License to Teach: Raising Standards for Teaching* was published in its second edition (Darling-Hammond, Wise, and Klein, 1999). In this book the authors report on the efforts of the Minnesota Board of Teaching to adopt performance-based standards in 1987. Based on their research in Minnesota and California, combined with the work of the NBPTS, the authors present a framework for assessing the knowledge, skills, and dispositions of future teachers. Much of their work focuses on what teachers should know and be able to do. Darling-Hammond et al. (1999) also discuss dispositions that affect teacher performance.

This standards movement, lead by various professional groups, promulgated various standards designed to improve the quality of teachers entering our nation's classrooms. In the case of the NBPTS, the standards were designed to encourage experienced and exemplary teachers to apply for a new national certification. The INTASC standards were organized into knowledge, performances, and dispositions. Although many teacher education programs understood the importance of candidates' knowledge base and specific skills, dispositions was a new dimension that had not always been overtly assessed by teacher educators. It was a term defined in various ways, including references to caring teachers; moral professionals; flexible, adaptive, or creative individuals; and communities and partnerships.

Teacher education programs are accustomed to developing conceptual frameworks that portray their core beliefs and elaborate on the connections between these beliefs and the research to support them. In deciding on the core values or dispositions for a teacher education program, it may also be helpful to establish a conceptual framework specifically for dispositions. Such a framework is presented in Figure 2.1. The knowledge base to support this conceptual framework will be discussed here.

MORAL CONDUCT OF TEACHERS

In response to an overly technical emphasis on preparing and assessing the effectiveness of classroom teachers, the 1990s brought an increased interest in the moral dimensions of teaching. The editors of the book titled *The*

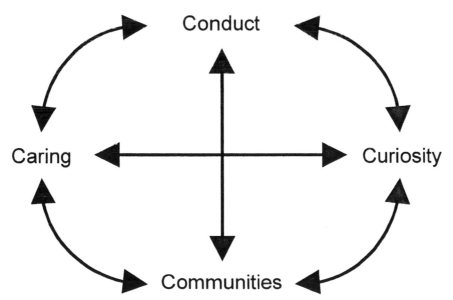

Figure 2.1. Conceptual Framework for Dispositions

Moral Dimensions of Teaching presented a series of essays that explored the professionalism of teachers, the ethical practice of teaching, and moral transactions in the classroom (Goodlad, Soder, & Sirotnik, 1990).

One author in that book (Fenstermacher, 1990) highlighted the importance of moral conduct and referred to this as the manner of the teacher. Moral conduct, according to Fenstermacher, included treating students justly while demonstrating compassion and care. Fenstermacher suggested that a teacher consistently personifies morality and even suggested that the manner of teachers was as critical to their work as their subject matter mastery.

In another chapter in that book, Soder (1990) discussed the moral obligation to ensure equality of treatment for all children, regardless of their gender, race, or social class. Soder argued that teachers are essential to promoting the humanity of children due to the low status that society gives to children. Soder states that a teacher's responsibility goes far beyond mastering the technical aspects related to teaching, but includes establishing trust and preventing harm.

In that same volume, Goodlad (1990a) wrote about the importance of producing educators willing to struggle with the critical moral and ethical issues related to schooling. Goodlad suggested that all teachers must cultivate habits of reflection as part of their moral mission. He also suggested that we should begin to recognize the "calling" of teachers. In another publication, *Teachers for Our Nation's Schools*, Goodlad (1990b) raised concerns about the moral conduct of teacher education programs. Goodlad described teacher education programs that include a component of moral teaching as having four dimensions: enculturating youth in a social and political democracy, providing all children with equitable access to knowledge, practicing pedagogical nurturing, and connecting with others beyond the school by engaging in responsible stewardship. Other educational leaders such as Lytle and Cochran-Smith (1992) also discussed the importance of preparing teachers to conduct research so that they may become change agents and leaders in schools and a variety of communities.

Finally, Clark (1990) raised questions about the values of honesty, respect, selflessness, and moral scrutiny of ends and means. He urged educators and community members to recognize the importance of the moral dimension of teaching and view it as equally important as students' test scores. Clark states, "To educate is to lead responsibly—to influence students' knowledge, skills, and dispositions in ways that will serve them and their society well and to do so in morally defensible ways" (pp. 251–252).

These concerns about the moral actions of teachers as they work and interact with students who are required to be in school are clearly reflected in standards describing dispositions. For example, in the INTASC Principle 3, related to diversity, the following dispositions are described: "The teacher believes that all children can learn at high levels and persists in helping all children achieve success" (Darling-Hammond et al., 1999, p. 187). Such descriptions of dispositions seem to reflect what many policy leaders were addressing in their writing about the moral dimensions of teaching. These same leaders often referred to the importance of caring on the part of classroom teachers. This disposition will be discussed in the following section.

AN ETHIC OF CARE

Nel Noddings (1984, 1992) is recognized for her writings about care. Noddings is a feminist scholar who developed the concept of an ethic of care and presented a different version of empathy. Noddings preferred to use the term engrossment rather than empathy, believing that it reflected the temporary nature of empathy, which must be nonselective on the part of a classroom teacher. Noddings eloquently explores this view in her book *Caring: A Feminine Approach to Ethics and Moral Education* (1984). In this book, Noddings discusses the importance of teacher education programs that produce ethical decision makers who display care and justice toward all students.

In 1992, Noddings applied her ethic of care to the school curriculum. She suggested that schools might be organized around themes of care rather than the traditional liberal arts curriculum. In doing so, Noddings proposed that such a curriculum must provide others with moral support, intellectual help, and friendship. When conversing about students, Noddings recommended that educators behave in a caring and professional manner.

Noddings' ideas are also incorporated in INTASC principles and reflected in codes of ethics for various professional organizations. For example, a review of the INTASC Principle 6 related to communication states: "The teacher is a thoughtful and responsive listener" (Darling-Hammond et al., 1999, p. 188). Such thoughtfulness and responsiveness certainly must come from an ethic of care as described by Noddings.

Others have also written about care and an ethic of social justice (Sirotnik, 1990). Sirotnik challenged the patterns of inequity often found in schools connected with curricular differences implemented with wealthy college-bound students verses those implemented with typically minority, poorer, noncollege-bound students. Along with writing about curriculum and social justice, Sirotnik also discussed the moral commitment to inquiry and the importance of modeling this activity to students. Such an inquiry is hard to conduct if teachers work in isolated classrooms and are not able to form respectful communities (Sirotnik, 1990).

COMMUNITIES AND PARTNERSHIPS

The belief that teachers must establish meaningful partnerships with others is not a new one. Leonard Covello wrote his autobiography *The Heart Is the Teacher* in 1958. He described his experience as a young boy in Italy and later as an Italian immigrant in New York City. His personal experience during his school-age years was significant in shaping his commitment to meeting the needs of all children in Benjamin Franklin Community High School in the New York City public school system. During his principalship at Benjamin Franklin Community High School, Covello recognized the importance of encouraging immigrant children to be proud of their native cultures as they tried to adapt to new environments. He worked tirelessly to build positive relationships with students and their families while recognizing the school's role in building community among families. Covello mobilized other teachers in his school to take a personal interest in the boys at Benjamin Franklin High School and served as an example for future generations of educators.

In 1998, Vito Perrone, a leading educational reformer on the faculty at Harvard, published a book titled *Teacher With a Heart: Reflections on Leonard Covello and Community*. Here Perrone connects the work of Leonard Covello with that of today's teachers working with new immigrants. Perrone stresses the importance of community schools, intercultural education, and advocating for students and families.

Perrone has also written extensively about the importance of collaborative climate and community within the school building, particularly in secondary schools. He expressed concern about a focus on teaching subject matter in secondary teacher education programs to the exclusion of highlighting the important role of high schools as social institutions (Perrone & Traver, 1996). He also stressed the importance of professional communities of teachers and the importance of promoting these in teacher education programs.

Perrone's work and the earlier work of Covello clearly emphasized the importance of forming partnerships with families and forming communities within school settings. Both authors began with a fundamental assumption that teachers must respect all students. These themes of communities, partnerships, and respect were also the basis for the extensive work of Joyce Epstein, director of the Center on School, Family and Community Partnerships. Epstein published extensively in the 1990s about the importance of parents, teachers, and students forming meaningful partnerships. Her work involved researching patterns relating to partnerships and resulted in a framework for involvement, interestingly referred to as "six types of involvement; six types of caring" (Epstein, 1995). Epstein stressed redefining traditional views of workshops, communication, and collaboration with others to take into account the changing needs of families and children. Her work connected with the ideas of Covello with its emphasis on meeting the needs of all families and establishing mutually respectful partnerships. Such themes are also prevalent in the dispositions associated with INTASC Principle 10, related to collaboration, which states: "The teacher is willing to consult with other adults regarding the education and well-being of his/her students" (Darling-Hammond et al., 1999, p. 188). It seems significant that the verb *consults* was selected for this particular disposition. Consults reflects a respect for the expertise that all individuals may be able to contribute about a child. Such experts include families, as espoused by Covello (1958) and Epstein (1995).

CURIOSITY AND INQUIRY

Paulo Freire (2004) states: "For apart from inquiry, apart from praxis, individuals cannot be truly human. Knowledge emerges only though invention, re-invention, through the restless, impatient continuing, hopeful inquiry human beings pursue in the world, with the world, and with each other" (p. 100). Sockett (2001) writes further that inquiry, reflection, and collaboration are critical habits of teachers who must recognize that a democratic education is based on the idea that teaching and learning must always be renewed.

Lifelong learning is another term connected with inquiry, originally used by those in the field of adult education or adult learning. Assumptions when working with adult learners include the notion that adult learners are largely self-directed and intrinsically motivated. Lifelong learners do not necessarily require an educational institution or setting to inquire into new areas. Instead, learning is viewed as a cognitive process internal to the learner, which can occur "both incidentally and in planned educational activities" (Merriam & Brockett, 1997, p. 6).

In the field of education, we often use the phrase *engaging in ongoing professional development* to refer to some of the incidental and planned activities that educators participate in to continually update knowledge and skills related to their discipline and their pedagogical content knowledge. Such activities include attending professional conferences, participating in workshops, attending lectures and other community events, joining professional organizations, and engaging in various professional study groups. All of these activities allow for a significant amount of autonomy, inquiry, and creativity on the part of educators (Sockett, 2001). Participation in these activities indicates an educator's curiosity about his specific discipline, his learners, and the field of education. This curiosity is an essential disposition for classroom teachers, as it is the intrinsic motivation underlying inquiry and their ability to engage in professional renewal.

This disposition of curiosity and inquiry is found in the INTASC Principle 1, which states: "The teacher is committed to continuous learning and engages in professional discourse about subject matter knowledge and children's learning of the discipline" (Darling-Hammond et al., 1999, p. 187).

The formation of a conceptual framework for dispositions precedes the decisions that teacher educators must make about how to assess and promote these values or attitudes. Identifying specific dispositions that are essential to future teachers is a necessary first step before assessment methods can be developed. A review of the literature reporting on methods of assessing dispositions reveals articles that might be grouped into three categories: (a) methods for monitoring dispositions, (b) methods for assessing dispositions, and (c) methods for enhancing specific dispositions. Each of these areas will be explored in the following paragraphs.

Methods for Monitoring Dispositions

St. Bonaventure University utilizes a yellow flag system for documenting interventions and early concerns about candidates' dispositions. The yellow flag form is completed by a member of the faculty when there is concern in an on-campus class and a field experience related to attitudes, demeanor, abilities, or preparation. After the form is filled-out, a conference is held with a student, followed by a conference with administrators. The student eventually signs a contract specifying the steps that will be taken to address the concern. Students who receive three yellow flag forms are not allowed to enter the student teaching experience. The yellow-flag system is described as a formative way to help students recognize and develop appropriate dispositions (Burke, 2002).

Indiana University South Bend also employs a monitoring system in the form of letters of concern. If a student displays problematic behaviors indicating unacceptable dispositions, a member of the faculty is encouraged to discuss the concern directly with the student. The discussion is then documented with a written letter. The letter becomes part of the student's advising record. If subsequent letters of concern are filed, a meeting is again held with the student to develop a remedial plan to change the disposition of concern. Students could be counseled out of the program as a result of multiple letters of concern.

Methods for Assessing Dispositions

Ryan and Kuhs (1993) posit that assessing preservice teachers holds many challenges as we struggle to reconceptualize effective teaching. They suggest that new assessments must be multidimensional and integrated. They write about various methods for assessing dispositions, including journals, logs, and written rationales for lessons and activities. Beyond the methods used, these authors implore teacher educators to be sure to employ integrated, multiple sources of information. Maylone (2002) also discusses the complexities of assessing dispositions and urges colleges to form dispositions committees. These committees should go beyond creating checklists with specific attributes listed and instead reflect on a list of 21 questions as educators struggle with appropriate assessments in this area.

Researchers at the University of Nevada used storybook prompts to assess preservice teachers' dispositions toward struggling students (Abernathy, 2002). In this study, Abernathy presented both early service and late service preservice teachers with a story about a first grader who is not feeling successful in her classroom. In the story, the character suggests that next year will be better because she will have a new teacher. Participants were asked to react to the student's prediction that she will have a more successful year in second grade. Surprisingly, the participants in the study profess the belief that the character in the story will not have a successful year the following year. In fact, this pessimistic outlook is more prevalent in the later service teacher education candidates than the earlier ones.

Additional work has been done assessing the dispositions of physical education students (McBride, Xiang, Wittenburg, & Shen, 2002). These researchers compared the critical thinking dispositions of American and Chinese preservice physical education teachers using the California Critical Thinking Dispositions Inventory (CCTDI). This instrument is based on a triadic theory for dispositions. The triadic theory suggests that dispositions include inclinations, abilities, and sensitivity. These traits can be measured using the seven subscales on the CCTDI.

Methods for Enhancing Specific Dispositions

Several researchers have offered ideas about methods to enhance desirable dispositions. Such ideas include using social inquiry strategies (Lamson, Aldrich, & Thomas, 2003), employing teacher work samples (Cartwright & Blacklock, 2003), engaging in reflective practice (Breese & Nawrocki-Chabin 2002), and using dialogue journals with goal setting (Goldstein & Freedman, 2003). Although there is limited research on any one of these methods, it is helpful to begin to review the available literature in these areas.

Lamson et al. (2003) used role playing, a social inquiry strategy, to enhance appropriate dispositions. The role plays were student-centered and required student teachers to apply theory as they responded to various situations. The researchers concluded that using the role plays engaged student teachers in higher-order thinking and self-reflection. Participants developed confidence, and appropriate dispositions seemed to emerge as a result of these activities (Lamson et al., 2003).

Cartwright and Blacklock (2003) involved 55 university students in developing modified teacher work samples. These work samples were the result of the interns' work with elementary students who were considered struggling readers. After 12 weeks of delivering individualized interventions, interns completed a questionnaire that measured their dispositions. The researchers report that certain dispositions toward struggling readers improved as a result of the intense work.

Breese and Nawrocki-Chabin (2002) conclude that dispositions must indeed be cultivated through intentional activities in order to ensure that teachers enter the field with acceptable dispositions. They used reflection and peer conferencing to identify specific actions and engage beginning education students in an analysis of those actions. Finally, Goldstein and Freedman (2003) explore enhancing an ethic of care by using dialogue journals. Although no definite conclusions are available from their study, these authors hypothesize that a caring relationship transcends specific activities in establishing an ethic of care.

CONCLUSION

This chapter examined the connection between various educational issues that had been scrutinized in the 1990s, and dispositions. This was done in an effort to establish a conceptual framework. Research to support this framework was also discussed. Conceptual frameworks should always reflect the uniqueness of a teacher education program; therefore, the one presented in this chapter is only one of many possibilities. Since the requirement of assessing dispositions is relatively new, this initial framework may be useful to others as they try to determine what dispositions should be assessed and how to carry out these assessments in a fair and equitable manner.

REFERENCES

Abernathy, T. V. (2002). Using a storybook prompt to uncover inservice and preservice teachers' dispositions toward struggling students. *Teacher Educator, 38*(2), 78–98.

Breese, L., & Nawrocki-Chabin, R. (2002, October). Nurturing dispositions through reflective practice. Paper presented at the meeting of The Association of Independent Liberal Arts Colleges for Teacher Education, San Diego, CA.

Burke, P. Y. (2002). A mechanism for monitoring dispositions in preservice teachers. *Childhood Education, 78*(4), 224K–224M.

Cartwright, D. D., & Blacklock, K. K. (2003). *Teacher work samples and struggling readers: Impacting student performance and candidate dispositions.* (ERIC Document Reproduction Service No. ED472395)

Clark C. M. (1990). The teacher and the taught: Moral transactions in the classroom. In J. Goodlad, R. Soder, & K. A. Sirotnik (Eds.), *The moral dimensions of teaching* (pp. 251–265). San Francisco: Jossey-Bass.

Covello, L. (1958). *The heart is the teacher*. New York: McGraw-Hill.

Darling-Hammond, L. (1996). What matters most a competent teacher for every child. *Phi Delta Kappan, 78*(3), 193–200.

Darling-Hammond, L., Wise, A. E., & Klein, S. P. (1999). *A license to teach raising standards for teaching*. San Francisco: Jossey-Bass.

Epstein, J. L. (1995). School/family/community partnerships: Caring for the children we share. *Phi Delta Kappan, 76*(9), 701–712.

Fenstermacher, G. D. (1990). Some moral considerations on teaching as a profession. In J. Goodlad, R. Soder, & K.A. Sirotnik (Eds.), *The moral dimensions of teaching* (pp. 130–151). San Francisco: Jossey-Bass.

Freire, P. (2004). The banking concept of education. In A. S. Canestrari & B. A. Marlowe (Eds.), *Educational foundations an anthology of critical readings* (pp. 99–111). Thousand Oaks, CA: Sage.

Goldstein, L. S., & Freedman, D. (2003). Challenges enacting caring teacher education. *Journal of Teacher Education, 54*(5), 441–454.

Goodlad, J. (1990a). The occupation of teaching in schools. In J. Goodlad, R. Soder, & K. A. Sirotnik (Eds.), *The moral dimensions of teaching* (pp. 3–34). San Francisco: Jossey-Bass.

Goodlad, J. J. (1990b). *Teachers for our nation's schools*. San Francisco: Jossey-Bass.

Goodlad, J. J., Soder, R., & Sirotnik, K. A. (1990). *The moral dimensions of teaching*. San Francisco: Jossey-Bass.

Lamson, S. L., Aldrich, J. E., & Thomas, K. R. (2003). *Using social inquiry strategies to enhance teacher candidate dispositions*. (ERIC Document Reproduction Service No. ED 474176)

Lytle, S. L., & Cochran-Smith. M. (1992). Teacher research as a way of knowing. *Harvard Educational Review, 62*, 447–473.

Maylone, N. (2002). *Identifying desirable pre service teacher dispositions: An intractable problem?* (ERIC Document Reproduction Service No. ED463258)

McBride, R. E., Xiang, P., Wittenburg, D., & Shen, J. (2002). An analysis of preservice teachers' dispositions toward critical thinking: A cross-cultural perspective. *Asia-Pacific Journal of Teacher Education, 30*(2), 131–140.

Merriam, S. B., & Brockett, R. G. (1997) *The profession and practice of adult education*. San Francisco: Jossey-Bass.

Noddings, N. (1984). *Caring: A feminine approach to ethics and moral education*. Berkeley, CA: University of California Press.

Noddings, N. (1992). *The challenge to care in schools an alternative approach to education*. New York: Teachers College Press.

Perrone, V. (1998). *Teacher with a heart: Reflections on Leonard Covello and community*. New York: Teachers College Press.

Perrone, V., & Traver, R. (1996). Secondary education. In J. Sikula (Ed.), *Handbook of research on teacher education* (2nd ed., pp. 392–409). New York: Simon & Schuster.

Ryan, J. M., & Kuhs, T. M. (1993). Assessment of preservice teachers and the use of portfolios. *Theory into Practice 32*(2), 75–81.

Sirotnik, K. A. (1990). Society, schooling, teaching, and preparing to teach. In J. Goodlad, R. Soder, & K. A. Sirotnik (Eds.), *The moral dimensions of teaching* (pp. 296–327). San Francisco: Jossey-Bass.

Soder, R. (1990). The rhetoric of teacher professionalization. In J. Goodlad, R. Soder, & K. A. Sirotnik (Eds.), *The moral dimensions of teaching* (pp. 35–86). San Francisco: Jossey-Bass.

Sockett, H. (2001). Transforming teacher education. In H. T. Sockett, E. K. DeMulder, P. C. LePage, & D. R. Wood (Eds.), *Transforming teacher education lessons in professional development* (pp.1–10). Westport, CT: Bergin & Garvey.

Wise, A. E. (1996). Building a system of quality assurance for the teaching profession: Moving into the 21st century. *Phi Delta Kappan, 78*(3), 190–192.

3

A Model for Defining the Construct of Caring in Teacher Education

R. Lee Smith and Lynda Emigh

There is a perception that the social and interpersonal aspects of teacher education are less important than the content, technical, and instructional methods taught in teacher preparation and graduate programs. The inclusion of interpersonal and affective aspects in teacher education pedagogy may be prudent. Increasingly, many families depend on schools to act as an extension of their social support system, including emotional support and guidance for their children (DeFord, 1996). Currently, only 88% of students finish 12 years of school (McMillen, Kaufman, & Klein, 1997), and there are increasing numbers of students who enter school from homes of low socioeconomic means (Grossman, 1995). These issues, and the increased attention to the efficacy of teacher training programs, provide impetus for teacher educators to examine contemporary curricula, instruction, and practices in teacher education.

Several contemporary researchers and authors have addressed the relational aspects of education and suggested that instructing teachers in aspects of care should be an important component of teacher preparation programs (Noblit, Rogers, & McCadden, 1995; Noddings, 1984, 1992, 1995b; Wolfgramm, 1995). Noblit et al. (1995) believe current forms of educational organization are a result of a belief system that values the technical dimensions of teaching and learning over relational aspects. Caring, in contrast to the technical dimensions of teaching, gives priority to relationships and how these relationships are socially constructed. Likewise, Noddings (1995b) contends that educators should strive for the development of caring people. She challenges contemporary educational thought by encouraging educators to consider it legitimate to spend time "developing relations of trust, talking with students about problems that are central to their lives, and guiding them toward greater sensitivity and competence across all the domains of care" (p. 679). Furthermore, caring may be an integral part of broader social interactions in schools. Behaviors homologous with caring may be considered vital outcomes associated with lifelong interpersonal functioning and subsequent quality of life.

There are several possibilities that may explain reasons why content regarding the social interaction aspects of schools has been diminished recently in teacher education. First, there has been a quest for efficiency of instructional method, most notably characterized by time on task. This emphasis on maximizing the on-task behaviors and orientation of teachers has sent a message to teacher educators that spending instructional time in building relationships has little value in education. Second, a primary focus of educational research has been to measure and improve aptitude treatment interactions (ATI). In the application of research methodologies that measure ATI, perhaps the less quantifiable aspects of teachers' interactions have been neglected. Concurrently, and most recently, there has been political and societal pressure to produce acceptable scores in high-stakes assessment programs. As such, inquiry activities in educational settings to document and research social or relational aspects in students have been depreciated and neglected. It is important to begin to develop curricula and continue to build a research basis for pedagogy that is more inclusive of the relational aspects of education. Instruction about caring and caring behaviors in teacher education programs may help current and future educators explicitly value caring and other relational aspects of teaching as having equal priority with academic achievement.

The purpose of this chapter is to propose a parsimonious model for use in teacher education. The model attempts to synthesize the many concepts and constructs associated with care and caring for use in teacher education programs. Such explanation may further lead to the development of curricula to teach about caring and caring behaviors for preservice and working teachers. Increased attention to the teaching, study, and research of caring and other relational attributes can legitimize interpersonal relationships and their associated values and ethics. The intent of the proposed model is to provide teacher educators with a pedagogical tool for presenting concepts relating to caring and caring behaviors in curricula.

A MODEL OF CARING FOR TEACHER EDUCATION

A model for teaching about caring is presented in Table 3.1. The model proposes four dimensions of care synthesized from concepts that are prevalent in the professional literature. The first dimension, the dynamics of care, addresses relationships that occur between teachers and students when an ethic of caring is valued. The second dimension, caring behaviors, refers to specific actions teachers perform that indicate caring. The third dimension of the model, construction of a caring environment, pertains to the social formation of physical and psychological safety in schools and classrooms. The last dimension of the framework, modeling and facilitating caring in others, is concerned with the educational processes to teach students to become caring individuals. This dimension helps to explain necessary practices to develop the interpersonal traits needed for a continuity of caring in Western society (Katzenmeyer, 1992). In the following pages, contextual and theoretical perspectives of each dimension in the proposed model of caring are explicated.

Table 3.1.   A Model for the Construct of Caring in Teaching for Use in Teacher Education Pedagogy

Components of Caring in Education	Examples
Dynamics of Care The dynamics of relationships that occur between teachers and students	• Positive regard toward students and their families • Mutual personal belief about the responsibility to nurture caring in relationships • The dual and reciprocal nature of caring
Caring Behaviors The specific acts that a teacher performs that may be considered to be caring	• Behaviors that attend to social, affective, and academic areas • A behavioral pattern consistently related to caring acts • Personal values of persistence, responsibility, and sacrifice
Construction of a Caring Environment The physical and social-emotional dimensions of classroom and school climate that a teacher develops	• Providing a safe and orderly classroom designed to meet student needs • Establishing a school and classroom climate of mutual trust, honesty, and respect • Providing psychological protection and care in institutional interactions
Modeling and Facilitating Caring in Others Process in the educational environment that shows children how to care	• Demonstrating caring thoughts and behaviors • Creating moral thoughts and behavior • Respecting differences in each individual

The Dynamics of Caring

The dynamics of caring refers to the psychological states and beliefs of a teacher that result in caring relationships between the teacher and students. Noblit et al. (1995) defined caring as "a value that is grounded in the kinds of relationships that good teachers have cultivated for years . . . and a belief about how we should view and interact with others" (p. 673). Furthermore, Noddings states that caring is "the glue that binds teachers and students together and makes life in classrooms meaningful" (p. 681). The dynamic of caring concerns the development of these relationships. In many cases, scholars consider caring a value or ethic, more a singular behavior, and as such, this dynamic presumes persistent activity.

Discussions of caring relationships in the literature yielded three concepts that can be utilized to further define the dynamic of caring. The first is a positive regard for others on the part of the caregiver. This means an individual acting out of a dynamic of care has a belief in the value, worth, and well-being of others. Martin Buber (1965) states that caring is an act of affirming and encouraging the best in others. Additionally, Noddings (1995a) asserts that when we care, we want to do our very best for the people in our care. Rogers (1994) found caring is evidenced by activities that demonstrate there are positive interactions between the teacher and students.

A second defining component of the dynamic of caring is a consistent personal belief about the responsibility to nurture caring and in caring for one another. Assuming another's point of reality or frame of reference leads one to take responsibility for her or him and to sense obligation to the relationship. This prominent point is found in literature on the ethic of care. Gilligan (1982) stresses that caring includes assuming responsibility for another, by acting responsively to nurture or lessen another's needs. Furthermore, Gilligan mentions the dynamic of the interaction as individuals being motivated to act responsibly toward another who also maintains his or her own needs for connections and relationships. Mayeroff (1971) considers a caring relationship to be one in which the caregiver is devoted, consistent and persistent over time. Mayeroff termed this dimension of caring as knowing. He believes that, to act responsibly, the caregiver must know the powers, limitations, and needs of the other, and how to respond in order to assist in growth and development. Additionally, caregivers must know their own powers and limitations to help understand and meet the other's needs. Ezzo and Ezzo (1993) discuss the responsibility of the caring person as having an other-oriented sensitivity that is not at the expense of the self, but a fulfillment of individual desires for gratification that comes from knowing another's needs have been met.

The last component of the dynamic of caring is concerned with the reciprocal nature of the attribute. Many who have explored the constructs of caring insist that caring is not a unidirectional relationship. Terms such as "interdependence and connectivity" (Gilligan, 1982), "reciprocal" (Noblit, 1993), "mutuality" (Chaskin & Rauner, 1995), and "ethic of relation" (Noddings, 1992) have been used by researchers to describe the interactive nature of caring relations. Gilligan (1982) describes the relational quality of interdependence. She writes that when interdependence exists between people, they are motivated to act responsively toward self and others, sustaining connectivity and an ethic of care.

Chaskin and Rauner (1995) discuss the reciprocal nature of caring in teacher-student relationships and the concern for mutuality and connection. They contend the most important influences in the social development of children are nurturance, empathy, and opportunities for mastery of tasks. Children deprived of such opportunities in the family may have a greater need to connect with a teacher, making teacher-student relationships all the more important. Through attempts at caring, responsive teachers recognize, understand, and respect their students and trust is established, creating caring interpersonal relationships in classrooms (Chaskin & Rauner, 1995). Teachers' values and beliefs for the dynamic of caring provide a psychological basis for caring behaviors.

Caring Behaviors

Caring behaviors are defined as the specific acts a teacher performs that may be considered to be caring. This includes behaviors that attend to affective and academic areas of learning, behaviors that follow patterns and consistency, and behaviors that emphasize responsibility, persistence, and sacrifice.

The first component of this dimension is a primary caring behavior in teachers: an ability to attend to academic, social, and emotional areas of students. McLaughlin (1991) found that caring teachers consider the academic needs of students by teaching them study skills, by challenging them to be better students, and by considering their interests and the relevance and challenge of the content matter. Likewise, Rogers (1994) mentions that one of the challenges of caring is meeting individual needs by designing the curriculum to excite and engage students and at the same time give them an opportunity to make choices. Beyond academics are the teacher's behaviors that attended to students' affective needs. Many teachers used affective skills to send the message, "I care about you, I like you, you are a worthy individual, and I understand and I want to help" (Thompkins & Thompkins-McGill, 1993, p. 68). Agne (1992) states that teachers send this message by exhibition of relational behaviors such as sharing information about themselves with students, establishing friendships, learning about students, and listening willingly, even to complaints. Caring includes behaviors like helping students with schoolwork without being demeaning, acting fair and unintimidatingly, exhibiting an eagerness to learn from students, showing interest in individuals, trying to get to know students outside of class time, making students feel good about themselves, and attributing the best possible motives to student actions (McLaughlin, 1991; Noblit et al., 1995; Rogers, 1994).

A second aspect of caring behaviors is a consistent behavioral pattern of caring acts. Although these may be isolated individual instances or many small, incremental acts of kindness, many caring behaviors require consistent actions over time for full expression (Chaskin & Rauner, 1995). Noblit et al. (1995) write of cases where children told them that good teachers talked with them and that the talk became the "currency of caring" (p. 684). Rogers (1994) noted this talk may take the form of simple words of recognition, praise, encouragement, or advice, but the specific situation and student dictates its form. Examples of behaviors that are best expressed over time have been elucidated as getting to know students well, being a good listener (Agne, 1992), acting fair and unintimidatingly, making students feel good about themselves (McLaughlin, 1991), being a committed learner, having passion for a subject, and communicating enthusiasm and excitement (Smith, 1995). Similarly, unrelenting devotion to a struggling student or helping a student to become socially accepted (Noblit et al., 1995) requires commitment and continuity.

A personal value of responsibility, persistence, and sacrifice is the last component of the dimension of caring behaviors. Caring is a constant willingness to respond when the situation demands. In her book *In a Different Voice*, Carol Gilligan (1982) suggests caring people are those who recognize they have a moral imperative to discern the real and recognizable trouble of this world and respond by meeting others' needs. Jones and Jones (1995) state that effective teachers recognize the influence they have on students by meeting their needs, and they use this influence positively. Noddings (1984) emphasizes that caring must be more than an attitude and result in responsive action. Agne (1992) believes caring teachers want to know their students well, which requires persistence and sacrifice. Sacrifice can be expressed in several ways: willingness on the part of teachers to expose a part of themselves (Smith, 1995), being real and spending time with students outside of class time (McLaughlin, 1991), and openly taking responsibility for human error or persisting with a difficult student (Noblit et al., 1995).

The actions of a teacher that may be considered caring do not exclude attention to academics but include behaviors in affective areas, behaviors with patterns and consistency, and activity that emphasizes responsibility, persistence, and sacrifice.

Construction of a Caring Environment

The construction of a caring environment is the third dimension in the proposed model of caring. In establishing a caring classroom community, a teacher must consider the physical and social-emotional atmosphere of the room's environment and how this is developed. The three components in this dimension of the model are the construction of a safe and orderly environment, the creation of a climate of mutual trust, honesty, and respect, and an emphasis on psychological protection and care in interpersonal interactions.

The creation of a safe and orderly environment is established through the development of a setting that is predictable. There are several features of a predictable classroom. Again, the acts of being consistently supportive over time (Noblit et al., 1995) and the creation of routines and rituals are emphasized. Noblit et al. (1995) believe classroom rituals help students and teachers understand the significance of everyday activities. Teachers and students in caring classrooms work together in constructing rituals to observe and celebrate relationships and actions that support moral responsibility, continuity, and constancy (p. 684). Rituals may also promote continuity in the curriculum and instruction and develop shared responsibilities for work in schools. Routines and rituals are primary ingredients in orderly environments, as are a continuity of the actions of people involved in the classroom and delivery of curriculum.

Another method of establishing a caring environment is through activities that promote collective responsibility and connectedness. Several researchers and authors (Byrd, Lundeberg, Hoffland, Couillard, & Lee, 1996; Lewis, Schaps, & Watson, 1995; Mecca, 1996; Noblit, 1993) write about caring environments as communities in which there is a connectedness or family-like environment and shared responsibility. Teacher actions may include involvement of the class as a collective entity (Noblit, 1993), involving students in decision making and in ensuring that students know one another and share a sense of purpose (Lewis et al., 1995). In examining practices of exemplary inner-city teachers, Byrd et al. (1996) noted that teachers described as caring were those who approached students as parental figures rather than in authoritarian roles.

The second concept in establishing a caring environment is developing a school and classroom climate of mutual trust, honesty, and respect. This climate fosters the belief that everyone should care about others' learning and show respect for one another (Mecca, 1996). In such classrooms, students often helped to shape the rules they would live by and discussed how they want to treat one another. The teacher did not impose values of fairness, kindness, and responsibility. Operating principles were selected and agreed upon collectively by the students. Students helped make decisions and valued and experienced connection with one another (Lewis et al., 1995).

Individual differences are respected and valued in a caring environment. There is open acknowledgment and discussion of individual differences and affirmation of diversity in caring environments. Classrooms that accept and are supportive of minority students and those where students with special needs feel part of the class help make those individuals' experiences safe and nurturing (Byrd et al., 1996; Noblit, 1993). Louis, Schaps, and Watson (1996) found a climate in which all students get to know and support one another's strengths and interests to be caring environments. Moreover, McLaughlin (1995) concluded from his study on caring in pre-service teachers that ethical caring requires some control by teachers over the social environment so certain individuals do not dominate classroom interactions.

Last, an emphasis on psychological protection and care in institutional interactions is critical to the creation of a caring environment. Bulach (1996) surveyed graduate students in education to determine the behaviors used to let students know they cared. They identified five categories: the ability to reduce anxiety, the willingness to listen, the rewarding of appropriate behavior, being a friend to students, and the appropriate use of positive and negative criticism. Bulach concluded that a caring learning community exists if teachers and administrators demonstrate actions in these five categories. Additionally, Thompkins and Thompkin-McGill (1993) state that the comfort and security of students can be met by providing nurturing responses to biological needs. Teachers provide a caring environment when they meet psychological, and in some cases, biological needs in sensitive ways. Students appreciate teachers who consistently provide psychological messages of concern, affection, and security.

Modeling and Facilitating Caring in Others

The development of caring in students is the fourth dimension in the model of caring. This dimension of the model is deeply embedded in teaching and can be defined as the processes where teachers communicate to students through actions that show how to care. Three significant attributes in teachers may facilitate the development of caring youth: the modeling of caring thoughts and behaviors, the valuing of expressions of differing moral thoughts and behaviors, and respecting individual differences.

Modeling caring is a significant behavior in the facilitation of the development of caring children. Noddings (1984, 1992, 1995a) argues that care should be a major purpose in responsible education. Not only should teachers develop caring relationships with students, but through these relationships, show children how to care by modeling. Agne (1992) also believes that caring must be demonstrated, not discussed. By example, teachers model such things as the desire to learn and understand and a constant desire for growth in all areas of knowledge. Caring teachers begin with sharing who they are, with the hope students will, in time, do the same.

The second area to foster caring in students is the creation of moral thoughts and behavior. Noblit and Rogers (1992) state that schools should be places where students construct moral lives. Furthermore, these researchers believe teachers should make caring an explicit value in their classrooms through helping and talking to students in ways they value. Lewis et al. (1995) found caring teachers helped students develop values by allowing them to collectively choose how they want to treat one another and to develop rules they will live by. Values such as fairness, kindness, and responsibility became living principles in the classroom. Noddings (1984) asserts the role of educators is to "encourage the actual growth of relational virtues and to establish learning conditions that permit people to contribute to their relational growth" (p. 237). Attitudes are shaped through experiences, so teachers should provide opportunities for students to practice caring. By providing a classroom dedicated to caring, teachers encourage students to support one another and interact in high-quality ways. The quality of interaction is as important as academic outcomes. The overall goal should be to produce caring, competent people. Additionally, Chaskin and Rauner (1995) and Wolfgramm (1995) express the need for children to see caring modeled and taught as a way to approach self, others, and society, so caring can be internalized as a value.

The last component in this dimension is the demonstration of respect for differences in each individual. In the study by Lewis et al. (1996), caring teachers were found to affirm diversity by making individual differences and similarities a part of the curriculum. Students were taught to get to know one another's strengths and interests. Additionally, Noblit (1993) concluded that caring teachers readily recognized that children with special education needs should become as connected to the class as children without disabilities. Concern for special children was modeled by commitment to the student, rather than by mandates, and demonstrated by the teachers' by searching for ways to ensure the students in special education participate and are included in multiple aspects of the class (Noblit et al., 1995). Caring teachers were also found to affirm diversity by making individual differences and similarities a part of the curriculum. Students were taught to get to know one another's strengths and interests (Lewis et al., 1996).

LIMITATIONS OF THE MODEL

The proposed model of caring in teacher education is intended as an entrée for a discussion of caring in teacher education programs. The present model is a linear and positivist explanation of an attribute that may be defined and described through differing philosophical traditions. A deficit of this style of model is that it may not adequately define the gestalt of caring. Caring may be further explicated by addressing the social construction and energetic interrelational aspects of the attribute. Additionally, the cognitive processes, the related emotional states, and the complex behaviors of caring and actions cannot be thoroughly explained linguistically within the scope of this chapter. The attribute of care and the related actions associated with caring in teacher education are in need of further investigation, utilizing a broad spectrum of inquiry techniques. However, the pragmatic benefit of this model is that it may prove useful as a catalyst for developing better pedagogical tools to use in teacher education.

IMPLICATIONS FOR TEACHER EDUCATION

Caring must be valued, taught, and explicitly modeled in teacher preparation programs as a utilitarian matter for school reform and success. Many teacher educators believe the best way to teach is to model. It has been said that novice teachers will emulate behaviors that they have experienced in their relationships with their previous teachers, college instructors, supervisors, and colleagues. If true, the demonstration of interpersonal skills by teacher educators who demonstrate such values and model those behaviors will impact future teachers. University and college students are influenced by the styles of instruction and choices that teacher educators make in their professional lives. The improvement in preservice teacher education to better provide knowledge and action in a wide variety of interpersonal skills, as well as methodological, technical, and instructional skills, will lead to better ethical decision-making processes to accommodate a truly heterogeneous society.

The study of caring should have particular meaning to educators. At its foundation, education has an implied ethic to recognize the unique abilities of all children, including those who are different from the norm. Addressing education solely as achievement by the technical and behavioral measures of academic subject areas is an insufficient aspect of school reform. Society, including teacher educators, should not preclude or minimize the reality or importance of education for purposes other than academic or vocational preparation.

The proposed model emphasizes the value of the individual and of relationships. Educating professionals to improve the quality of life in recognizing and solving philosophical, ethical, and moral dilemmas should have equal precedence with the technical and positivist rationalist goals predominant in educational systems. Balancing these aspects in teacher education programs may help future educators better envision an intertwining relationship between academic achievement and moral development in education.

In the study and research of teacher preparation, there is a need to develop techniques and methods of study for caring and its related constructs. Both qualitative and quantitative methodologies, and ideally mixed method designs, should be utilized. Beyond the current proposed model, there may be several constructs related to the attribute of caring: teacher beliefs about caring and the study of caring indicators and their relationship with achievement are examples.

An elucidated model of caring could potentially clarify the role of caring in education as it has in the field of nursing, where its long-term benefit is clearly recognized. Educators may then look beyond the short-term goal of academic achievement to the long-term outcome of producing productive, capable, and relational skilled individuals. Teacher educators must recognize the role of caring in education to the point that caring concepts are included as outcome goals in teacher preparation programs and pedagogy is developed.

CONCLUSION

There are several inferences that may relate to the current proposal. First, the literature includes many examples of values and behaviors considered caring by various scholars and researchers. Second, although many have written about caring behaviors, most scholars agree caring is more than an isolated repertoire or activity. It is an ethic and dynamic in relationships that considers both the caregiver and the one receiving the care. Attributes such as connectedness, community, and collectivity are used to describe the social and emotional relationships that are present in caring classrooms. Last, there appears to be a quiet but persistent call for caring to become an integral part of teacher education. More attention to research in caring and pedagogy for caring must be part of the current efforts to improve education as a whole, and special education in particular.

REFERENCES

Agne, K. J. (1992). Caring: The expert teacher's edge. *Educational Horizons, 70*(3), 120–124.

Buber, M. (1965). Education. In M. Buber (Ed.), *Between man and man* (pp. 83–103). New York: Macmillan.

Bulach, C. (1996, October). *Behaviors that create a caring learning community.* Paper presented at the annual meeting of the Southern Regional Council on Education

Administration, Savannah, GA. (ERIC Document Reproduction Service No. ED 401 641)

Byrd, J., Lundeberg, M., Hoffland, S., Couillard, E., & Lee, M. (1996). Caring, cognition, and cultural pluralism: Case studies of urban teachers [online]. *Urban Education.* Retrieved www.bart.prod.oclc.org:3050/fetc...tml/fs_fulltext.htm%22:/fstxt47.htm

Chaskin, R. J., & Rauner D. M. (1995). Toward a field of caring: An epilogue. *Phi Delta Kappan, 76,* 718–719.

DeFord, M. S. (1996). *A comprehensive literature review in valuing the concept of caring in middle and secondary level schools.* Unpublished master's exit project. Indiana University, South Bend, IN. (ERIC Document Reproduction Service No. ED 404 041)

Ezzo, G., & Ezzo, A. M. (1993). *Growing kids God's way.* Chatsworth, CA: Growing Families International.

Gilligan, C. (1982). *In a different voice: Psychological theory and women's development.* Cambridge: Harvard University Press.

Grossman, H. (1995). *Special education in a diverse society.* Boston: Allyn & Bacon.

Jones, V. F., & Jones, L. S. (1995). *Comprehensive classroom management: Creating positive learning environments for all students* (4th ed.). Needham Heights, MA: Allyn & Bacon.

Katzenmeyer, W. (1992). *Inventing the schools of tomorrow.* Tampa, FL: University of South Florida.

Lewis, C., Schaps, E., & Watson, M. (1995). Beyond the pendulum: Creating challenging and caring schools. *Phi Delta Kappan, 76*(9), 547–554.

Lewis, C., Schaps, E., & Watson, M. (1996). The caring classroom's academic edge. *Educational Leadership, 54,* 16–21.

Mayeroff, M. (1971). *On caring.* New York: Harper & Row.

McLaughlin, H. J. (1991). Reconciling care and control: Authority in classroom relationships. *Journal of Teacher Education, 42,* 182–195.

McLaughlin, H. J. (1995). Wanting to care and hoping to control: The exploration of student teachers' relationships with students. In A. R. Prillaman, D. J. Eaker, & D. M. Kendrick (Eds.), *The tapestry of caring: Education as nurturance* (pp. 109–150). Norwood, NJ: Ablex.

McMillen, M. M., Kaufman, P., & Klein, S. (1997). *Dropout rates in the United States: 1995.* Washington, DC: U.S. Government Printing Office.

Mecca, M. E. (1996). Classrooms where children learn to care. *Childhood Education, 72,* 72–74.

Noblit, G. W. (1993). Power and caring. *American Educational Research Journal, 30,* 23–38.

Noblit, G. W., & Rogers, D. W. (1992, February). *Creating caring in schools.* Unpublished paper prepared for the Lilly Endowment Research Grants Program on Youth and Caring Conference in Key Biscayne, FL.

Noblit, G. W., Rogers, D. L., & McCadden, B. M. (1995). In the meantime: The possibilities of caring. *Phi Delta Kappan, 76,* 680–685.

Noddings, N. (1984). *Caring: A feminine approach to ethics and moral education.* Berkeley, CA: University of California Press.

Noddings, N. (1992). *The challenge to care in schools: An alternative approach to education.* New York: Teachers College Press.

Noddings, N. (1995a). A morally defensible mission for schools in the twenty-first century. *Phi Delta Kappan, 76,* 365–368.

Noddings, N. (1995b). Teaching themes of care. *Phi Delta Kappan, 76,* 675–679.

Rogers, D. L. (1994). Conceptions of caring in a fourth-grade classroom. In A. R. Prillaman, D. J. Eaker, & D. M. Kendrick (Eds.), *The tapestry of caring: Education as nurturance* (pp. 33–47). Norwood, NJ: Ablex.

Smith, B. (1995). That's no techno-fix. *Phi Delta Kappan, 76,* 659.

Tompkins, J. R., & Tompkins-McGill, P. L. (1993). *Surviving in schools in the 1990's: Strategic management of school environments.* Lanham, MD: University Press of America.

Wolfgramm, H. F. (1995). Needed: An ethic of caring in our schools. *Education, 115,* 516–521.

4

Dispositions and Multicultural Education

Kwadwo Okrah and Meryl Domina

The world is undergoing constant and rapid change that is unprecedented in human history. Most areas of the United States have had a recent influx of people of different cultures (Pipher, 2002). Most of the manufactured goods and food sold in the United States were produced in other countries of the world. The United States participates in a global economy, and this affects the daily lives of people living in each of the 50 states. This diversity affects teachers in all regions of the United States; it also affects workers in business, government, and the private sector. It will affect our students as they graduate and seek employment. The world of education needs to reflect these changes. Schooling must be equally accessible to all. Every student needs to know how to work with members of other cultures.

Multicultural education seeks to provide an equitable education for all students, regardless of their background or culture, and to provide all students with the tools necessary for taking on a role in this global society. James A. Banks (2002), one of the leaders of the multicultural education reform movement, explained:

> Multicultural education assumes that race, ethnicity, culture, and social class are salient parts of U.S. society. It also assumes that ethnic and cultural diversity enriches the nation and increases the ways in which its citizens can perceive and solve personal and public problems. This diversity also enriches a society by providing all citizens with more opportunities to experience other cultures and thus to become more fulfilled as human beings. When individuals are able to participate in a variety of ethnic cultures, they are more able to benefit from the total human experience. (p. 9)

There are educational theorists who would like to see the power imbalance between the rich and poor and between whites and peoples of color eliminated (Giroux & McLaren, 1989), thereby creating a socially just world. There is certainly overlap between those concerned about multicultural education and social justice; however, multicultural education will not topple the powerful or disrupt the social fabric of U.S. life. Rather, multicultural educational dispositions and curriculum will allow all students to participate to their full abilities in the educational and economic opportunities our country offers. A multicultural education achieves this in three ways. It sees that every student receives equitable schooling. It provides students with the attitudes, behaviors, skills, and knowledge for understanding and interacting with cultural and ethnic differences. It encourages an acceptance and appreciation of the richness of both their own and other cultures. Hopefully, this will go far in eliminating the limitations and hurt caused by prejudice and negative stereotypes.

The purpose of this chapter is to discuss the dispositions that teachers need to provide a multicultural education and to achieve the goals of INTASC Principles 2, 3, 6, 9, and 10 (see Appendix B). These dispositions include caring, tolerance, acceptance, empathy, adaptability, and dedication. There are numerous reasons why these particular dispositions are needed to provide multicultural education. First, recent research has reinforced the ideas that positive relationships are mandatory for learning and that the whole person needs to be addressed in the classroom. These relationships are dependent on the type of behaviors and attitudes these dispositions foster. Second, it is important to balance the cognitive domain, which includes knowledge, and the affective domain, which includes personal values. This is important in order to achieve a more ethical society.

The goals of multicultural education are discussed early in this chapter along with the true range of diversity that is found in our students. Universal U.S. values are briefly discussed, with examples of the different manifestations these values receive in specific cultures. This is followed by a brief history of ethnic and cultural differences in the United States. The role of culture in the achievement gap in test scores and how multicultural dispositions can address this problem are then discussed. Guidelines are offered for language, materials, and instructional strategies as well as for teacher dispositions that promote learning in all students. Suggestions are given to teachers concerning how they can learn more about the cultures of the children they serve.

Teachers' dispositions make a tremendous impact on students and their achievement. Students must feel they are full members of their classrooms in order to receive the full benefits of the education they are offered. Students remember how teachers treated them and how much they liked or disliked their teachers long after they have forgotten the specifics of the subjects they were taught.

MULTICULTURAL EDUCATION HAS TWO GOALS

Multicultural education has two goals. The implementation of each depends heavily upon the teacher's dispositions and attitudes. Multicultural education addresses knowledge and issues that apply directly to INTASC Principle 2—Development, Principle 3—Diversity, Principle 6—Communication, Principle 9—Professionalism, and Principle 10—Community. Multicultural education also affects the other principles. Teachers become more effective in their instruction, classroom management, and assessment when they are familiar with the cultures and individual differences of the students they teach.

Multicultural education is a reform movement that is concerned with providing an equitable education for all students to promote student learning (Nieto, 1999). This includes both having teachers accept, respect, and encourage achievement in all their students, and incorporating information into classroom curricula about the many cultures that have contributed to U.S. society (Banks, 2002). Banks and Banks (2001) have stated multicultural education is a field of study designed to increase educational equity for all students. Multicultural education incorporates purposes, concepts, principles, theories, and paradigms from the fields of history, the social and behavioral sciences, and particularly from ethnic studies and women's studies. The primary goal of multicultural education is to increase educational equality for both gender groups, for students from diverse ethnic, cultural, and language groups, and for exceptional students (Banks & Banks, 2001; Gay, 2000; Grant & Sleeter, 1998). Multicultural education in classrooms accepts that there are differences that are the result of race, culture, ethnicity, gender, religion, socioeconomic class, sexual orientation, mental ability, and physical ability. These differences need to be respected and addressed but must not be the rational for lowering expectations or limiting opportunities.

A major assumption of multicultural education (Banks, 2001; Nettles & Perna, 1997) is that the cultural and language characteristics of some groups of students are more consistent with the school's culture, norms, and expectations than the cultural and language characteristics of other groups of students. Students whose cultures are more consistent with the school culture have an easier time in school and greater opportunities for academic success than students whose cultures are in conflict with the school culture. An example of this is that low-income African American males tend to have more problems in school than middle-class Anglo American males (Meier, 2002; Wang & Kovach, 1996).

The second goal of multicultural education is to help all students, including middle-class white students, develop the knowledge, skills, and attitudes they need to survive and function effectively in a culturally diverse society (Banks, 2002). As more groups of people are taught together in the same classes, it is important that all students feel comfortable working with such diverse classmates as recent immigrants and children with special needs. As teachers, we must assume the responsibility of educating students in the micro-world of the school so they will be able to function effectively and appropriately in an increasingly global U.S. society. Today's students will soon be adults seeking employment. Often, this will involve the need to demonstrate that they can work well with supervisors, coworkers, and clients who represent diverse backgrounds.

Teachers, both individually and as a large profession, must serve as guides, models, and counselors for our students. Teachers must become active participants in the diverse societies they represent. Students will achieve both goals of multicultural education through teachers who model and teach the dispositions of caring, dedication, tolerance, acceptance, empathy, and adaptability.

When teachers make a serious mistake, it passes on to other people at a geometric rate. Unlike the physician who can bury a serious mistake or the newspaper editor who can retract it, recipients of teachers' mistakes grow up, marry, and have children who carry on the mistaken behavior (Henderson & Bibens, 1970). No other profession is in such a critical position. It is a well-known fact that teacher attitudes have the most significant impact on pupil achievement, including intelligence test scores, and can determine the failure or success of their students (Henderson & Bibens, 1970). In the past, teachers' attitudes have played a role in perpetuating negative stereotypes and prejudiced behavior. Now, teachers can encourage acceptance for people of all abilities and cultures (Zeichner, 1996).

Diversity

Diversity begins with the very characteristics that make individuals different from one another: temperaments (Keirsey & Bates, 1984); artistic, cognitive, and physical abilities (Armstrong, 1994; Gardner, 1993), interests that affect attitudes and abilities; and personal challenges and disabilities (Osman, 1982). Diversity continues with people's family and community experiences (Payne, 1998), background knowledge gained through their interests and experiences, and their ways of looking at the world. Differences in family and community stem from the individual members; from heritage and traditions; from economic states; from public acceptance of one's racial, religious, or ethnic group; and from the level of ethnic and religious identity one has internalized. Diversity in each of these areas is constantly increasing in our society (Pipher, 2002).

Teachers need to be dedicated to their students, their profession, and to their subject field. They need to care deeply about their students. This should be demonstrated by taking the time to understand the cultures their students represent. Teachers need to show acceptance of their students' differences in abilities and skills as well as cultural capital and cultural differences (Banks, 2000; Ladson-Billings, 1994; Smith, 1999). Teachers do this by showing empathy toward their students who need individual attention and by being curious about the conditions behind their students' needs. They act upon these dispositions by developing adaptability to meet their students' differing classroom needs.

Teaching Whole Individuals

Although it was once thought that the teacher's affect was unimportant in the learning process, researchers are finding that relationships are important to learning (Perry, 2002; Sylwester, 2003) and to self-discipline (Cothran & Ennis, 2000; De La Rosa, 1998; Noddings, 2002; Phillips, 2001). Research in biology, psychology, and education has shown that humans comprise a social species that learns through common activity with other people, including parents, other relatives, teachers, and peers (Gurian, Henley, & Trueman, 2001). Humans learn and behave in order to please the people who care about them—their families and teachers. Students know the characteristics they want in their teachers—the characteristics that encourage them to behave and do their best work. They want teachers (Henderson & Bibens, 1970) who are kind, helpful, fair, and are willing to listen and have fun with them. In contrast, students dislike teachers they perceive as mean, cross, rude, and unfair. When a group of contemporary high school students were asked what advice they had for teachers (Cushman, 2003), they responded that teachers must like their students, be trustworthy, and treat students as smart and capable of challenging work. In addition, the high school students said that teachers should show that they like and care about the material they teach.

Dispositions refer to attitudes, behaviors, or inborn traits that are characteristic of one's relationship with other individuals. Dispositions that teachers need to provide a multicultural education include dedication, caring, tolerance, acceptance, empathy, and adaptability. As the principal aim of education is to develop the whole individual, this should include the cognitive, psychomotor, and affective domains—the mind, the body, and the heart respectively. The dispositions teachers bring to their relationships with students are especially important, as too often curricula place undue emphasis on the cognitive and the psychomotor aspects at the expense of the affective domain (Dewey & Dewey, 1915; Noddings, 1992). The affective domain needs equal attention, as it comprises the emotional, spiritual, moral, attitudinal, and character development of the individual. The fact that these aspects of students' lives have been ignored for too long is filling our society with intellectual giants who are ethical dwarfs. We see examples of the problems this causes on our nightly news broadcasts in accounts of burglary, rape, murder, corporate misconduct, embezzlement, and stock fraud. Teachers who model dedication, caring, tolerance, acceptance, empathy, and adaptability touch students' affective domains and provide the first steps back to a more comfortable—and moral—society.

VALUES

Educators need to inculcate in students attitudes that contribute to the universal good. Without imposing any religious denomination on our students, we need to assist them in gaining virtues. Tolerance, acceptance, care, understanding, love, cooperation, generosity, and, above all, sympathy and empathy are values that are accepted by all religions. Teachers have the professional obligation to model these virtues in the classroom and to tailor their instructional objectives to advance these values. Recognition of the place these values hold in cultures and in all people's lives is a basic part of multicultural education. Attention must always be given to the different roles these values have in the different cultures and to the diverse norms and customs that surround these values. One of the strengths of a multicultural curriculum is that it can provide ample opportunities for discussing values through reading the stories or the history of any culture, by reading the biographies of people important in each field of study, and through discussion of news stories that connect to the subject being studied (Ladson-Billings, 1994).

Variations on Similar Values

People from all cultures share important U.S. values such as concern for one's family, participation in community life, responsibility, and respect for each person (Pipher, 2002). But how these values are acted upon in daily life depends on one's culture (Rogoff, 2003). The family provides an excellent example. Some European and European-descended American cultures focus on individualism centered around the nuclear family. The stereotypical picture of the nuclear U.S. family consists of a working father, a stay-at-home mother, and two or three sons or daughters. Relatives constituting the extended family consist of grandparents, aunts and uncles, and cousins; however, contact with many of these relatives is not regular. Many of the other world cultures practice collectivism, which centers on interdependence within an extended family. In many Asian American, African American, and Latino American families the immediate family consists of more people, and exact descriptive relationships and roles are defined differently. Cousins are considered brothers and sisters. In some groups, all individuals of the parents' age are considered to be uncles and aunts. In African societies, paternal uncles are considered to be fathers. Teachers need to become familiar with and accepting of these and other differences in families and to share this knowledge with their students.

This knowledge is important for teachers since many schoolbooks and many of our instructional practices conflict with this difference in values. Many textbooks, such as basal readers, assume the nuclear family is the norm, even though this is changing rapidly. Today there are many single-parent and blended families (Rice & Dolgin, 2002). Most classrooms promote individual, competitive learning, even though this contradicts the upbringing many children have at home and contributes to the achievement gap (Ladson-Billings, 1994; Nieto, 1999). This type of information about other cultures can be learned through interaction with people, by reading histories, biographies, and novels, and by viewing films produced by the people one wishes to study (Diaz, Massialas, & Xanthopolous, 1999).

A BRIEF HISTORY OF CULTURE IN THE UNITED STATES

During the first half of the 20th century, there was the impression that the United States was a melting pot and that each group of newcomers gave up their original culture for a common "American culture" (Hilliard, 2001). Every immigrant group, including those who did not come voluntarily, did assimilate many of the characteristics of the U.S. culture. This was often accomplished through the school system (Kliebard, 1987). However, many of these groups still retained much of their cultural inheritance. Large metropolitan areas had enclaves or neighborhoods that consisted of one, or a few, groups of people. For example, Chicago had separate Polish, Greek, Italian, Jewish, Lithuanian, African American, and Chinese neighborhoods (Culter, 1995). The local grocery stores carried ethnic foods, the restaurants catered to different tastes, there were community centers that taught ethnic music and dance, and there were subtle differences in the churches even within the same denomination.

These varied neighborhoods thrived. However, because they contradicted the myth of one U.S. culture, they were not recognized as having a significant role in society. This changed after the Civil Rights movement. Once recognition was given to African American cultures, it became more acceptable to recognize and celebrate all the other ethnic cultures that contributed to our U.S. culture (Zinn, 1980). New groups of immigrants are continually enriching our nation (Pipher, 2002). Today, just a few of these many groups include the Bosnians and Croatians from Europe; Mexicans, Nicaraguans, and Chileans from the Americas; the Eritreans from Africa; and Koreans, Pakistani, and Cambodians from Asia. Each of these groups shares in the democratic traditions and sense of personal responsibility that are the hallmark of U.S. values while maintaining positive aspects of their own cultures (Pipher, 2002).

Another critical point is that most groups of Americans faced strong prejudice when they first arrived here, and some groups of Americans still face that prejudice (Zinn, 1980). There was widespread discrimination against Irish, Ukrainian, Czech, Slovak, Serbian, Croatian, Lithuanian, Hungarian, Polish, and Jewish people who came to the United States because of harsh economic and political conditions in their native lands. In spite of the hardships and difficulties they faced, many immigrants thrived here. Most groups were accepted in time, and within a few generations, memories faded of the difficulties their relatives had faced when they first arrived.

This acceptance of diverse cultures was not universal. Native Americans lived all over the land that now comprises the United States before the rest of our ancestors arrived here. They did not choose the difficulties that befell them or the negative stereotypes that still cause them problems today. Chinese, Japanese, and Filipinos were welcomed as laborers when their work was needed in the 19th and 20th centuries to lay the tracks for railroads and to work in factories (Zinn, 1980); however, they were not welcomed as equal members of U.S. society. Although most members of these cultures have joined the middle class, today they are still considered "different" and are labeled "people of color."

African Americans did not come to the United States by choice. Millions of African people were captured by merchants with superior weapons and brought as prisoners to be slaves. Yet, they made important contributions as their labor brought prosperity to the Southern states, their inventions offered improvements to all, and many aspects of their African cultures permeated U.S. life (Asante, 1995; Zinn, 1980). When the slaves were freed after the Civil War, the economic conditions in the Southern states were that of destitution. Blacks were not welcomed as equals and little schooling was provided. In spite of acute discrimination, Blacks continued to work and make contributions to U.S. life. When government schools were established in the 1800s Blacks were not allowed to enroll with White people. Separate, inferior schools were established (Watkins, 2001), with a curriculum that focused on citizenship, appropriate social practices, and vocational education (Kliebard, 1987). For a century after the Civil War, Blacks worked to improve their economic conditions, to educate themselves, and to participate in the democratic system. As conditions were not keeping up with those for Whites and Asian Americans, by the 1940s, Blacks were taking action to make changes (Lewis, 2001). The Civil Rights movement had a strong impact on U.S. politics, and attitudes and efforts were made to correct the problems slavery and prejudice caused (Teaching Tolerance, 1989). Conditions sufficiently improved but prejudice and discrimination were not eliminated. Although educational opportunities improved for many Black children, it has not been adequate. Many Black children still attend poor quality schools (Kozol, 1991; Ladson-Billings, 1994; Wang & Kovach, 1996) and do not receive instruction and curriculum materials that acknowledge their cultural and socioeconomic needs (Lewis, 1998; Meier, 2002).

THE SITUATION TODAY

Today's achievement gap between the standardized test scores of White students and students of color is caused by the effects of discrimination over generations of unequal schools and economic opportunities. Few people of color are in places of power in schools to be involved in policy making and to serve as role models. Many well-meaning teachers have unconscious low expectations for their students of color (Lewis, 2001). In recent years, there have been efforts in the Black community to improve schooling for their children. Researchers such as Gloria Ladson-Billings (1994), Lisa Delpit (1995), Phillip Murrell (2002), and Carol Lee (2001) have many ideas on how teachers can best teach Black students. Other researchers have written on Native American and Latino children. Culturally relevant teaching (Ladson-Billings, 1994) suggests that teachers use cultural referents to impart knowledge, skills, and attitudes in order to help students develop in ways that enhance their intellectual, emotional, and social abilities and foster a strong sense of their personal and cultural identity. To achieve this, teachers should do the following:

- Legitimize students' real-life experience;
- Use culturally relevant literature and biographies;
- Draw on community examples and problem solving in all subject areas;
- Encourage students toward excellence with critical thinking and college-bound literacy;
- Use cooperative learning and other interactive instructional techniques;
- Provide instructional scaffolding;
- Allow students to view knowledge critically;
- Accept only high performance and acknowledge students' efforts; and
- Bring in guest speakers from the students' community. (Ladson-Billings, 1994)

MULTICULTURAL DISPOSITIONS

The most important of the concerns and issues brought up by multicultural educators is the necessity of assuring all students that their teachers care about, trust, and believe in them. When teachers work with students from a

culture that differs from theirs, they need to become bicultural (Klug & Whitfield, 2003). This allows teachers to share knowledge of how education has
helped this culture's people historically and has helped individual members
from their students' communities. Some of the specific information that
teachers need to learn includes the culture's value of and experience with
education, expectations of teachers, how much parents can participate in
helping with schooling, views of history, and the alignment between the cultural values of the home and of the school (Meier, 2002). A diverse and pluralistic U.S. culture must be honest in recognizing where discrimination still
exists, as this still limits opportunities. Honoring the dispositions of dedication, tolerance, caring, acceptance, empathy, and adaptability are important
steps in eliminating discrimination.

Cultural differences show up in various ways. An example comes from a
master's level class on adolescent development and behavior. Students were
assigned a project to learn about a culture different from their own. One student, a learning disability resource teacher in a high school, indicated she
wanted to learn more about the Cambodian culture. She had a student who
always responded enthusiastically to her help when he was scheduled time
in the resource room. However, the IEP for his junior year indicated that he
was to initiate requests for help rather than be regularly scheduled to receive
her help. He did not request any help, and he began to fail his courses.
Through working on her cultural project she learned that according to Cambodian culture, children were not to bother adults or to directly request their
attention. When she asked her student about this he admitted that was why
he never requested help. She immediately called a new IEP conference and
was able to change his IEP to allow her to offer help on a regular basis. When
educators understand the cultural reasoning and influences behind students'
and their parents' actions they are better able to serve their students.

MULTICULTURAL ISSUES IN THE CLASSROOM

Language and Terms

When teachers project dedication, caring, acceptance, and empathy they
show recognition and respect for their students' affective domain. Teachers
with these dispositions are careful in how they describe students, how they
talk with other individuals, how they refer to groups of people, and how
they joke with students. These communication practices are important because how teachers treat students can have two major effects on students.
The first effect is teachers' personal impact on students' self-esteem (Berlak
& Moyenda, 2001). The second effect is that teachers' words, actions, and attitudes can cause positive or negative stereotypes that students carry with

them. This can influence how these students act toward others (Ginott, 1972). To achieve equity in human society in general we need to encourage and engage in self-identification, critical thinking, and acceptance of all forms of diversity. Thus, we need to work toward a general model that will include, tolerate, and accept all students in our microworld, the school. In the classroom, teachers can help children arouse their interest in and develop their sense of empathy for other groups by only using positive names, referents, and labels. When children of one group come to know and love the stories, history, systems, and nomenclatures of others, they have made an important beginning toward multicultural understanding and appreciation (Diaz et al., 1999).

Our world is socially constructed (Henslin, 1991), and humans learn through their interactions, particularly through language and attitude. When students are negatively labeled or treated meanly, their imagination and aspirations are hurt and the possibilities for their personal growth are disabled to the degree that they accept the label (Berlak & Moyenda, 2001). Word meanings are arbitrarily assigned by common use over generations. This has allowed some people to dehumanize others through terminology that is deliberately consigned to debase these "others," their family members, and the events and objects of their culture (Hilliard, 2001). Jahn (1961) points out that prejudice causes people's thinking to interpret what they see and believe. When one expects their fellowmen to be fools, blockheads, or devils, one will find evidence to confirm their prejudices. Through vocabulary alone one can easily turn gods into idols, smiles to grimaces, votive images into fetishes, discussions into palavers. Concrete objects and factual events can be similarly distorted. Language can perpetuate bigotry and prejudice. Jahn further explained that it is prejudice that has caused people to believe that only a "European" can be highly cultivated, cosmopolitan, and enlightened, while those who are not "European" cannot be highly cultivated, cosmopolitan, or enlightened. This prejudiced thinking continues to imagine Africans as naked, carefree bush dwellers, happily illiterate, carving primitive sculptures. This view ignores the possibility that although Africans might be part of a pastoral tribe or a small village, they could also be from a modern, cosmopolitan city.

One may wonder why it is important to discuss the subjugation of a group other than one's own. A Ghanaian proverb provides the answer: "It is only the fool that convinces himself that what affects the other person does not have an impact on him." Since the time of slavery, Africa and many African ideas and artifacts have been viewed as inferior because only derogatory and disempowering terminologies have been used to describe them (Thairu, 1975). Education and life in the United States today are less than optimal because of the prejudice and discrimination faced by African Americans and other people of color (Nieto, 1999). Teachers are among those who can create the changes needed to live in a world without prejudice. The first step to help end the devaluation of powerless people is to eliminate linguistic misrepresentation.

Multicultural Guidelines

All cultures and all people need to be viewed through their own lenses rather than the cultural lenses of their victimizers (Smith, 1999). Recognition of each cultural group's self-identification is necessary to put into place the full multicultural and global education that is needed in our U.S. schools and society today. Dedicated, caring, and accepting teachers may ask how they can tell when statements or reading materials reflect bias, stereotypes, or inaccurate information and what they should look for. We should use the following multicultural guidelines.

1. "Stop words" are words that imply inferior status, ability, or skill. They are patronizing terms that arouse stereotypes and tend to embarrass or hurt members of the referred to group. "Stop words" include terms that treat people as objects (Oyate, 2003) and refer to a group of people as "not human." Examples of this include implying that a person is playing a role or is an animal. We need to substitute less value-laden words (Oyate, 2003). Table 4.1 gives examples of these "stop words" and more appropriate terms to substitute.
2. Language and pejorative terms that promote numbing and dehumanization need to be eliminated (Smith, 1999). Lifton (as cited in Markusen, 1991) has stated that psychic numbing is a powerful factor facilitating mistreatment toward other people. "It is probably impossible to kill another human being without numbing oneself toward the victim" (p. 356). Psychic numbing is to regard the victim as somehow less than human and, therefore, not capable of evoking empathy or moral restraint. In *Home From the War*, Lifton (1973) stated that "some dehumanizing terms [as "gook" or "slope" to depict Vietnamese people] are always necessary to the numbing of widespread killing—it is much easier to annihilate 'Huns' or 'Communists' or 'Imperialists' (or rebels, mutineers, dissidents) than it is men, or women or children" (p. 356). Teachers need to recognize when words cause one to label a group rather than to notice individuals. Substitute the ethnicity of the people or use neutral words to describe them.
3. In the political realm, it is easier to look down on citizens when we refer to their countries as "third world," "developing," "underdeveloped," or "fourth world, hopeless have-nots." Instead, teachers need to use each country's official name. Teachers can speak of Cuba and Haiti rather than the underdeveloped Caribbean world.

4. The assignment of colors to individuals can be dehumanizing and dis-empowering unless the victims self-identify themselves as such. The following examples are misnomers that have been negatively used in the United States: Negroes, Afro, colored, minorities, blue, black, yellow, red, white, Hispanics, Chicanos, Indians, and Natives. Individuals do not fit these colors or the identifications assigned to the different races. These terms are demeaning and unacceptable. Educators need to foster the development of a positive attitude toward all Americans by referring to citizens as Americans and by dropping all hyphenated identifiers, for example, African-Americans, Native-Americans, Asian-Americans. Some people do choose to use labels for themselves, but that is in a very specific context, so we need to be careful in general use.

5. Treating a group of people or a culture as an extinct species is not appropriate. To refer to the "vanishing Indian" implies that they do not exist as contemporary Americans (Oyate, 2003). Instead, teachers need to name specific groups such as the Navaho, the Seminole, or the Potowatomi and give information concerning their histories.

6. Materials that give the impression that Europeans or White Americans brought civilization to native people and improved their way of life should not be used (Oyate, 2003). Watch for terms such as conquest, civilization, ignorant, simple, advanced, customs, superstitions, and dialects. These tend to demean other cultures and imply the futility of their traditional ways. Again, teachers should use more specific words and refer to the way each group names itself and its practices.

Multicultural Classrooms and Teachers' Attitudes

In *Savage Inequalities*, Kozol (1991) asserted that poor children will continue to fail until we address their lack of motivation and the very real problems they face daily. We cannot meaningfully confront the problem of educational equality without confronting the problem of social and economic equality (Ladson-Billings, 1994; Tesconi & Hurwitz, 1974). In order for students to engage in their learning, they need to feel they are full members of their school community *and* full citizens of the United States. The significant contributions their ancestors gave to the world and the contributions their families and they can now make need to be recognized and addressed. Otherwise they will always feel they are not part of the school, their city, their state, or their country.

To build on children's innate motivation, it is imperative we use culturally relevant practices (Ladson-Billings, 1994) and establish a classroom atmosphere in which students' healthy emotional growth and development are supported as part of a natural process (Starko et al., 2003). Teachers should not be "color blind" and pretend that differences do not exist. Rather they

Table 4.1.   Words That Should Not Be Used

Stop Words	Substitute	Notes
Jungle	Rainforest	Only 5% of Africa is rainforest
Tribe	People, ethnic group, nation	We do not call the Welsh a British tribe, the Canadians a French tribe
Backward or primitive	Indigenous or traditional	These words are patronizing and are used to imply inferior status
Savage, native	African or Ghanaian, Tanzanian, Kenyan	These words are patronizing and are used to imply inferior status
Native costume	National dress	Incorrect use of the word costume
Pagan, fetish, heathen, ancestral worship, animism, polytheism	Traditional religion	These words are used to lessen the importance of other religious beliefs

must *recognize* and *accept* their students' cultures (Berlak & Moyenda, 2001; Ladson-Billings, 1994).

Even something as simple as praise must be examined carefully. Teachers must be cautioned to avoid giving judgmental praise (Faber & Mazlish, 1995). General global statements of correctness have the tendency of becoming associated with goodness. Students' ability to do schoolwork *correctly* is no guarantee that they are *good* people. If the teacher—consciously or unconsciously—connects the traits of correctness and goodness, some students may begin to take advantage of being "the best" students and may seek to exercise more liberties than are reasonably allowed. Conversely, students whose work does not measure up will arrive at the conclusion that they are "not good people" and, therefore, "bad" (Ginott, 1972). Descriptive praise, which acknowledges the effort put forth and exactly what was accomplished, allows all students to develop pride in themselves.

Teachers need to use the multicultural dispositions discussed earlier to ensure that children develop a healthy attitude that promotes emotional well-being (Ladson-Billings, 1994; Noddings, 1992). Teachers should be *sensitive* to students who are having problems and *curious* enough about the problems' source to probe for its causes: Are the problems due to conditions in the classroom or instruction? Do they arise from personal or family circumstances or from socioeconomic conditions of students' lives? Do the problems stem from cultural differences between home and school?

Are there other determining factors? Teachers should consider how information they learn about their students and their cultures can be useful in their teaching and interaction. In accepting the reasons behind the difficulties, teachers should be understanding, not to execute learning but to better facilitate learning. Teachers should be *flexible* and willing to adjust their plans to better serve the needs of their students. A flexible attitude toward the course curriculum, lesson outlines, examples, instructional strategies, seating arrangements, and wall decorations can go far toward meeting their students' needs and contributing to the success of all their students. Children have to feel *cared for* in order to feel enough motivation to make an effort. Teachers are reminded that the most outstanding qualification for teaching is *dedication*. Teachers must be dedicated to their subject, their students, and their profession. Why, other than dedication, would we continue to teach?

Instructional Planning and Strategies

In order to instill healthy attitudes in all students, teachers' instructional strategies should go beyond the lecture mode in both elementary and secondary schools. Experiential and reflective methods allow children to practice academic skills, to engage in critical thinking, and to reflect on real-life issues that are relevant (Dewey, 1938; Ladson-Billings, 1994). For experiential models teachers may consider using skits, simulations, role playing, newspapers, hands-on activities, authentic opportunities, speakers from the community, games, art, and the creation of class magazines and visuals such as posters and charts. Cooperative learning is an important instructional strategy that allows students to use and engage in discussion on what they are learning, to show caring and practice social skills with their classmates, to participate in democratic discussions, and to feel an integral part of a classroom learning community (Johnson, Johnson, & Holubec, 1988). Additional reflective instructional practices teachers can incorporate into their teaching include discovery learning, problem solving, inquiry, and jurisprudential methods (Banks, 2002).

Teachers need to encourage participation in class discussions by all students. Rather than ignore African American students because "they might have an 'attitude'" or girls because they might be shy, teachers purposely engage them in order to dispel stereotypes. Teachers must be careful not to direct math questions only to males or Asian students. Instead, they should develop strategies that distribute questions evenly, provide helpful scaffolding, and welcome personal opinion in order to motivate and set students at ease. They should include all students fairly, be caring, show tolerance, acceptance, and adaptability.

Teachers who wish to show the dispositions needed for multicultural education go beyond the classroom; they are concerned with all aspects of school-community relations. They make sure that the standardized tests and textbooks that are selected have minimal bias. They recognize that parents want to feel welcomed in their children's classrooms. Caring teachers encourage all school committees, including parent-teacher associations, to involve as many parents as possible. They must also find ways to involve all students in classroom decisions (Henderson & Bibens, 1970).

Another factor that contributes to building positive attitudes in the classroom concerns the discipline or management model used. Teacher behaviors that are conducive to student failure include being too strong an authoritarian, using intimidation or sarcasm, and demanding more regimentation than is necessary for organization and discipline. Another poor practice is showing little warmth or maintaining too great a distance between themselves, their students, and parents. Teachers who are too permissive, who are not consistent, who have low expectations of students, or who convey the attitude that they are not concerned about their students also contribute to student failures. On the other hand, teachers who provide democratic discipline with concern for the social and emotional climate in the classroom guide most of their students to success. They reflect on students who are not successful to determine if there are changes they can make to assist these students. Teachers should be genuine, have high expectations, and show sincere empathy for students from all backgrounds regardless of their skill and social ability (Cushman, 2003; Zeichner, 1996).

To achieve these dispositions teachers should strive for continual learning about their students. They need to talk to students. At the least, they can ask friendly questions of one or two students per period. They can ask parents questions about how they encourage learning and discourage misbehavior at home; they listen closely to *hear* parents' responses. Teachers should cultivate a deeper understanding about differences in temperaments (Keirsey & Bates, 1984), multiple intelligences (Armstrong, 1994), thinking styles (Sternberg, 1997), and disabling health conditions (Osman, 1982). Study the backgrounds, philosophies, and daily life of the different socioeconomic classes (Payne, 1998) and ethnic groups you teach (Klug & Whitfield, 2003; Nieto, 1999). This can be accomplished by reading histories, biographies, novels, or multicultural theory (Banks, 2002), by informal interviews with group members, and through movies and videos. There are many Internet websites and publishing companies that focus on multicultural education, social justice, and/or a specific ethnicity. The reference list for this chapter provides some resources that teachers can use to start their search. This studying models learning, shows concern for a democratic way of life, and allows teachers to apply appropriate culturally relevant illustrations.

CONCLUSION

Teachers are expected to work with an increasing number of diverse students. The number of cultures represented in the United States keeps growing yearly. Students who were often educated in different classrooms or schools in the past are now being included with their peers. There are five keys to using multicultural education with this diversity through a multicultural education. The first key is to use the appropriate dispositions: dedication, caring, tolerance, acceptance, empathy, and adaptability. Second, teachers should learn about the cultures and other factors that contribute to the diversity of the students being served. The third key is to apply culturally relevant pedagogy. The fourth key entails evaluating classroom materials based on the six multicultural guidelines and eliminating inappropriate classroom material. The fifth key for teaching a multicultural population is to rely on a variety of instructional strategies and a democratic classroom discipline style.

Although multicultural education may seem like an overwhelming task to teachers new to multicultural teaching and student teachers, in reality, it is not. Students are quite forgiving of mistakes when their teachers are making a true effort to understand and work with them. Students welcome the opportunity to share their own experiences, their needs, and their cultures with their teachers. When teachers are dedicated, caring, and show empathy, when they model tolerance, acceptance, and adaptability, students respond. Students return their teachers' caring and empathy. They accept and adapt to their teachers' efforts. Together, teachers and students become more tolerant and more dedicated to learning as they work to sustain a multicultural democracy.

REFERENCES

Armstrong, T. (1994). *Multiple intelligences in the classroom.* Alexandria, VA: ASCD.

Asante, M. K. (1995) *African-American history: A journey of liberation.* Saddle Brook, NJ: Peoples Publishing Group.

Banks, J. A. (1991). *Teaching strategies for ethnic studies* (5th ed.). Boston: Allyn & Bacon.

Banks, J. A. (2001). Multicultural education: Goals, possibilities, and challenges. In C. F. Diaz (Ed.), *Multicultural education in the 21st century* (pp. 11–22). New York: Longman.

Banks, J. A. (2002). *An introduction to multicultural education* (3rd ed.). Boston: Allyn & Bacon.

Banks, J. A., & Banks, C. A. M. (Eds.). (2001). *Multicultural education: Issues and perspectives* (4th ed.). New York: Wiley.

Berlak, A., & Moyenda, S. (2001). *Taking it personally: Racism in the classroom from kindergarten to college.* Philadelphia: Temple University Press.

Cothran, D. J., & Ennis, C.D. (2000). Building bridges to student engagement: communicating respect and care for students in urban high schools. *Journal of Research and Development in Education, 33*(2), 106–117.

Culter, I. (1995). *The Jews of Chicago: From shtetl to suburb.* Champaign: University of Illinois Press.

Cushman, K. (2003). *Fires in the bathroom: Advice for teachers from high school students.* New York: New Press.

De La Rosa, D. (1998, April–May). Why alternative education works. *High School Journal,* 268–272.

Delpit, L. (1995). *Other people's children: Cultural conflict in the classroom.* New York: New Press.

Dewey, J. (1938). *Experience and education.* New York: Simon & Schuster.

Dewey, J., & Dewey, E. (1915). *Schools of to-morrow.* New York: Dutton.

Diaz, F. C., Massialas, B. G., & Xanthopolous, J. A. (1999). *Global perspectives for educators.* Boston: Allyn & Bacon.

Faber, A., & Mazlish, A. (1995). *How to talk so children will learn.* New York: Simon & Schuster.

Gardner, H. (1993). *Multiple intelligences: The theory in practice: A reader.* New York: Basic Books.

Gay, G. (2000). *Culturally responsive teaching: Theory, research and practice.* New York: Teachers College Press.

Ginott, H. G. (1972). *Teacher and child: A book for parents and teachers.* New York: Macmillan.

Giroux, H. A., & McLaren, P. L. (Eds.). (1989). *Critical pedagogy, the state, and cultural struggle.* Albany: State University of New York Press.

Grant, C., & Sleeter, C. (1998). *Turning on learning: Five approaches for multicultural teaching plans for race, class, gender, and disability* (2nd ed.). New York: Macmillan.

Gurian, M., Henley, P., & Trueman, T. (2001). *Boys and girls learn differently!: A guide for teachers and parents.* San Francisco: Jossey-Bass.

Henderson, G., & Bibens, R. F. (1970). *Teachers should care: Social perspectives of teaching.*New York: Harper & Row.

Henslin, J. M. (1991). *Down to earth sociology: Introductory readings.* New York: Free Press.

Hilliard, Asa G., III. (2001). "Race," identity, hegemony, and education: What do we need to know now? In W. H. Watkins, J. H. Lewis, & V. Chou (Eds.), *Race and education: The roles of history and society in educating African American students* (pp. 7–34). Boston: Allyn & Bacon.

Jahn, J. (1961). *Muntu: The new African culture.* New York: Faber & Faber.

Johnson, D. W., Johnson, R. T., & Holubec, E. J. (1988). *Cooperation in the classroom* (rev. ed.). Edina, MN: Interaction Book.

Keirsey, D., & Bates, M. (1984). *Please understand me: Character and temperament types* (5th ed.). Del Mar, CA: Prometheus Nemesis.

Kliebard, H. (1987). *The struggle for the American curriculum: 1893–1958.* New York: Routledge & Kegan Paul.

Klug, B. J., & Whitfield, P. T. (2003). *Widening the circle: Culturally relevant pedagogy for American Indian children.* New York: Routledge.

Kozol, J. (1991). *Savage inequities: Children in America's schools.* New York: Harper-Trade.

Ladson-Billings, G. (1994). *The dreamkeepers: Successful teachers of African American children.* San Francisco: Jossey-Bass.

Lee, C. D. (2001). Comment: Unpacking culture, teaching, and learning: A response to "the power of pedagogy." In W. H. Watkins, J. H. Lewis, & V. Chou (Eds.), *Race and education: The roles of history and society in educating African American students* (pp. 89–99). Boston: Allyn & Bacon.

Lewis, J. (1998). *Walking with the wind: A memoir of the movement.* New York: Harcourt Trade.

Lewis, J. H. (2001). The search for new answers. In W. H. Watkins, J. H. Lewis, & V. Chou (Eds.), *Race and education: The roles of history and society in educating African American students* (pp. 1–6). Boston: Allyn & Bacon.

Lifton, R. (1973). *Home from the war: Vietnam veterans—neither victims nor executioners.* New York: Simon & Schuster.

Markusen, E. (1991). Genocide in Cambodia. In J. M. Henslin (Ed.), *Down to earth sociology: Introductory readings* (pp. 355–364). New York: Free Press.

Meier, D. (2002). *In schools we trust: Creating communities of learning in an era of testing and standardization.* Boston: Beacon.

Murrell, P. C., Jr. (2002). *African-centered pedagogy: Developing schools of achievement for African American children.* Albany: State University of New York Press.

Nettles, M. T., & Perna, L.W. (1997). *The African American educators data book.* Fairfax, VA: Patterson Research Institute.

Nieto, S. (1999). *The light in their eyes: Creating multicultural learning communities.* New York: Teachers College Press.

Noddings, N. (1992). *The challenge to care in schools.* New York: Teachers College Press.

Noddings, N. (2002). *Educating moral people: A caring alternative to character education.* New York: Teachers College Press.

Osman, B. (1982). *No one to play with: The social side of learning disabilities.* New York: Random House.

Oyate. (2003). Books to avoid. Retrieved August 1, 2003, from www.oyate.org

Payne, R. (1998). *A framework for understanding poverty* (rev. ed.). Highlands, TX: RFZ Publishing.

Perry, B. D. (2002, April). Childhood experience and the expression of genetic potential: What childhood neglect tells us about nature and nurture. *Brain and Mind: A transdisciplinary Journal of Neuroscience and Neurophilosophy, 3*(1), 70–100.

Phillips, V. (2001). *Empowering discipline: An approach that works with at-risk students.* Carmel Valley, CA: Personal Development Publishing.

Pipher, M. (2002). *The middle of everywhere: The world's refugees come to our town.* New York: Harcourt.

Rice, P. F., & Dolgin, K. G. (2002). *The adolescent: Development, relationships, and culture.* Boston: Allyn & Bacon.

Rogoff, B. (2003). *The cultural nature of human development.* Oxford: Oxford University Press.

Smith L. T. (1999). *Decolonizing methodologies: Research and indigenous peoples.* London: Zed Books.

Starko, A. J., Sparks-Langer, G. M., Pasch, M., Frankel, L., Gardner, T. G., & Moody, C. D. (2003). *Teaching as decision making* (3rd ed.). Upper Saddle River, NJ: Merrill Prentice-Hall.

Sternberg, R. J. (1997). *Thinking styles*. New York: Cambridge University Press.

Sylwester, R. (2003). *A biological brain in a cultural classroom* (2nd ed.). Thousand Oaks, CA: Corwin Press.

Teaching Tolerance. (1989). *Free at last: A history of the civil rights movement and those who died in the struggle*. Montgomery, AL: Author.

Tesconi, C. A., Jr., & Hurwitz, E., Jr. (1974). *Education for whom? The question of equal educational opportunity*. New York: Dodd, Mead.

Thairu, K. (1975). *The African civilization (Utamanduni Wa Kiafrica)*. Nairobi: East African Literature Bureau.

Wang, M., & Kovach, J. (1996). Bridging the achievement gap in urban schools: Reducing educational segregation and advancing resilience-promoting strategies. In B. Williams (Ed.), *Closing the achievement gap: A vision for changing beliefs and practices* (pp. 10–26). Alexandria, VA: Association for Supervision and Curriculum Development.

Watkins, W. H. (2001). *The white architects of black education: Ideology and power in America, 1865–1954*. New York: Teachers College Press.

Zeichner, K. (1996). Educating teachers to close the achievement gap: Issues of pedagogy, knowledge, and teacher preparation. In B. Williams (Ed.), *Closing the achievement gap: A vision for changing beliefs and practices* (pp. 56–76). Alexandria, VA: Association for Supervision and Curriculum Development.

Zinn, H. (1980). *A people's history of the United States*. New York: Harper & Row.

5

School Counselors as Models and Teachers of Dispositional Attitudes and Behaviors: Within and Beyond the School Setting

Constance Deuschle

The main task of this chapter is to offer theoretical perspectives that help construct the meaning of dispositions, as they are understood, practiced, observed, and assessed by school counselors. This chapter will also offer strategies on how school counselors move from theory to the actual praxis of dispositional behaviors and attitudes. The chapter begins by examining the structure and content of a person's thoughts, behaviors, and feelings and how they contribute to the development of characteristics that are identified as "self"—the core of the counselor (Baldwin & Satir, 1987; Ivey, 1986; Noddings, 1995; Rogers, 1965; Wittmer, 2000). The integration of these characteristics and how school counselors within and outside the school community perform them will be described and identified in order to appreciate the complexity of dispositional theory.

School counseling requires its practitioners to be individuals who emulate the "values, commitments, and professional ethics" that affect student learning, motivation, and development as well as the educator's own professional identity within the school community (inside and beyond the school building). A discussion of dispositions involves a dialogue of how to educate school counselors to demonstrate the dispositional attitudes and behaviors that are embedded within the highest standards of practice for effective school counseling programs. The school counselor is at the helm of school counseling programs and services, and as part of the leadership team, is expected to teach, model, and implement the principles of dispositions that promote positive communication, a caring school environment, networking and collaboration, and advocacy for all students.

Further, the discussion requires exploration of the complexity of the elusive definition of dispositions. Although included in the school counseling standards, ethical guidelines, and standards of practice, and presumed to be an internal mode of behavior for effective counselors, the word *disposition* is rarely defined or referenced in counseling literature. For example, the Ethical Standards for School Counseling Programs' guidelines established by the American School Counselor Association (ASCA) delineate the responsibilities of school counselors to the school students, the staff, the families, the community, the counseling profession, and the school counselor him- or herself (ASCA, 1998). The document refers to the principles of ethical behaviors and responsibilities and reinforces the high standards of integrity, leadership, and professionalism among the ASCA members, but does not include dispositions.

Individual states may have identified dispositions through their licensure requirements. The Indiana Professional Standards Board (IPSB) refers to dispositional behaviors and attitudes and describes the behaviors that are part of the knowledge and performance of effective school counselors (IPSB, 1998). The descriptions included in the document are open to individual counselor interpretations and perceptions are reflective of the counselors' dispositional way of believing, way of seeing, way of hearing, and way of "being." Given this fact, this chapter will focus on the development of the school counselor as a person, and how the self of the counselor is instrumental in meeting the standards for school counselors. This chapter defines the element of self as stated by Rogers in his person-centered therapeutic approach: "In using myself, I include my intuition and the essence of myself, whatever that is" (as cited in Baldwin & Satir, 1987, pp. 45–46). Through this knowledge of self, the dispositions of school counselors are manifest in the multiple roles within and beyond the school setting.

Although many school counselors enter the profession because of a love for children or adolescents and a desire to make a difference in the lives of students, they soon discover the role of the school counselor is very broad, deep, and complicated (Erford, 2003). The ability of the counselor to respond and adapt to the complexities within schools requires knowledge and dispositions that provide a balance or centering to sustain the counselor over time—feeling entirely secure as a person, and with that feeling the counselor becomes fully authentic (Baldwin & Satir, 1987).

The very core of self and the dispositions that are reflected through the beliefs, behaviors, and very essence of the person are considered to be the "center" of the total personality and "this new centre might be called the self" (Jung, as cited in Storr, 1983, p. 19). This self that Jung speaks about becomes the personality that is shaped and guided by the inner voice. The importance of this concept is related to the very essence of school counseling dispositions. It is the individual's internal compass, manifest in one's personality, that determines how a school counselor makes decisions, solves problems, and thinks critically about students and families, which ultimately are reflected in the daily activities of that counselor.

Ivey (1986) describes the importance of understanding how people construct reality. Rather than seeing reality construction as an individual journey, Ivey suggests the idea of "co-construction of reality." Ivey's term "dialectics" is a search for more workable answers and truth, involving two (or more) people constructing truth or knowledge through interactions. Occurring together with this co-construction, each individual experiences an internal construction within the self.

O'Farrell (1999) describes the importance between this connection of the inner core of the self and the outer world:

> Our behavior is to a large extent an acting-out of the way we actually feel about ourselves and the world we inhabit. In essence, what we do is often a reflection of how we evaluate ourselves, and if we have come to the conclusion that we are inept, worthless, and unacceptable, it is more than likely that we shall behave in a way which demonstrates the validity of such an assessment. (O'Farrell, 1999, p. 24)

This description offers the perspective that the external behaviors and attitudes of a person reflect the inner self and act as a mirror to the values and beliefs of the person (counselor).

The awareness of oneself at a conscious or even an unconscious level produces reactions to situations. All individuals have within themselves what seems to be connections between their personal constructions of dispositions, which depend upon their unique personal history, along with cultural and social factors that contribute to the awareness of the self (Ivey, 1986). Therefore, the cognitive processes involved in moral and behavioral development influence the abilities and sensibilities of caring for others and reinforces the self or the inner core of oneself. The inner core, being the compass that guides reactions and responses to the external world, is instrumental in the responses critical to the meaning of interactions and situations—whether or not they have positive and growth-producing outcomes.

DISPOSITIONS AS A WAY OF BELIEVING

Myrick (1987) outlines his perceptions of the valuable approaches to guidance and counseling in this changing world. Included in his approaches are developmental guidance, individual counseling, small- and large-group counseling, response services, and program management. All of the prescribed roles for the school counselor require interactions with others within and outside the school. The outcome of such interactions is based upon the facilitative conditions and positive working relationships purposefully orchestrated by the school counselor. There is a weight of responsibility placed upon the school counselor as someone with the knowledge and tools to construct effective communication and understanding even in the most difficult of circumstances. Myrick refers to the facilitative relationship based upon six guiding conditions: caring, understanding, acceptance, respect, friendliness, and trustworthiness. Each of the guiding conditions contributes to the dispositional attitudes of the school counselor. Wittmer (2000) concurs in his comments about the importance of the school counselor building and maintaining relationships:

> A developmental school counselor cannot be effective standing alone; everyone's involvement in the school is needed, sought, and appreciated. Involving the administration, school staff, parents, and teachers provide needed support and backing. Interested, involved individuals will defend the program and the counselor and will play a vital role within the program. (p. 6)

The counselor is expected to treat the total school community respectfully, with a high regard for confidentiality, and by inviting collaboration in the design and implementation of school programs and services. Wittmer (2000) emphasizes the importance of counselors functioning within the boundaries of their individual professional competencies and with behaviors reflective of the prescribed standards of practice and ethical guidelines. It is through the intentions of school counselors, how they approach relationships, how they offer and receive communication, how and when they initiate interactions and conduct themselves both professionally and personally that their beliefs and values are reflected.

Understanding how school counselors make choices and their own knowledge of themselves plays an important part in teaching and assessing the self that can be observed through dispositional behaviors. How school counselors view students and perform their responsibilities toward students reveal the inner intentions and motivations of counselors referred to as dispositions. Whether the counselor accepts the worth of all students, responds with sensitivity to their needs, and accepts their different learning styles and cultural backgrounds are factors that reveal the self of the counselor. How counselors choose to communicate with the entire school community and the way they interact with students and families are thought to be indicators of the level of proficiency of performance and disposition standards. Whether the interactions are positive or negative helps to identify the congruency of the inner self and outer behaviors.

DISPOSITIONS AS A WAY OF CARING

Noddings (1984), in her research on caring, writes from many perspectives that speak about the person giving the caring and the one receiving the caring. Noddings's sense of caring describes a regard for another's views and interests. She explains that ethical caring requires one to extend beyond the traditional sense of caring into an ethic of virtue that is built in relationships and that reaches out to the other person and grows in response to the other. This "caring," based upon an obligation to others, is not an easy endeavor, but rather challenges the caring person to act in accordance with that which is good within the person, and therefore, requires the person to know the depth of oneself (Deuschle, 1999).

Seen as one of the guiding conditions in relationships, it is important to thoroughly understand the impact of a commitment to caring. As education becomes more accountable to all of the stakeholders, how education is defined in the 21st century and a realization that academic achievements cannot occur unless "...our children believe that they themselves are cared for and learn to care for others," Noddings (1995) suggests that education be centered around the "ethic of care" (Noddings, 1995, p. 71). Effective school counselors demonstrate this caring attitude by promoting individual strengths of all people in the school community. This requires certain actions at certain times, dependent upon the circumstances and situations that need to be assessed by the counselor. Without a specific set of dispositions that can be taught or prescribed for all circumstances, the school counselor is challenged to be able to determine the actions to take based upon the dispositional thinking, feelings, and the environment at the time. The counselors' perspective of the observations and cues of different situations are processed through an inner filter and view of self, thereby producing accompanying dispositional attitudes and behaviors.

Nunner-Winkler (1993) described characteristics that show the ethic of care and responsibility to be part of a person's orientation to duties that can be either perfect or imperfect, as postulated by Gilligan (1982). Reflections about ethical responses to duties are based upon one's perceptions of whether the duty requires actions of omission (duties that require one not to act) or imperfect duties that require commission of positive actions (Larrabee et al., 1993). Dispositions are reflective of these responses through the thinking process that tells a person how to act under certain circumstances. As school counselors are part of the fabric of the school environment, a core belief of caring and responsibility toward others becomes the underpinning for thought construction that leads to caring responses and ethical actions.

The counselor who is comfortable and caring for him- or herself would be able to receive caring from others with the same positive dispositions as those evident when giving to others. Even during times of conflict, the school counselor would be able to come from a position of confidence in self, receiving and accepting from others responses that could be hurtful or derogatory. Dispositions in this context embody the sense of mutual love and forgiveness extended to self and others. "Forgiveness is not intended to mean the abandonment of moral standards, but the context in which one reflects upon a situation and chooses to exemplify the good rather than the bad" (Bellah, Madsen, Sullivan, Swindler, & Tipton, 1996, p. 116).

The construct of caring, truly caring for another, weaves together the concepts of an "ethic of care" and can result in dispositions yielding actions of a deeper reflective dimension about how we treat others. The deeper counselors choose to reflect upon and are aware of their own beliefs and values that determine and frame their caring responses, the deeper the understanding of the self and the external performance of dispositional beliefs and behaviors. Together the choice of self-awareness and knowledge and the concept of caring are the covert supports for the overt dispositional behaviors and attitudes.

DISPOSITIONS AS A WAY OF SEEING

The "I" in seeing, rather than the eye through which one "sees," was proposed by Buber, as one totally with the other (as cited in Noddings, 1984, p. 32). Buber believed that the teacher, or in this case the counselor, receives the student through acts of caring, through his or her commitment to the student. The "I–Thou" relationship, proposed by Buber, presents the possibility that one person can be changed by the other. The opposite, the "I–It" relationship, in which others are treated as objects to be used and manipulated, diminishes both persons by limiting the encounter to purely external responses of utility, rather than coming from an internal core of caring and a moral commitment to others.

This internal "I" has a way of seeing and not seeing. What the person values, as determined by perceptions of past and present experiences, becomes the internal eye for viewing life. If one sees someone or something, inevitably there are other people or parts of the environment that are not seen. It is simply impossible to see everyone and everything at the same time. The human filter may become the dispositional stance of the person and guides what the person has chosen or learned to focus upon because of his or her past beliefs and values. Counselors who approach students and focus only upon their problems, dress, cleanliness, or posture miss the gestalt of the total student. The counselor who sees only the "figure" and not the "background," or mutes the interplay between them as unimportant, misses the totality of human nature that contributes to self-awareness and ones responsibility for making changes.

A major responsibility of school counselors is to offer opportunities and possibilities for change with students, families, and within the school environment (Nelson-Jones, 2001). School counselors are required to not only micromanage changes with students and families, but are also involved in macromanagement of school systems and communities. Through consultation opportunities, school counselors can educate and update others on topics of interests, as well as offer valuable information and insights. Whether through informal or formal methods of consultation, the school counselor is a pivotal figure in advocating for changes that affect the learning environment and home situations. Seeing these as opportunities for improving the entire school community, rather than overwhelming challenges that keep people paralyzed in negative situations, reflects the views and dispositions of school counselors—the desire to care about and help people at all levels.

School improvement strategies inevitably involve changes promoted by some people and resisted by others. Approaching change with a positive attitude and assisting people and systems through changes and transitions are actions embraced by school counselors as "change agents" and school leaders who model the content and substance for schools that help to sustain people through changes. School counselor dispositions can serve as the catalyst and offer confidence through the steps required for interventions purposefully designed to benefit all students and promote student learning and success.

In systems theory, families and communities are seen as "living systems," with implications that change in the status quo are inevitable, as life is never static (Goldenberg & Goldenberg, 1990). The school counselor, with a background in theoretical approaches to counseling, can assist families and school systems to develop balance and reduce the stress that occurs during transitions, changes, stress-related experiences, and other uncontrollable events. Assistance may be more accepted if approached through behaviors that are reflective of positive dispositions; meaning there is an underpinning of care, respect, commitment, and ethics that surrounds the counselor's way of "being" in such circumstances. The assistance is presented as a way of empowering families rather than from misplaced charity or piety.

DISPOSITIONS AS A WAY OF LISTENING

It is as though he listened
and such listening as his enfolds us in a silence
in which at last we begin to hear
what we are meant to be (written by Lao-Tse, as cited in Nelson-Jones, 2001, p. 98)

Gathering data through listening requires the school counselor to be cognizant of the way we respond to information. Usually we seize upon information that is sifted through our conscious hearing (Reik, 1952). If psychoanalysts must learn to listen "with the third ear," than it follows that school counselors must learn to listen "with the third ear" placed in their hearts and not only in their heads. The voice that may be heard by counselors often is not the verbal words that are spoken, but the unspoken words that are said in other ways. It is the way in which school counselors are encouraged to look at the voids and to resist first impressions. The third ear is the same that was understood by Freud when he spoke of the capacity of the unconscious for fine hearing—not only what someone does not say, but what the person may feel or think (Reik, 1952).

Reik (1952) speaks to the ability to be turned inward to oneself and to hear the voice from within rather than just the "noise of our conscious thought-processes" (p. 147). As Reik further explains through his wisdom, "The night reveals to the wanderer things that are hidden by day" (p. 147). Pondering this valuable insight into how we listen to others, counselors are conscious of the complexities of truly listening to someone, and that messages are often sent and understood unconsciously before they are processed consciously. The processing speaks to how the mind sorts through all of our messages. Although certain messages and perceptions may elude us, others refuse to be ignored. They convey a meaning that we have already experienced and accept, or may convey a message that moves from unconsciousness to consciousness. Riek speaks to the process of "catching" these elusive signs and trusting our senses.

Once again the question of the development of the internal self is important in understanding how we care, listen, and respond, which becomes the framework for dispositions. These are the dispositions that contribute to the transformation of counselors and help with the progression and development of the sensibilities to grasp the entirety of this complex means of seeing, hearing, interpreting, and responding to others. (Goethe has expressed it beautifully: "If the eye were not something sunlike itself, it could never see the sun" [as cited in Reik, 1952, p. 154].)

DISPOSITIONS AS A WAY OF BEING

Rogers, in his philosophy of person-centered therapy, captures the ideal of a way of "being." Through the eyes of Rogers, the person-centered approach is primarily a way of being that finds its expression in attitudes and behaviors that enhance a growth-promoting climate. Person-centered counselors do not simply use techniques or structured methods of counseling, but focus upon the development of core conditions of empathy, genuineness, and respect. These can offer greater self-acceptance and positive behavior change (as cited in Peterson & Nisenholz, 1999). The relationship between the counselor and client explores the way of "being" of both client and counselor and focuses upon the person rather than the client's problem (Peterson & Nisenholz, 1999).

A way of "being" is about how an individual perceives, processes, and contributes to life. Life includes cycles of activities, how individuals see, hear, think, feel, and behave, as well as cycles of rest, production, consumption, and interactions (Csikszentmihalyi, 1997). As life is lived daily, personal characteristics, rather than situational ones, may determine the emotional and cognitive responses experienced. "In other words, over time some people come to think of themselves as happy regardless of external conditions, while others will become used to feeling relatively less happy no matter what happens to them" (p. 21). The similarity to be drawn here is reflective of the characteristics and mental constructs of individuals and their corresponding dispositional beliefs, attitudes, behaviors. This concept places a high value on self-knowledge and how individuals choose to view themselves and their lives.

Maslow's hierarchy of needs outlines life's journey toward self-actualization (Maslow, 1962). Based upon his research, individuals who are self-actualizing experience harmony between self and environment. They are congruent with their inner and outer selves. Nietzsche's philosophy looks at a life that embraces and loves everything (Csikszentmihalyi, 1997). These theories speak to the importance of the integration and harmony of the inner and outer self, and the self-awareness possessed by individuals who reflect these beliefs through caring for self and others. The "I" in being is not just "what kind of person do I want to be," but more about "who and how am I being."

DISPOSITIONS AND COGNITIVE DEVELOPMENT

The profession of school counseling and the multifaceted roles of the counselor within a school setting include interactions with a diverse culture of school staff, students and their families, and businesses within the surrounding community. Effective school counselors demonstrate positive dispositional attitudes and behaviors that help to build and support the many relationships that promote student success and positive school climates.

The standards of practice and the ethical guidelines for school counselors focus on students and learning (Wittmer, 2000). It is important to consider what students find helpful in learning and to appreciate what connects them to teachers and others within the school setting, as school counselors also teach developmental guidance lessons in the classrooms. Bluestein (1995) sees her mission as offering stories from children and their perspectives on who influenced them positively about learning, about themselves, and about life. Included are a few of the comments made by children about someone who was a "really great teacher":

- lets you work at your own pace;
- knows who you are;

- listens to you when you need to tell her something, even if you're interrupting;
- will make the students learn the lessons without the students ever knowing they are studying;
- has a sense of humor and is united with the students;
- always cares and understands you;
- teaches you not only about school, but about life in general;
- treats you the way you want to be treated. (pp. 314–315)

The children emphasized the value of being listened to, of teachers having a sense of humor, of learning about school and life, and having someone who cares about them. The children identified the essence of positive dispositions. An integral part of developmental school counseling is that school counselors also wear many "hats," but whether counselors wear the "hat" of a teacher, of an administrator, of the nurse, of the parent, or of the school counselor they are challenged to perform all tasks with positive dispositions. Whether teaching is related to choices and decision making, problem-solving skills, conflict resolution, anger management, communication, or general life skills, the dispositional behaviors of the school counselor can effectively affect the climate for learning.

School counselors who are also effective teachers engage students in learning through active and invested participation and multicultural activities (Danielson, 1996). Through creativity and diversity of instruction, counselors enhance core curriculum instruction by the juxtaposition of life skill goals and the engagement of students both mentally and affectively. Dispositional behaviors that emulate the values, commitments, and beliefs that reflect the respect and support of cultural diversity integrate into teaching those strategies and multicultural education that embraces the primary goal effective teachers, "the development in all students of an understanding of and appreciation for the human potential of persons of all backgrounds" (Redman, 1999, p. 4).

How school counselors demonstrate dispositions is reflected in the language and behavior that result from our thoughts. Understanding the stages of cognitive and moral development, the critical thought process, involves movement through stages of moral development. Kohlberg's three levels of moral development progress from preconventional reasoning to postconventional reasoning when "morality is completely internalized and is not based on others' standards" (as cited in Santrock, 2002, p. 317). Critical thinking about positive dispositions contributes to the deeper understanding and value of knowing oneself, predicting responses, observing cues, sensitivity toward others and circumstances, and the core values of dispositional attitudes and behaviors. The question is: How do we prepare school counselors with sensitive antennae and thinking skills necessary for giving and receiving the highest standards and expectations of dispositions?

Appreciating the joint construction of knowledge and truth, the relationships between persons and their environments, becomes a critical concept in the development of dispositional behaviors and attitudes. Influencing the way people think about themselves and their situations requires a safe environment in which perceptions and beliefs can be expressed, discussed, and explored. Ivey (1986) suggests the way that individuals receive information, process and organize the data, and reflect through formal operations or abstract thoughts results in a heightened awareness and synchronism of responsive actions.

The responsive actions and behaviors of an individual can be observed overtly, and yet they begin within the self rather than solely as responses to external obligations. "The individual must find and assert his or her true self because this self is the only source of genuine relationships to other people" (Bellah et al., 1996, p. 97). The development of dispositions that contribute to the validation and autonomy of one's self is encouraged in this quote: "Before one can love others, one must learn to love one's self" (p. 98).

The roots of giving and receiving reflective of one's dispositional attitudes, beliefs, and ways of seeing and listening come from oneself and then spill over into the thinking, behaviors, and feelings toward others. O'Farrell (1999) refers to the integration of these characteristics as "self-concept."

> Self-concept is our attitude towards our self. Like any attitude it has three components, commonly referred to as the cognitive component (our knowledge and beliefs about our self); and affective component (our feelings and evaluations about our self); and a behavioral component (our tendency to behave in ways that reflect our thoughts and feelings about our self). (p. 23)

The counselor who is comfortable and caring for himself would be able to receive caring from others with the same positive dispositions as those evident when giving to others. Even during times of conflict, the school counselor would be able to come from a position of confidence in self, receiving and accepting from others responses that could be hurtful or derogatory. It is with the understanding that taking responsibility for self can result in expressions of caring, compassion, and benevolent responses to others. Dispositions in this context embody the sense of mutual love and forgiveness extended to self and others. "Forgiveness is not intended to mean the abandonment of moral standards, but the context in which one reflects upon a situation and chooses to exemplify the good rather than the bad" (Bellah et al., 1996, p. 116).

School counselors who come from this position of centering or stability can be role models for school-age students, school staff, and the entire school community. As the mental health expert in the school environment, the school counselor is expected to remain calm, even in the midst of turmoil and crisis, and to behave within the confines of the ethical standards for school counselors held as the yardstick as the standards of practice for all school counselors (ASCA, 1998).

DISPOSITIONS IN TEACHING AND PRACTICE

The actual process of implementing the connections between thoughts and behaviors happens so instantly, that without having positive dispositions as part of an individual's inner core, the synapse between thinking and behaving would be prolonged and could interrupt the demonstration of a caring disposition toward the other person. How we teach, monitor, and assess caring dispositions of school counselors is seriously affected by the way the counselors are able to purposefully respond to different people and in different situations.

Some learning theories are based upon the principles that knowledge is created and learned through active involvement, and that learning occurs through interactions among persons, behaviors, and environments (Foote, Vermette, & Battaglia, 2001; Johnson, 2000; Schunk, 1996; Strong, 2002). Whatever the mode of instruction, the intentional design, and implementation of the teaching strategies, all involve the whole student in the learning process—the affect, behaviors, and cognitions of the students. It is through this complex appreciation of how individual students learn that school counselors become effective "counseling teachers," and their classroom curriculum is delivered with an emphasis upon the total child. The dispositional behaviors and attitudes of school counselors are reflected through their direct classroom teaching, mentoring, practicing, and assessing procedures.

What are the pieces of the dispositional puzzle that need to be included in the instructional teaching to promote the development of positive dispositions? There are many pieces to be included in the teaching of positive dispositional attitudes and behaviors. The developmental stages of cognitions, behaviors, moral and affective development, and social development are all integrated into the internal and external elements of dispositions. Juxtaposed upon the complexity of individual differences, it is no wonder that the picture on the puzzle box is not always clear. There are multiple ways of assembling the puzzle that could present a picture of dispositional attitudes and behaviors depending upon a multitude of influences. But this reality does not eliminate the need to determine the desired dispositional characteristics that describe an effective school counselor and teacher. It is important to construct a framework for the puzzle to prevent pieces from being unnoticed or lost.

The challenge of teaching dispositions and assessing the outcomes of dispositional attitudes and behaviors reinforces the need to create a structure and design to assist students through the maturation of dispositional development. Borrowing from the classic framework of multicultural competencies, the counselor must first be aware of self-perspectives and then move through acceptance and celebration of others' perceptions. There are specific domains related to dispositional growth. Each designated domain is interrelated and has incremental and identifiable steps from early development of positive dispositions to a mature stage or mastery of positive dispositions (Erford, 2003).

Some of the elements to include in teaching dispositional thoughts and behaviors would include: values, commitment, ethics, caring, listening, relationships, seeing, self and being. Accepting the main modes of learning as observational and interactive, a structured teaching model would be beneficial for the assessment of the level of mastery and professional growth of the school counselor. Sergiovanni (1992) offers this formula as part of his model of teaching:

- Say it. Define and communicate the core values
- Model it. Act on the core values
- Organize for it. Put it into resources, dialogues, personal contact
- Support it. Provide resources to promote core values
- Enforce it. Embody core values in personal assessments
- Express it. Tell people why and what is important—repeatedly. (p. 74)

As counseling and teaching educators, the position requires a teaching model that provide a means of assessment to correlate with the learning, skills, and abilities of the student. If the dispositions of school counselors and teachers are as valued as believed and proved from the theories addressed in this chapter, then it is imperative to proceed with purposeful teaching strategies that require demonstration of dispositional attitudes and behaviors. The teacher with the dispositional stance described in this chapter should be able to demonstrate positive dispositional attributes before expecting students to meet the dispositional standards. The responsibility for teaching students requires that educators define and talk about the core values of dispositions.

Say it "out loud" when discussing situations and cases and the dispositional responses that would be appropriate, and embrace the core beliefs expressed in this chapter. Through written, verbal, and nonverbal communication, the school counselor needs to approach persons and circumstances within the framework of caring, respect, and ethical practices. Observations of the counselor would reflect a favorable attitude toward others, respect for ideas and academic requirements, a sensitivity to individuals of diversity, and characteristic that contribute toward positive communications and actions.

Model dispositional characteristics that are reflective of attitudes about self as well as others. While teaching and instructing, counselors utilize positive skills in communication, thinking, and outcomes of cognitive process, expression of feelings, anticipation of others' behaviors, attention to cues from people and the environment, acting in ways that bring the counselors into real life situations and ways to deal with them. Observers can then imitate the positive behaviors and attitudes by transferring the learning into actual situations. Modeling also demonstrates self-monitoring to others. Through tangible ways of processing, verbally and nonverbally, counselors are more prepared to respond appropriately in different situations. After all, school counseling is not about the life of the school counselor, but about how the school counselor can affect the lives of others as observed by others.

Modeling also offers opportunities to emphasize the need for care of self. Although much time is spent on how school counselors are responsible to others, the ethical standards also stress the importance of school counselors taking care and protecting themselves. According to Siebert, (as cited in Davis, 2004):

> As a school counselor, a big part of your job is that of caregiver. You provide people in need with a shoulder to cry on, someone to listen to their concerns and advice on how to deal with adversity. However, it can be a fine line to walk between helping others with their problems and letting others' problems have a negative impact on your own mental health. You not only owe it to yourself but to your students to be a role model for resiliency. (p. 315)

Organize and structure learning scenarios and situations for students to observe, practice, and receive feedback to allow for mistakes and encouragement for continued efforts and expectations. Organize for the present, but also for the future, appreciating that school counselors will be teaching others through staff development, parenting classes, and community networking. Counselors will need to be prepared and articulate about the profession of school counseling, as leaders and advocates for all students and families.

Support school counseling programs through continuous professional development and leadership. The reality of the current economics and tightened school budgets promotes a message that school counselors are dispensable and interprets that the No Child Left Behind legislation does not require counseling support. As a professional, it rests upon school counselors to heighten the awareness of their role in the school and how they are valued in the academic, career, social, and personal success of all students. A united voice speaking for practitioners in the field can confront the comments that prevail without interruption. Without a clear vision of why counselors are an integral part of the educational enterprise that is understood by others and their role in the academic mission of schools, support will likely be only lukewarm and not of the intensity to make a viable difference (Johnson, 2000).

Enforcement of positive dispositions and attitudes is necessary for the alignment of counseling program objectives and needs to be part of the total school evaluation to identify and support the growth and development of the core values outlined in this chapter. Dispositional characteristics of the school counselor may be part of a checklist or informal tools of assessment, or they may be measured through more qualitative methodologies of interviews, observations, and multiple responses from school staff, students, and families. Self-reporting narratives can help in identifying how school counselors perceive themselves and are perceived by others. Specific items being measured need to be included throughout the assessment tools and categories. Self-examination of personal strengths and weaknesses are part of the process for the development of self-knowledge and awareness (Peterson & Nisenhohlz, 1999, p. 51). The more open and honest the counselor is in assessing oneself, the more opportunities for self-examination of integrity and personal growth.

Both the university and site supervisor would have valuable input in assessment of the school counselor's dispositional behaviors and attitudes if the counselor were enrolled in a master's level program. The school administrator, along with the other leadership team members, would also be able to offer feedback to the school counselor practitioner as a way of providing information about dispositions that may not be evident to the counselor. Extending beyond self-examination, school counselors who invite feedback from others receive it as a means of professional growth and increased self-knowledge, and they adapt behavior and attitude changes reflective of a counseling professional and are better able to model for others the dispositional qualities that are beneficial for the students and the entire school climate.

Express the meaning, beliefs, value, and ethics of positive dispositions throughout school counseling materials and resources. It is important to take advantage of opportunities to network with other professionals and speak about the standards of accountability for school counseling; including the knowledge, performance, and disposition requirements (ASCA, 2002).

Taken from Ivey's (1986) text, the story of a Samurai swordsman provides a metaphor for this concept of moving from a way of thinking or theory into an integration of theory with practice—praxis:

Japanese master swordsmen learn their skills through a complex set of highly detailed training exercises. Through theoretical analysis and examination, the process of masterful swordsmanship is broken down into specific components and studied carefully, one at a time. In this process of technical mastery, the naturally skilled person often finds handling the sword awkward. The skilled individual may even find his performance dropping during the practice of single skills. Being aware of what one is doing can interfere with coordination and smoothness. Once the individual skills are practiced and learned to perfection, the Samurai retire to a mountaintop to meditate. They deliberately forget about what they have learned. When they return, they find that the distinct skills have been naturally integrated into their style of way of being. The Samurai then seldom have to think about skills at all. They have become the Samurai swordsmen. (p. 27)

This same model that was utilized in the teaching of the Samurai learning model can be transferred into the construction for teaching other skills. Identification of the puzzle pieces (divided into teaching modules and coaching students to reflect upon intrapersonal and interpersonal learning gained during experiences of working through the modules) are the first domain of dispositional growth. Each puzzle piece or dispositional characteristic would be accompanied by explanations and activities to allow students to construct personal learnings and appreciation of the inner and outer self. Practicing with the puzzle pieces (domains) leads to integration and a natural way of being, acting, thinking, and feeling, resulting in dispositional behaviors. Praxis evolves, and the skills and theories become so well integrated that it is no longer necessary for artificial simulations. Practice leads to integration and a natural way of being, acting, thinking, and feeling, resulting in dispositional behaviors—the picture on the cover of the puzzle box becomes clearer and defined for each individual.

CONCLUSION

School counselors are professionals who enter public and private school buildings throughout the world every day. They are faced with multiple tasks relegated to school counselors by school administrators and other external forces, many outside the control of the counselor. School counselors are also burdened by their own personal concerns and issues, unseen pressures, and demands, often unshared and unnoticed by others, but they must still be prepared to effectively handle positive and negative interactions and relationships. Working daily with the realities of human nature, the school counselor, seen as the mental health expert in the school, should be included in all issues in the school related to any mental health issues. This means one school counselor may be responsible for several hundred children, a school staff, families of the students, and community resources.

School counseling practice is characterized by a high level of ambiguity and a need for spontaneous responses and flexibility in dealing with a variety of school situations. The willingness of school counselors to self-monitor and to critically self-reflect upon situations as part of their dispositional development embraces the sensibility for construction of an inner compass that guides and instructs the counselor during the calm, as well as the crisis, situations that inevitably surface in schools. Stress and burnout among counselors may result for many reasons, and self-awareness and self-maintenance become more important to the dispositional behaviors demonstrated by counselors.

The Ethical Standards for School Counseling Programs established guidelines for the role of the school counselor, including prevention, interventions, crisis activities, and program management as part of the job description for successful school counselors (ASCA, 1998). The National Model for School Counseling Programs strengthened the profession by the development of exemplary school counseling programs, with the purpose of improving student achievement (ASCA, 2002). Additionally, the school counselor is often the single person offering mental health services, and he or she functions as a solitary care provider. The reality is not to excuse behaviors, accent or diminish the multiple roles of the school counselor, but to postulate there are internal dimensions needed to sustain the external demands of the counselor.

The internal dimensions are the foundation of the development of dispositional attitudes, behaviors, beliefs, thoughts, and feelings that prepare and sustain school counselors through the pressures of the profession. Simultaneously being aware and in touch with the internal fabric of his "being," the counselor is then able to perform the "art" of school counseling, not in spite of the pressures, but rather, because of the way the counselor views life based upon his or her internal foundation.

It seems that new approaches and understandings in the fields of school counseling and teaching are being recognized and implemented. The changes cannot be seen as a *revolution* but rather as an *evolution* of how educators and other school staff work within and outside of the school community. Hopefully, the focus of this book on the importance of dispositions in the professions of teaching and school counseling will contribute to these approaches and help to usher in new ways of dispositions as seeing, listening, thinking, behaving, and feeling about the weighty responsibilities to be upheld by educational professionals.

> The more in touch I am with my beliefs and acknowledge them, the more I give myself the freedom to choose how to use those beliefs. In other words, there is a close relationship between what I believe, and how I act. (Baldwin & Satir, 1987, p. 24)

REFERENCES

American School Counselor Association (ASCA). (1998). *Ethical standards for school counseling programs*. Alexandria, VA: Author.

American School Counselor Association (ASCA). (2002). *National model for school counseling programs.* Alexandria, VA: Author.

Baldwin, M., & Satir, V. (1987). *The use of self in therapy.* New York: Haworth.

Bellah, R., Madsen, R., Sullivan, W., Swindler, A., & Tipton, S. (1996). *Habits of the heart.* Berkley and Los Angeles, CA: University of California Press.

Bluestein, J. (1995). *Mentors, masters and Mrs. MacGregor: Stories of teachers making a difference.* Deerfield Beach, FL: Health Communications.

Csikszentmihalyi, M. (1997). *Finding flow: The psychology of engagement with everyday life.* New York: Basic Books.

Danielson, C. (1996). *Enhancing professional practice: A framework for teaching.* Alexandria, VA: Association for Supervision and Curriculum Development.

Davis, T. (2004). *Exploring school counseling: Professional practices and perspectives.* Boston: Lahaska Press.

Deuschle, C. (1999). *Transformational leadership: Theory to practice.* Unpublished doctoral dissertation, Indiana University of Bloomington, IN.

Erford, B. (2003). *Transforming the school counseling profession.* Upper Saddle River, NJ: Merrill Prentice-Hall.

Foote, C., Vermette, P., & Battaglia, C. (2001). *Constructivist strategies: Meeting standards and engaging adolescent minds.* Larchmont, NY: Eye on Education.

Gilligan, C. (1982). *The contributions of women's thought to developmental theory.* Washington, DC: National Institute of Education.

Goldenberg, H., & Goldenberg, I. (1990). *Counseling today's families.* Pacific Grove, CA: Brooks/Cole.

Indiana Professional Standards Board (IPSB). (1998). *Standards for school services professionals.* Indianapolis, IN: Author.

Ivey, A. (1986). *Developmental therapy: Theory into practice.* San Francisco: Jossey-Bass.

Johnson, D. (2000). *Reaching out: Interpersonal effectiveness and self-actualization* (7th ed.). Needham Heights, MA: Viacom.

Larrabee, M., Baier, A., Brabeck, M., Blum, L., Flanagan, O., Jackson, K. et al. (1993). *An ethic of care: Feminist and interdisciplinary perspectives.* New York: Routledge, Chapman & Hall.

Maslow, A. (1962). *Toward a psychology of being* (2nd ed.) New York: Van Nostrand Reinhold.

Myrick, R. (1987). *Developmental guidance and counseling: A practical approach.* Minneapolis: Educational Media Corporation.

Nelson-Jones, R. (2001). *Theory and practice of counseling & therapy.* New York: Continuum.

Noddings, N. (1984). *Caring: A feminine approach to ethics & moral education.* Berkeley and Los Angeles, CA: University of California Press.

Noddings, N. (1995). Teaching themes of care. *Phi Delta Kappan, 76*(9), 675–680.

Nunner-Winkler, G. (1993). Two moralities? A critical discussion of an ethic of care and responsibility versus an ethic of rights and justice. In M. J. Larrabee (Ed.), And ethic of care. Feminist and interdisciplinary perspectives (pp. 143–156). New York: Routledge.

O'Farrell, U. (1999). *Courage to change: The counseling process.* Dublin: Veritas Publications.

Peterson, V., & Nisenholz, B. (1999). *Orientation to counseling.* Needham Heights, MA: Viacom.

Redman, G. (1999). *Teaching in today's classrooms: Cases from middle and secondary school.* Upper Saddle, NY: Prentice-Hall.

Reik, T. (1952). *Listening with the third ear: The inner experience of a psychoanalyst.* New York: Farrar, Straus and Company.

Rogers, C. (1965). *Client-centered therapy.* Cambridge, MA: Riverside Press.

Santrock, J. (2002). *Life-span development.* Boston: McGraw Hill.

Schunk, D. (1996). *Learning theories* (2nd ed.). Englewood Cliffs, NJ: Prentice-Hall.

Sergiovanni, T. (1992). *Moral leadership: Getting to the heart of school improvement.* San Francisco: Jossey-Bass.

Storr, A. (1983). *The essential Jung.* Princeton, NJ: Princeton University Press.

Strong, J. (2002). *Qualities of effective teachers.* Alexandria, VA: Association for Supervision and Curriculum Development.

Wittmer, J. (2000). *Managing your school counseling program: K–12 developmental strategies.* Minneapolis: Educational Media.

6

Dispositions in the Helping Professions

James R. Hurst

Over the past 10 to 15 years, the field of teacher education has increasingly emphasized the importance of the assessment and facilitation of dispositions for preservice teachers. This emphasis is evident in the standards (see Appendix A) articulated by the Interstate New Teacher Assessment and Support Consortium (INTASC) and the National Council for the Accreditation of Teacher Education (NCATE). However, when the construct of dispositions is examined in helping professions outside of education, one encounters professional literature that utilizes different terms and heuristics while still addressing the same applied concepts. The term "disposition" itself is rarely used by those involved in medical, nursing, or psychotherapeutic training and licensure to describe the same types of skills, attitudes, and behaviors as when the term is applied to teacher education. On the other hand, terms and constructs such as "values," "professional ethics," and "empathy" are heavily emphasized throughout most of the helping professions, and especially in the training process of those other professionals. In short, once one gets past some minor semantic differences, it would be reasonable to think that teacher educators might benefit from integrating the knowledge and dilemmas faced by those responsible for training other helping professionals and by those who have extensively studied some of the more circumscribed concepts, such as empathy, that directly relate to the educational conceptualization of dispositions.

Many, but not all, helping professionals, such as physicians, nurses, psychologists, social workers, and counselors, enter into their respective professions with certain attributes that predispose them to want to care for others. Such attributes are often described by those in the early stages of training with descriptions that evoke a "caring" personality, a "good listener," "wanting to help others," and being able to "place oneself into another's shoes." These descriptors are typical examples of lay definitions of empathy. Much of this chapter will discuss the role of empathy in assisting others across various helping professions. Some researchers theorize that empathy can be learned as a skill and refined with each new encounter with a client. However, it has also been suggested in the literature that the ability to offer empathy is too often lacking among the very same professionals who are presumed to possess it in abundance (Reynolds, 2000). Along these same lines, Carkuff and Berenson (1967) stressed that those individuals in our society designated as "more knowing" (i.e., teachers, ministers, nurses, doctors, and psychologists) often create feelings of impotence among those who are supposed to be receiving their help. This chapter will examine some of the similarities and differences regarding how various helping professions outside of education conceptualize and operationalize dispositions, as well as the various challenges that impact how these dispositions are manifested in the delivery of direct patient or client care. The specific professions considered here are medicine, nursing, and psychotherapy, with the latter group comprised of psychologists, social workers, and counselors. Although these professions are in many ways indicative of practices and trends throughout the health/mental health sector, it is important to note that they do not represent all health care professions and specialties.

CARING AND EMPATHY

The concept of caring has a significant place in teacher education, as other chapters in this volume more fully describe. Among the fields of medicine, nursing, or psychotherapy, it is mainly the nursing profession and its literature that invoke the term. However, even within nursing, there are a variety of emphases and interpretations of caring. Due to these differences, it is difficult to pinpoint a definition for caring. Watson (2002) discusses the concept of caring for health professionals. At times, some advocate for "caring" to be defined as an ethical/moral principle. Yet others do not want the concept defined in a manner that implies emotional attachment and dependency. A common ground on the concept of caring is that it involves the expression of openness, receptiveness, and authenticity. These characteristics of "caring" are also the backbone of Carl Rogers's person-centered therapy, which is mainly identified as a psychotherapeutic theory, but also one with broad applications to all helping professions including education. Rogers (1957) noted that the main quality of effective therapists included "sensing the world as if it were one's own," which would require the therapist to suspend his or her own personal views, thoughts, and feelings and delve into another's world. However, it is often the inability to put aside one's tendency to judge, disapprove, or evaluate that becomes a barrier to helping clients (Rogers, 1961). In Wheeler and Barrett (1994), a content analysis of caring paradigms within nursing revealed that empathy is the quality most responsible for creating a "caring" environment. In this chapter, the construct and characteristic of empathy will be utilized to define a "caring" disposition in the helping professions.

An important aspect of the concept of empathy concerns how it is developed, nurtured, and taught. Many theorists have viewed empathy as a personality trait. This perspective assumes that some people intrinsically have more empathy than others. Feshbach (1975) stated that, as with other personality traits and abilities, the ability to empathize is a product of development. Other predictors of empathy include a number of personal characteristic istic variables that include gender, sex-role orientation, cognitive complexity, personality types, communication style, and cultural values (Duan, Rose, & Kraatz, 2002). If empathy is a personality trait, is it possible to learn how to empathize? From the nursing literature, Alligood (1992) hypothesizes that there are two types of empathy. "Basic empathy" is seen as a human attribute, "a universal human capacity" that is similar to the natural ordinary feelings for others. According to Alligood, this type of empathy cannot be taught; it is involuntary. The second type of empathy can be taught by identifying appropriate responses to clients, reinforcing and refining these responses to develop an empathic expertise. The concept of "trained empathy" is empathy that is learned in relation to professional practice. Trained empathy, in opposition to basic empathy, is viewed as a deliberate process and is a learned clinical skill. Trained empathy includes the cognitive selection of the best response (Kunyk & Olson, 2001). Patterson (1984) suggested that a therapist's empathic abilities could be acquired and improved through vicarious, participative, and personal experiences. In order to learn how to be empathic, it is crucial for one to have enough self-awareness to develop (a) a repertoire of interactions between emotions and cognitions, (b) an understanding of congruency between feelings and behaviors, and (c) a strong self-concept that enables one to enter another's experience without fear of losing oneself (Duan et al., 2002).

PSYCHOTHERAPY DISPOSITIONS

Even among helping professions, empathy has various meanings. Empathy is defined as a cognitive attribute, as opposed to an affective state, in most health care settings. Physicians and nurses view empathy as involving an understanding of a patient's experiences and perspective, combined with the ability to communicate this understanding to the patient (Hojat, Fields, & Gonnella, 2003). Psychologists, social workers, and counselors place empathy as "the most fundamental principle" in their work as therapists in trying to understand their patient's goals and needs (Strupp, 1995). For psychotherapists, empathy goes to another level that is deeper than just sensing another's emotions. Empathy for therapists requires that the therapist is sensitive to the range of emotions and each individual situation in order to work through the client's thoughts, provide accurate analysis, and helpful feedback (Goldstein & Michaels, 1985).

The disposition of the therapist has to be one that draws him or her into the world of the patient, as well as conveying to the patient that there is genuine interest and receptivity (Bennett, 2001). A basic requisite of the empathic therapist is the concept of sharing. Therapists must maintain a balance between attitudes of detachment and involvement in their patients' lives. Often, therapists fall into extremes of these two concepts—either being too detached toward their patients or too involved (Greenson, 1960). There are multiple factors that can affect a therapist's ability to empathize with his or her patient: (a) therapist mood, (b) knowledge of the client, (c) awareness of the client's culture, (d) the nature of the client's emotions, (e) client/therapist values and differences between the two, (f) therapist's motivation and attitudes toward empathy, (g) therapist's emotions toward clients, and (h) cultural values (Duan & Hill, 1996).

Therapists' identification with specific theoretical orientations often defines their specific meaning and use of empathy. Therapists who align themselves with humanistic/experiential and psychodynamic theories tend to view empathy as "feeling" focused as well as a communicative process (Carlozzi, Bull, Stein, Ray, & Barnes, 2002). From the humanistic/experiential perspective, the client feeling "understood" is the most helpful outcome arising from the therapeutic relationship (Duan et al., 2002). Client-centered or Rogerian therapists utilize empathy in their responses to clients to convey genuineness and unconditional positive regard. Adlerian therapists would use empathic responses to "reflect the acknowledgment of the client's lifestyle" (Scharf, 1996).

Whatever the therapist's theoretical orientation, it is common to utilize "standard" empathic responses that are learned during clinical training. Bozarth (1984) suggests that therapists employ idiosyncratic empathy by trusting their own intuition and formulating responses that are individualized to each client. Therapist communication style often plays a key role in conveying empathy to clients. Factors such as timing, posture, and voice quality, as well as the use of metaphor and imagery to convey meaning, are crucial to the therapeutic empathic response (McLeod, 1999).

MEDICAL DISPOSITIONS

In medicine, the concept of empathy has changed over the years and has been redefined in modern times. Premodern physicians believed that being emotionally affected by patients was a part of being an effective "healer." Originating from the Hippocratic Oath, the healing role has emphasized sympathy and compassion toward patients. Hippocratic writings suggested that the goal for physicians was to eliminate destructive and selfish feelings and focus their emotions into compassionate feelings that would guide their thinking with patients (Halpern, 2001). The scientific advances of the modern age and expanding knowledge about diseases and their causes and remedies have altered the humanistic tradition in medicine. Over the years, physicians have changed from physician-healers to physician-scientists (Bennett, 2001). Physicians believe that they need to detach themselves from their patients in order to prevent burnout due to having to care for a larger number of patients under time constraints imposed by the managed care system (Halpern, 2001). Physicians represent their sense of detachment from their patients by describing empathy in an intellectualized way. Reflecting this traditional view, Aring (1958) asserted that the role for physicians' empathy does not involve emotional interactions with patients. Instead, physicians utilized previously acquired emotional knowledge that is intellectualized to interpret what the patient is feeling. This acquired emotional knowledge impacts a physician's ability to be empathic toward his or her patients. The physician's own emotional experiences are the basis for inner perception, intuition, and the ability to understand one's own feelings and relationships as well as others (Halpern, 2001).

A physician cannot will him- or herself to empathize, but can develop curiosity that can then result in increased empathy toward patients. According to Halpern (2001), physicians who cultivated curiosity about others, sensitivity to their own emotional reactions, and an ongoing capacity to see the patients' situations, motives, and reactions as distinct from their own are more likely to develop increased empathic skills. This curiosity that can assist in cultivating empathy is an affective experience of connecting and wanting to relate to another person as another self.

Although physicians are able to learn to empathize with their patients, they often do not exhibit this trait due to the lack of recognition and importance accorded by professional peers and health administrators. During the professional "socialization" process in medical school, students are not graded on the manner in which they relate to patients. In addition, once students become physicians, compassion and empathy are not among the top criteria of professional recognition that lead to promotions within medical organizations. In a study by Carmel and Glick (1996), the concept of compassionate-empathic physicians was examined. They found that compassionate-empathic physicians tend to be younger and have fewer years of medical practice experience. More compassionate-empathic physicians are found in the primary care specialties of internal medicine and pediatrics than in surgery. These more empathic physicians also have high self-esteem and feel more at ease in emotional situations, as well as having more pro-social, nonstereotypic attitudes toward patients.

NURSING DISPOSITIONS

The field of nursing also views empathy as a cognitive attribute, instead of an affective one, that involves understanding the experiences and perspective of patients combined with the ability to communicate this understanding to the patient (Hojat et al., 2003). A significant factor in the delivery of care by nurses is the ability to identify imaginatively with the patient as a basis for gaining accurate insight into what the patient needs (Scott, 1995). This type of identification is more central to the provision of nursing care than physician care due to the much higher amount of time that nurses spend in direct patient care. At a time when health care has been rapidly changing due to increased technology, it has become even more important for nurses to "humanize" care by relating empathically to their patients. However, like physicians and therapists, nurses have come up against environmental expectations through the managed care system that have impacted their tendency to offer empathy to patients (Reynolds, 2000). Due in part to external factors such as understaffing issues and time constraints from the managed care system, nurses often are found to have low levels of empathy. In a study conducted by MacLeod-Clarke (1983), it was found that nurses often manipulate conversations with patients to suit their own needs. Many nurses were observed to ignore the concerns of patients in order to stay on their own clinical agenda. These findings suggest that some of the negative stereotypes regarding nonempathic physicians can also be applied to nurses.

Despite the external constraints placed on nursing, Liaschenko and Davis (1991) argue for the need to focus on the whole person, which is a distinguishing factor between nurses and physicians. By focusing on the patient as a whole person, recognition is made by the nurse that a patient is more than the disease or illness that brought him or her into the health care system. A study by Hudson (1993) found that when patients perceive that their nurses understand them, effective nursing has taken place. Moreover, it is better when empathy equates to caring as opposed to "curing" when practiced by nurses. Nursing actions that are described as "caring" actions include listening, "being with," comforting, and talking. "Curing" actions of nursing refer to the more technical clinical skills such as physical observation, treatment, and biotechnological maintenance. Nurses often view empathy as being valuable, but only after the patient's basic needs are met.

In many nursing education programs, it is often thought that nursing students learn empathic communication skills; however, this has been found to be false. Kunst-Wilson, Carpenter, Poser, Verker, and Kushner (1981) discovered that students' empathic ability did not increase because of their educational program. Mynatt (1985) also found an inverse relationship between empathy level and work experience in the nursing field. Several models are utilized in nursing education to promote the development of empathy. One such model is the active listening model, which emphasizes the communication component of empathy. This component keys into understanding what the patient is saying and feeling and then being able to communicate this back to the patient. In nursing education, the focus is not on exploring the students' feelings, but on providing a therapeutic context in which the nursing instructor communicates high levels of empathy to the students and in turn, the students practice communication skills aimed toward empathic responses (Wheeler & Barrett, 1994).

CROSS-DISCIPLINARY ISSUES

Across disciplines, a crucial component in developing empathy is self-awareness. Students must first learn to "be in touch" with their own emotions before they can begin to understand another's. It is important for students to be able to sort out their own personal feelings, as differentiated from those of their patients. Being able to recognize emotional cues in others varies with each person, and helping students gain understanding into their own individualized emotional responses increases one's capacity to empathize with others (Wheeler & Barrett, 1994). Various helping professions require the use of students keeping "process logs" or "process recordings" to assist students to better understand their perceptions and responses to patients. These process recordings encourage self-awareness, which is the cornerstone of empathy. Other educational programs also utilize audio/videotaping of clinical sessions and interactions with patients to provide students the opportunity to critique themselves as well as to receive feedback on their clinical skills, including empathic responses.

One aspect that was not mentioned in the preceding factors is the role of external factors on the levels of empathy in psychotherapists, physicians, and nurses. One such external factor is the managed care environment, which often dictates what is considered "acceptable" for the helping professional regarding their patients (Karon, 1995). The managed care system often creates time constraints on the therapeutic relationship, where therapists may find themselves planning strategies of intervention prematurely based on a limited understanding of the patient's problem. In order to meet the demands of time constraints, therapists may also feel compelled to demonstrate that their patients are "making progress" by pressing too hard, or limiting their interventions to what they feel competent to treat, often avoiding deeper and more complex aspects of patients' problems in order to comply with the restrictions of managed care (Bennett, 2001). To illustrate this point, one counselor stated:

> In this second session I had wanted to do some real counseling, move him toward action, appease my own impatience, and write a progress note that testified to his specific identifiable behavioral changes. I wanted something tangible to prove to myself that I was making a difference. (Kottler, 1998, p. 40)

The external pressures due to managed care in the health professions is similar in some important ways to the pressures faced by educators in implementing mandatory testing and other governmental directives. In both cases, the helping professional is expected to achieve a patient or student outcome with limited funding and resources. Although it is reasonable to conclude that these external pressures would consistently reduce therapeutic empathy, Mitchell (1998) found that clients' perception of therapist empathy did not appear to be negatively impacted by managed care. Future research in this area might benefit from considering such factors as severity of clients problems and therapist skill level as variables that could mediate the impact of managed care on therapist empathy.

In addition to managed care impacting levels of empathy, other external forces play a role in decreased levels of empathy in helping professionals. Reynolds, Scott, and Austin (2000) report that in nursing literature, the barriers to empathy may include the way in which nursing work is traditionally organized and a fear of risk-taking on the nurse's part when the patient's emotional distress is too overwhelming. Other external factors in health care, such as staffing levels (mostly understaffed), workloads, expectations and pressure of rapid patient discharge from the hospital, and a lack of understanding of the therapeutic potential of empathy, often prevent empathy from being regarded as a norm (Reynolds et al., 2000). As seen through the eyes of each discipline, empathy can take on different interpretations that signify each profession's core values, beliefs, as well as external constraints such as managed care, staffing issues, and the age of consumerism.

RECENT DEVELOPMENTS

Recently, the medical profession has taken significant and substantive measures to ensure that all newly trained physicians can demonstrate proficiency in the interpersonal skills necessary for typical patient contact by instituting a new clinical skills examination. This "bedside manner" test began in October 2004 for all graduating medical students and is now required as part of the national licensing exam. One of the three subcomponents of the exam specifically evaluates the student's ability to ask questions and share information in a clear, responsive, and effective manner. The examinees are also assessed regarding their skills in conveying concern and sensitivity as a way of building rapport with the patient (U.S. Medical Licensing Examination, 2004). These aspects of the exam reflect an applied conceptualization of empathic skills for the medical profession. The other two subcomponents of the overall clinical skills examination assess the ability of the student to accurately gather patient data, appropriately document the information, and speak English in an understandable manner.

The national medical licensing authorities have implemented this exam over the strong objections of the main professional organizations for physicians (American Medical Association) and medical students (American Medical Students Association). Papadakis (2004) has concisely reviewed this controversy and, as a leading medical educator, she concludes that in the interest of professional accountability as well as maintaining the public's trust, the new exam is warranted. Despite this intraprofessional controversy, the medical profession should now be recognized as the only helping profession that requires a nationally uniform experiential exam that directly evaluates professional interpersonal skills. There is strong evidence that the public supports the requirement for physicians to demonstrate professional interpersonal skills (U.S. Medical Licensing Examination, 2004), and anecdotes of doctors with poor bedside manners are legion. It stands to reason that the public would also want to ensure that psychotherapists, nurses, and other health professionals demonstrate the interpersonal skills commensurate for their helping roles. This is especially relevant for psychotherapists, who often recognize the psychotherapeutic relationship as the main curative agent in and of itself. However, while individual degree programs and state licensing boards throughout the health professions may institute different degrees of "dispositional gatekeeping," none currently utilize a nationally administered experiential exam similar to the one instituted by physicians. Perhaps other helping professions, including education and teacher education, can benefit from closely following the implementation and evolution of the new physicians' exam. Although the challenges and obstacles to implementing a similar type of exam for teachers would undoubtedly be fertile ground for controversy, the importance of ensuring that teachers can demonstrate the requisite dispositions to teach is much less open to debate.

REFERENCES

Alligood, M. R. (1992). Empathy: The importance of recognizing two types. *Journal of Psychosocial Nursing, 30*, 14–17.

Aring, C. (1958). Sympathy and empathy. *Journal of the American Medical Association, 167*(4), 448–452.

Bennett, M. J. (2001). *The empathic healer: An endangered species.* San Diego: Academic Press.

Bozarth, J. (1984). Beyond reflection-emergent modes of empathy. In R. E. Levant & J. M. Shlien (Eds.), *Client-centered therapy and the person-centered approach: New directions* (pp. 59–75). New York: Praeger.

Carkuff, R., & Berenson, B. (1967). *Beyond counseling and therapy.* New York: Praeger.

Carlozzi, A. F., Bull, K. S., Stein, L. B., Ray, K., & Barnes, L. (2002). Empathy theory and practice: A survey of psychologists and counselors. *Journal of Psychology, 136*(2), 161–171.

Carmel, S., & Glick, S. (1996). Compassionate-empathic physicians: Personality traits and social-organizational factors that enhance or inhibit this behavior pattern. *Social Sciences and Medicine, 43*(8), 1253–1261.

Duan, C., & Hill, C. E. (1996). The current state of empathy research. *Journal of Counseling Psychology, 43*(3), 261–274.

Duan, C., Rose, T. B., & Kratz, R. A. (2002). Empathy. In G. Tryon (Ed.), *Counseling based on process research: Applying what we know* (pp. 197–231). Boston: Allyn & Bacon.

Feshbach, N. D. (1975). Empathy in children: Some theoretical and empirical considerations. *Counseling Psychologist, 5*, 25–30.

Goldstein, A. P., & Michaels, G. Y. (1985). *Empathy: Development, training, and consequences.* Hillsdale, NJ: Erlbaum.

Greenson, R. R. (1960). Empathy and its vicissitudes. *International Journal of Psychoanalysis, 41*, 418–424.

Halpern, J. (2001). *From detached concern to empathy: Humanizing medical practice.* Oxford: Oxford University Press.

Hojat, M., Fields, S. K., & Gonnella, J. S. (2003). Empathy: An NP/MD comparison. *Nurse Practitioner, 28*(4), 45–48.

Hudson, G. R. (1993). Empathy and technology in the coronary care unit. *Intensive and Critical Care Nursing, 9*, 55–61.

Karon, B. P. (1995). Provision of psychotherapy under managed care: A growing crisis and national nightmare. *Professional Psychology, 26*, 5–9.

Kottler, J. (1998). Three variations on a theme: The power of pure empathy. *Journal of Humanistic Education and Development, 37*(1), 39–47.

Kunst-Wilson, W., Carpenter, L., Poser, A., Verker, I., & Kushner, K. (1981). Empathic perceptions of nursing students' self-reported and actual ability. *Residential Nursing Health, 4*, 283–293.

Kunyk, D., & Olson, J. K. (2001). Clarification of conceptualizations of empathy. *Journal of Advanced Nursing, 35*, 317–326.

Liaschenko, J., & Davis, A. J. (1991). Nurses and physicians on nutritional support: A comparison. *Journal of Medicine and Philosophy, 16*, 259–283.

MacLeod-Clarke, J. (1983). Nurse-patient communications: An analysis of conversations from surgical wards. In J. Wilson-Barnett (Ed.), *Nursing research: Ten studies in care* (pp. 25–56). Chichester: Wiley.

McLeod, J. (1999). A narrative social constructivist approach to therapeutic empathy. *Counselling Psychology Quarterly, 12*(4), 377–395.

Mitchell, C. G. (1998). Perceptions of empathy and client satisfaction with managed behavioral healthcare. *Social Work, 43*(5), 404–412.

Mynatt, S. (1985). Empathy in faculty and students in different types of nursing preparation programs. *West Journal Nursing Resources, 7*, 333–348.

Papadakis, M. A. (2004). The step 2 clinical-skills examination. *New England Journal of Medicine, 350*(17), 1703–1705.

Patterson, C. H. (1984). Empathy, warmth, and genuineness: A review of reviews. *Psychotherapy, 21*, 431–438.

Reynolds, W. J. (2000). Do nurses and other professional helpers normally display much empathy? *Journal of Advanced Nursing, 31*(1), 226–235.

Reynolds, W., Scott, P. A., & Austin, W. (2000). Nursing, empathy, and perception of the moral. *Journal of Advanced Nursing, 32*(1), 235–243.

Rogers, C. R. (1957). The necessary and sufficient conditions of therapeutic personality change. *Journal of Consulting Psychology, 21*, 95–103.

Rogers, C. R. (1961). *On becoming a person*. Boston: Houghton Mifflin.

Scharf, R. S. (1996). *Theories of psychotherapy and counseling concepts and cases*. New York: Brooks/Cole.

Scott, P. A. (1995). Care, attention trod imaginative identification in nursing practice. *Journal of Advanced Nursing, 21*, 1196–1200.

Strupp, H. H. (1995). The psychotherapist's skills revisited. *Clinical Psychology: Science and Practice, 2*, 70–74.

U.S. Medical Licensing Examination. (2004). Scoring of the step 2 examination. Retrieved October 14, 2004, from http://www.usmle.org/step2/Step2CS/Step2CS2005GI/scoring.asp

Watson, J. (2002). *Assessing and measuring caring in nursing and health science*. New York: Springer.

Wheeler, K., & Barrett, E. (1994). Review and synthesis of selected nursing studies on teaching empathy and implications for nursing research and education. *Nursing Outlook, 42*, 230–236.

7

Using Moral Development Theory to Promote the Growth of Ethical Dispositions Within K–12 Students

Judith Oates Lewandowski

Children today face a very different world from that of their parents. A recent television commercial exemplifies this point when a young teen, who after disobeying her parents, is grounded from the use of the telephone. The teen jokes with her friend, through the use of an Internet-based phone, about the "punishment" she has received. Much to the chagrin of the teen, her mother enters the room and overhears the conversation. Without hesitation, the mother extends the punishment to include banishment from the computer.

Technology, it seems, has permeated into virtually all aspects of our lives. Its incorporation has influenced the way in which we communicate, travel, work, learn, and raise our children. Consider the lifespan of teenagers born in 1988. For them, it is common practice to chat with friends from around the world, watch news events as they happen, interact with experts via the Internet, capture photos digitally, and manipulate historical recordings of events. The environment in which these children will grow up is quite different from that of their parents. All of these differences resonate the divide between the skill set that will be required of these children as they mature into adults as opposed to the skills that were needed by previous generations. In addition to the acquisition of technical skills, it is critical that children acquire the disposition to use technology in a productive, equitable, and ultimately ethical manner. If children are not encouraged to develop the disposition to utilize technology in a positive and productive manner at the same time that they are introduced to technical skills, the burden of ethical growth becomes an even more daunting task for schools and industry alike.

ACQUISITION OF ETHICAL GUIDELINES IN THE WORKPLACE

Familiarity with and utilization of new technical advances are critical components of an educated 21st-century workforce. However, the development of a new skill set goes far beyond simple technical know-how. The information technology (IT) workforce must also understand the ethical implications of the programs they write, the actions they take, and the criticality of protecting intellectual property in the online environment. Individuals who learn only the technical side of technology are missing an integral part of the new skill set.

Unethical behavior can be a costly mistake for industries to counteract on several levels. Fines, public embarrassment, negative publicity, professional reputation damage, low employee morale, and difficulty in employee recruitment are all examples of common costs associated with unethical business practices (Nash, 1993). Lands' End, a prominent clothing manufacturer, offers a dramatic example of a commitment to include ethical training as part of the new skill set required of its employees. Members of the Lands' End IT team are routinely placed under security audits, which include technical attacks on its information security practices as well as individual ethical tests of the team members (Wilder & Soat, 2001). By utilizing this type of spontaneous performance check, Lands' End is actively working to develop and maintain a workforce that is both secure and ethical in its daily practice. Additionally, a recent *Information Week* survey indicated that 62% of the reporting corporations monitor their employees' use of the Internet, and 54% monitor the e-mail of their employees (Wilder & Soat, 2001). These monitoring practices are deemed both ethical and common by most IT professionals, yet it is not clear as to where the employees are to acquire these skills for discerning appropriate use of the technology.

The nature of the IT world changes the use of ethical behavior for some. In the invisible online world, where you can interact almost anonymously, some individuals experience difficulty in translating their real-world ethical guidelines into the online environment. When individuals interact in a direct face-to-face manner, they can see the impact their dialogue is creating. In the online environment, individuals can send a dramatic, painful, and derogatory response without having to witness the pain the receiver endures (DeMaio, 1990).

ACQUISITION OF ETHICAL GUIDELINES IN SCHOOLS

In an effort to promote the development of ethical dispositions within children, it is imperative that students understand the implications that their online behavior may have upon others. If they are unable to draw the connection between real-world ethics and the online environment, the students will need to be guided in this transition by role models, parents, and teachers. Ethical training can benefit students by "increasing their awareness and sensitivity to important issues surrounding ethical problem solving" (Windsor & Cappel, 1999, p. 288). To this end, it is critical that cyber ethics be addressed as part of the regular curriculum of our K–12 schools. As we teach students the skills to use technology, we must also teach them the proper guidelines for appropriate use.

ETHICS AND CYBER ETHICS DEFINED

According to the American Heritage Dictionary, "ethics" refers to the set of principles of right conduct. It is "concern with what we consider to be 'right' or 'just' behavior" (Gibney, 1999, p.19). Ethics refers to the guiding principles or ideals of good versus evil. Ethics are not based in law, religion, or standardized beliefs; rather, ethics refer to a general conception of right and wrong that transcend both religion and law. Cyber ethics refers to the application of ethics into the online or virtual environment (Ethics Connection, 2000).

Justification of Cyber Ethics at the K–12 Level

When promoting the disposition to utilize technology in an ethical manner, it demands attention at a young age. The majority of children begin developing significant use of their ethical principles between the ages of 10 and 12 (Geide, Crystal, & Salpeter, 2000). To hesitate in teaching ethical principles until adulthood is not only ineffective but also risky. There are countless examples of the horror stories of students who, once empowered with technical skills, feel the need to practice them in inappropriate ways. Distribution of pornography, sexual harassment, credit card theft, destruction of governmental websites, modification of grades, counterfeiting rings, and software piracy are just a few of the technically based illegal activities with which students in our schools have been involved (Marsh, 2000).

In addition, common classroom distractions have even been impacted by technology, often with a more vicious twist. One prominent example involves the illegal use of others' e-mail accounts to send inappropriate, threatening, or mean e-mail to fellow classmates. This practice has become so commonplace in schools that many middle school teachers trivialize it by making it analogous to passing handwritten notes about the "un-cool kids" in class (Marsh, 2000).

As technology integration has progressed throughout society over the past several years, it is also interesting to note that the frequency of computer crimes and misuse has also dramatically risen. Specifically, the 2000 Computer Security Institute/FBI Computer Crime and Security survey indicates that computer crime and other information security breaches are on the rise, with 90% of the responding 585 participants reporting computer security violations within the previous 12-month period (Smith, 2000). Many experts agree that this trend in increasing rates of computer crime will escalate even further. The consensus from a recent Department of Justice conference on computer-related crime was that, due to the increased integration of computers into the K–12 learning environment, the number of potential perpetrators of this type of crime will rise dramatically (Smith, 2000). According to this group, the basic adventurous nature of technology can lead undirected users to misuse the equipment (Sivin & Bialo, 1992).

It appears that schools are providing students with the opportunity to develop and learn the skills to use technology; yet, at the same time failing to teach the students the principles surrounding the acceptable use of technology. It is the lack of instruction on these soft skills in the curriculum that has many experts worried about the propagating culture of young Internet users (Geide et al., 2000).

Other research echoes this sentiment on a more youthful level. In April 2000, Scholastic, Inc. conducted a survey asking 47,235 elementary and middle school students if hacking should be considered a crime. Alarmingly, 48% of students reported that it was not criminal (Geide et al., 2000). Additionally, in a study of 729 high school students conducted by Vincent and Meche (2001), 19% of the students indicated that they felt that personal use of company e-mail, which was designated for company use only, was ethical, and 49% said that they would use it for personal mail.

Society is a dynamic system. It must, by nature, evolve in order to survive. As we develop the new definitions of appropriate behavior in the online environment, it is imperative that many members of society be engaged in this ongoing dialogue. An informed community and active discussion of ethical issues will enable society to determine civil and just manners to deal with the nuances of technological advancement (Rezmierski, 1992). By opening this dialogue within the K–12 environment, teachers will be able to prepare students to understand the proper use of technology and explore the issues that will continue to unfold. Unfortunately, many educators are not equipped with the skills to effectively integrate ethics into their classrooms. In order to successfully blend ethical instruction into the K–12 curriculum, educators must develop an understanding of moral development principles, recognize age-appropriate moral dissonance, and learn to advocate for the moral growth of the students' perspectives (Clare, Gallimore, & Patthey-Chavez, 1996).

ALIGNING K–12 CYBER ETHICS CONTENT WITH MORAL DEVELOPMENT THEORY

The teaching of cyber ethics and the promotion of dispositional growth goes far beyond the simple memorization of a "code of conduct" or guidelines for acceptable use. The basis of cyber ethics is grounded within the moral development of children and requires an adherence to the findings of researchers on the most effective and appropriate methods of dissemination.

Determining Cyber Ethic Age Appropriate Activities

According to Deni Elliott (1997), director of the Practical Ethics Center, moral development is very similar to the physical development of humans; just as infants must learn to crawl before they walk, they must go through the process of learning how to "develop a sense of caring for oneself before one can take others' needs into consideration" (p. 71). Many educators feel overwhelmed at selecting both the appropriate cyber ethical content and the developmental strategy to be incorporated into their classrooms. The following section of this chapter offers a synthesis of the foundational theories of moral development and the prominent issues of age-appropriate cyber ethics activities.

A Synthesis of Moral Development Theories

Piaget's Theory

Within his prominent research on the cognitive development of children, Jean Piaget included focus upon the moral development of children. His belief was that once children developed cognitively, they were then able to formulate opinions and beliefs regarding social dilemmas. Piaget argued that as the children aged, their moral development would predictably occur at specific stages, beginning with an egocentric level (heteronymous morality) and transposing into a more sophisticated judicious level (autonomous morality) (Slavin, 2000). "Heteronymous morality" refers to the first stage of moral development through which a child progresses and focuses upon the adherence to rules created by others. At this stage, children believe that "bad" people will always be punished, justice will always prevail, and the "morality" of a decision is determined by its impending consequence (Lamb, 1978).

Piaget believed children remained in the heteronymous stage from approximately age 6 through age 10, at which time they entered into the autonomous morality stage (Slavin, 2000). Within this second stage, children understood the concept of rules, but often based their moral judgment upon the "intent" of a person, as opposed to the consequences of the action as well as the overall establishment of fairness for all involved (Lamb, 1978). Piaget noted that children in this stage of development often question hypothetical situations and the resulting impact upon the established rules (Slavin, 2000).

Piaget argued that in order for children to refine and increase the sophistication of their ability to conduct moral analysis (critical for reference as adults), they must engage in conflict resolution with peers in which they must work together collectively in order to redefine the appropriate response for the situation (Piaget, 1965). Piaget believed that this growth was constructivist in nature and demanded problem-based learning activities rather than strict memorization or adherence to a particular set of social norms (Piaget, 1965). The ability to act from an analysis of intent and fairness is associated with a shift in the child's cognitive structure from heteronymous morality to autonomous morality (Murray, 2001). As Mary Elizabeth Murray of the University of Illinois summarizes:

> Coordinating one's own perspective with that of others means that what is right needs to be based on solutions that meet the requirements of fair reciprocity. Thus, Piaget viewed moral development, as the result of interpersonal interactions through which individuals work out resolutions which all deem fair. Paradoxically, this autonomous view of morality as fairness is more compelling and leads to more consistent behavior than the heteronymous orientation held by younger children. (p. 2)

Kohlberg's Theory

Building on Piaget's beliefs of moral development, Lawrence Kohlberg elaborated the stages and developed a new theory of moral development. Kohlberg argued that Piaget's description of moral stages was not thorough. He believed that the attainment of moral development was much more gradual and occurred in several distinct stages (Murray, 2001). Through his research, Kohlberg identified six stages of moral development that were contained equally within three separate levels of reasoning (see Table 7.1.). Kohlberg believed that children developed through an invariant sequence of his defined stages (Crain, 2000).

The first level of Kohlbergian theory is the preconventional level. This first level, containing Stages 1 and 2, deals primarily with reactions of individuals on the basis of fear and the establishment of morality as an external set of principles defined by society (Crain, 2000). Within Stage 1, individuals react to moral dilemmas by focusing upon fear and punishment. Individuals at this stage simply want to obey all rules in order to avoid punishment. In Stage 2, individuals choose their reaction in hopes of a reward. Kohlberg believed

Table 7.1. Kohlberg's Six Stages of Moral Development

Level	Stage
Preconventional	Stage 1: Fear and punishment
	Stage 2: Hope for a reward
Conventional	Stage 3: Peer approval
	Stage 4: Adherence to law and order
Postconventional	Stage 5: Inherent social contract
	Stage 6: Universal ethical principles

Source: Kohlberg & Turiel, 1971.

that individuals functioned within this level from anticipation of a positive reinforcement.

Kohlberg's second level, containing Stages 3 and 4, is known as the conventional level, which emphasizes the importance of societal needs over individual needs (Kohlberg & Turiel, 1971). Within Stage 3, the individual seeks peer approval to determine moral decisions. Beliefs of what is right or wrong are based solely upon the acceptance of others (Elliott, 1997). Stage 4 focuses on the individual's establishment of formal law and order. The individual defines his or her perspective of right and wrong based upon the established social mandates (Murray, 2001).

The postconventional level, containing Stages 5 and 6, requires individuals to define their own values and ethical principles and demands the highest level of sophisticated thought (Kohlberg & Turiel, 1971). Stage 5 focuses on the individual as a component of the inherent social contract that enables the development of a strong society. Due to this contract, individuals must make ethical decisions based upon the "broad benefit" of society (Crain, 2000). Stage 6 builds on the depth of Stage 5 and requires individuals to determine ethical decisions on the basis of universal principles, including individual worth, democratic processes, and justice (Crain, 2000; Elliott, 1997). These two postconventional stages demand an extremely high level of moral sophistication.

Kohlberg (Kohlberg, 1981; Kohlberg & Turiel, 1971) believed these stages were not the direct result of chronology or maturation. Rather, Kohlberg argued that these stages emerged from individual thinking, reflection, and analysis of moral dilemmas (Crain, 2000). As others actively challenge personal beliefs through discussion and debate, the individual must respond with a more comprehensive analysis of the perspective resulting in the progression through Kohlberg's stages (Kohlberg, Kauffman, Scharf, & Hickey, 1975). Kohlberg encouraged the incorporation of these types of moral analysis activities within the curriculum of K–12 education as a means to help the students identify, clarify, and analyze their personal moral beliefs and development (Crain, 2000).

Gilligan's Theory

Carol Gilligan, a former student of Kohlberg's, believed that his theory of moral development was incomplete due to the gender bias inherent within his male-only studies (Murray, 2001). Gilligan does not promote the establishment of gender-based moral development; rather, she underscores that a "mature individual" would exhibit both masculine and feminine characteristics (Elliott, 1997). Through her research of women's experiences, Gilligan found that a "morality of care can serve in the place of the morality of justice and rights espoused by Kohlberg" (Murray, 2001, p. 4). Gilligan argues that females will often focus upon altruistic and self-sacrificial choices rather than individual rights or justice (Gilligan, 1982).

Gilligan's (1982) theory, also known as the "Morality of Care," focuses on the feminine perspective of moral development (Murray, 2001). This theory is based on the sequential development of women from the care of self (Level 1) to the care of others (Level 2) to the integration of the care of self and others (Level 3).

Within Level 1 (Orientation to Individual Survival), the individual reacts as a victim and perceives that she is incapable of caring for herself or others (Elliott, 1991). As the individual progresses to Level 2, a firm recognition of "responsibility" must occur. As the individual enters into Level 2 (Self-Sacrifice), she still is not capable of caring for herself; however, she recognizes the social benefit of sacrificing herself for the sake of others (Elliott, 1997). Within this stage, the individual focuses on the care of others as a means to gain positive reinforcement from peers and/or society. As the woman enters Level 3 (Nonviolence), she is able to move beyond the perceived conflict between her role as a caregiver and her own personal care. Within this final stage, the woman reacts to dilemmas with the insight of what is best for herself as well as for others. At this level, the individual "accepts nonviolence as the ultimate principle; being moral means minimizing pain and harm for everyone" (Elliott, 1991, p. 22).

Application of Kohlbergian Theory to the Instruction of Cyber Ethics

There is much to be learned and researched on the moral development process. None of the three theories discussed contains the conclusive set of best practices for the development of morality within children. At this point in time, those overall best practices have yet to be identified. According to Slavin (2000), all three theories have received substantial criticism: Piaget's is said to be too vague and general; Kohlberg's is said to be too structured, too idealistic, and both gender and culturally biased; and Gilligan's theory has come under intense scrutiny due to the lack of findings regarding divisional results of gender-based moral processes.

For the context of cyber ethics, Piaget's theory of moral development lacks the structure needed by K–12 educators to easily align the theory with the needs of their students. For the purpose of classroom integration, Piaget's work is simply too vague to be practical. Likewise, Gilligan's work seems to focus too minutely upon the perspective of the female within the process of moral development. Additionally, Gilligan's focus upon the "interpersonal relationships of daily life" does not lend itself to the study of the broad topic of cyber ethics.

On the contrary, Kohlberg's six stages of moral development seem to provide a balanced, structured guideline for incorporating the content of cyber ethics within the K–12 learning environment. The simplicity and chronological nature of the stages lend themselves well to the structure of current K–12 curricular practices. The use of Kohlberg's stages within the K–12 learning environment has been advocated by several groups of researchers (Clare et al., 1996). At this point, no formal research has been conducted to justify the use of Kohlberg's stages within the context of K–12 cyber ethics; however, the common principles of moral development inherent within the issue seem to imply a direct transfer of practice. According to Perry (1970), "Kohlberg's theory of moral judgment can thus be considered to be widely applicable in discussing moral education in a variety of fields and with a variety of age groups" (p. 90).

The inclusion of cyber ethics content must be aligned with the active learning strategies suggested by Kohlberg. In a 1971 study conducted by Turiel, children who listened to the moral viewpoints of adults demonstrated little overall change. This finding is in line with Kohlberg's beliefs that moral development, on any topic or issue, will only occur if the children are provided with an opportunity to explore their own moral reasoning and perspectives (Crain, 2000).

CYBER ETHICS INTEGRATION STRATEGIES

Due to the lack of research, there is not much information readily available to describe the current state of inclusion of cyber ethics within the U.S. K–12 curriculum. Despite this lacking, experts do have several suggestions for the incorporation of cyber ethics within the curriculum.

In selecting strategies, it is imperative that educators determine those that will work most effectively with their students. Additionally, it is critical that the examples, scenarios, or case studies that are used are both relevant and realistic to the learners. Failing to select realistic settings will make the transition of ideas more difficult for the students.

First and foremost, a commitment must be made to include the topic of cyber ethics as a yearlong component of the curriculum. Programs of dispositional development must be integrated within the regular classroom curriculum and should not be labeled as a special unit or focus (Nucci, 1987). Designating an "ethics" day and handing out ribbons and pencils will not do much for creating and sustaining an environment of acceptable use. According to Sivin and Bialo (1992), the first step in creating such an environment relies upon the ability of the teachers, administrators, and school officials to model strong cyber ethics attitudes as a method of teaching the concept vicariously to students. The integration of ethical discussions must be conducted regularly and focus upon issues that are relevant to the lives of the student (Perry, 1970). By demonstrating the importance of making ethical decisions on a daily basis, the students will learn directly from the positive dispositional role models they encounter.

Furthermore, the topic of ethics transcends individual subject areas. As technology is integrated throughout the curriculum, so must the discussion of ethics (Pligas, 2000). Utilizing such tools as the Computer Ethics Institute's "Ten Commandments for Computer Ethics" (see Table 7.2), teachers can easily create lessons and activities that focus upon the acceptable use of technology in conjunction with using technology as a tool for another class (Computer Ethics Institute, 2004).

A Moral Development Model for Cyber Ethics Integration

Moral development pedagogy must be both founded in theory and reflective of practice (Leming, 1997). By dividing the topic of cyber ethics into developmentally appropriate, engaging activities, educators will be able to more easily implement the recommended cyber ethics content identified earlier. The model presented in Table 7.3 contains a sample result of the blending of Kohlberg's six stages of moral development and the basic cyber

Table 7.2.   The Ten Commandments of Computer Ethics

1. Thou Shalt Not Use a Computer to Harm Other People.
2. Thou Shalt Not Interfere with Other People's Computer Work.
3. Thou Shalt Not Snoop around in Other People's Computer Files.
4. Thou Shalt Not Use a Computer to Steal.
5. Thou Shalt Not Use a Computer to Bear False Witness.
6. Thou Shalt Not Copy or Use Proprietary Software for which You Have Not Paid.
7. Thou Shalt Not Use Other People's Computer Resources without Authorization or Proper Compensation.
8. Thou Shalt Not Appropriate Other People's Intellectual Output.
9. Thou Shalt Think about the Social Consequences of the Program You Are Writing or the System You Are Designing.
10. Thou Shalt Always Use a Computer in Ways That Ensure Consideration and Respect for Your Fellow Humans.

Source: Computer Ethics Institute, 2004.

Table 7.3. Blending Kohlbergian Theory with Computer Ethics

Kohlbergian Stage	Sample Cyber Ethic Concepts	Example Activities*
Stage 1: Fear and punishment	Do not interfere with other people's work.	K–2: Using an age-appropriate analogy, conduct a minilesson with students comparing the destruction of artwork made in art class with the destruction of art made on the computer. Emphasize the resulting consequence to such behavior (rules).
	Do not use the computer to harm others.	3–5: Using a case study, identify a scenario in which a student deletes another's files for malicious purposes. Highlight the similar ties between this deletion and theft. Discuss appropriate consequences.
Stage 2: Hope for a reward	Do not copy software illegally.	3–5: Using a case study, develop a situation in which a student alerts school officials to the unauthorized use of software. As a result, the student is commended and receives praise and positive reinforcement.
Stage 3: Peer approval	Refrain from "snooping" in other people's files.	3–5: Using an analogy, conduct a minilesson in which students compare the reasons why they wouldn't snoop in the backpacks of their peers. Relate this to snooping into computer files. Emphasize the need for the students to base these decisions upon mutual respect/approval.
		6–8: Discuss the concept of privacy. Relate increased privacy needs (lockers, purses, backpacks) of the students to their maturation as young adults. Relate this to privacy protection of computer files. Emphasize the need for young adults to respect each other's privacy as a sign of maturity. Additionally, emphasize the peer-approval of privacy.

(continued)

Table 7.3. *(continued)*

Kohlbergian Stage	Sample Cyber Ethic Concepts	Example Activities*
Stage 4: Adherence to law and order	Respect copyright laws and intellectual property.	6–8: Using a case study, identify a situation in which a student's work is copied and turned by a peer. Relate this to copyright and discuss potential school-based consequences.
		9–12: During a unit on web page development, discuss the importance of copyright as it relates to web page design. Highlight the need for designers to be aware of legal principles as a means of avoiding violation.
Stage 5: Inherent social contract	Use a computer to show respect for others.	10–12: Within the context of a web design project, discuss with the students the ability of the Internet to serve as a springboard for global understanding and appreciation. As part of the project, have the students reflect upon their ability to positively impact society through the development of the project.
Stage 6: Universal ethical principles	Think about the social consequences of the programs you create.	11–12: Within the context of a programming course, ask students to reflect upon the inherent beneficial components of the programs they create. Discuss the value in pursuing opportunities with a positive impact as well as the resulting consequences of those with a negative impact.

*Note: This identification of grade level is subject to modification based upon the ability, environment, technical skills/access, and social structure of the classroom. Educators are encouraged to personalize the use of this mode for inclusion within their curriculum.

ethics content indicated from the Computer Ethics Institute's "Ten Commandments of Cyber Ethics."

APPLICATION OF THE MODEL

In an effort to promote dispositional growth, educators are encouraged to regularly develop student-based activities on the topic of cyber ethics. Throughout discussions and case studies, the teachers should attempt to lead their students to the next level in an attempt to challenge the students and aid in the development of their moral capabilities (Elliott, 1991). It is not enough for students to be provided with a list of classroom or computer lab procedures; students must actively engage themselves in the process of discovering the moral issue involved within realistic, yet diverse situations. The development of cyber ethics educational materials should focus upon simplistic scenarios that the students can readily understand and apply to their daily lives (Pollock, 1988).

Many of these topics naturally occur within the learning environment and simply need to be addressed with a more formal pedagogical approach. For example, at the start of the school year, many schools assign students a generic password to accompany their unique student log-in. Rather than just allowing the students to use a generic password that could threaten the overall security of the school's network, students should be guided in creating a unique and "strong" password to better protect their work and the system.

To teach respect for intellectual property, teachers could utilize an age-appropriate analogy and conduct a minilesson with students comparing the destruction of artwork made in art class with the destruction of art made on the computer. Additionally, when discussing the increased privacy needs (lockers, purses, backpacks) of the students, teachers could work to establish a similar connection to the protection of privacy via computer networks and storage media.

Short, concise discussions and natural teaching moments coupled with a strong role-model system will help to establish the foundational level of the importance of making decisions in conjunction with the standards of cyber ethics. By infusing ethical teachings within the instructional process, the students will benefit from the daily importance of the topic (Sivin & Bialo, 1992).

CONCLUSION

In choosing to incorporate these types of activities, educators will be actively promoting the development of cyber ethics, a critical skill that our students will need in order to propagate a productive and strong society (Eiermann, 1997). As technology becomes an increasingly more prominent component of society, the workforce must adapt and acquire both the technical skills and the ethical framework for utilizing these tools in a productive, respective, and equitable manner. The model of integration provided will hopefully serve as a springboard for the willing inclusion of cyber ethics content within individual classrooms. Teaching these concepts throughout the K–12 curriculum will help to establish the long-term importance of the principles and the promotion of a positive disposition for use. It will also provide the students with an opportunity to participate in a dialogue of discovery in which they can help to interpret and define the ever-changing face of ethics in society.

REFERENCES

Clare, L., Gallimore, R., & Patthey-Chavez, G. (1996). Using moral dilemmas in children's literature as a vehicle for moral education and teaching reading comprehension. *Journal of Moral Education, 25*(3), 325–343.

Computer Ethics Institute. (2004). *Ten commandments of computer ethics.* Retrieved July 20, 2004, from http://www.brook.edu/dybdocroot/its/cei/overview/Ten_Commanments_of_Computer_Ethics.htm

Crain, W. (2000). *Theories of development: Concepts and applications.* Upper Saddle River, NJ: Prentice-Hall.

DeMaio, H. (1990, April 27–28). *Information ethics, a private perspective.* Invited paper presented to the National Institute of Justice, Professional Conference on Information Technology Ethics, Washington, DC.

Eiermann, P. (1997). A teacher's postmodern guide to ethics in the video production laboratory. *Journal of Research on Computing in Education, 29*(3), 215–226.

Elliott, D. (1991). Moral development theories and the teaching of ethics. *Journalism Educator, 3,* 18–26.

Elliott, D. (1997). Universal values and moral development theories. In C. Christians & M. Traber (Eds.), *Communication ethics and universal values.* London: Sage.

Ethics Connection. (2000). *What is ethics?* Retrieved November 7, 2000, from http://www.scu.edu/SCU/Centers/Ethics/practicing/decision/whatisethics.shtml

Geide, C., Crystal, J., & Salpeter, J. (2000). The concerned educator's guide to safety and cyber-ethics. *Technology and Learning, 21*(4), 24–31.

Gibney, M. (1999). Missing the forest for the trees. *Humanist, 3,* 19–22.

Gilligan, C. (1982). *In a different voice: Psychological theory and women's development.* Cambridge: Harvard University Press.

Kohlberg, L. (1981). *Essays on moral development.* San Francisco: Harper & Row.

Kohlberg, L., Kauffman, K., Scharf, P., & Hickey, J. (1975). *The just community approach in corrections: A manual.* Niantic, CT: Connecticut Department of Corrections.

Kohlberg, L., & Turiel, E. (1971). Moral development and moral education. In G. Lesser (Ed.), *Psychology and educational practice.* Glenview, IL: Scott Foresman.

Lamb, M. (1978). *Social and personality development.* New York: Holt, Rinehart, & Winston.

Leming, J. (1997). Whither goes character education? *Journal of Education, 179*(2), 11–33.

Marsh, M. (2000). *Piracy, pornography, plagiarism, propaganda, privacy* (White paper). Retrieved May 4, 2000, from Computer Learning Organization website http://www.computerlearning.org/ARTICLES/Ethics98.htm

Murray, M. (2001). *Moral development and moral education: An overview.* Retrieved October 1, 2001, from http://tigger.uic.edu/~Inucci/MoralEd/overview.html

Nash, L. (1993). *Good intentions aside: A manager's guide to resolving ethical problems.* Boston: Harvard Business School Press.

Nucci, L. (1987). Synthesis of research on moral development. *Educational Leadership, 2,* 55–60.

Perry, W. (1970). *Forms of intellectual and ethical development in the college years.* New York: Holt, Rinehart, & Winston.

Piaget, J. (1965). *The moral judgment of the child.* New York: Free Press.

Pligas, L. (2000). Learning IT right from wrong. *Info World, 22*(40), 39–41.

Pollock, L. (1988). Evaluating moral theories. *American Philosophical Quarterly, 25*(3), 229–240.

Rezmierski, V. (1992). Managing information technology issues of ethics and values: Awareness, ownership, and values clarification. *Cause/Effect, 15*(3), 12–19.

Slavin, R. (2000). *Educational psychology: Theory and practice.* Boston: Allyn & Bacon.

Sivin, J., & Bialo, E. (1992). *Ethical use of information technologies in education: Important issues for America's schools.* U.S. Department of Justice Report. Retrieved May 4, 2000, from http://csrc.nist.gov/training/ethics.txt

Smith, P. (2000). *The cybercitizen partnership: Teaching children cyber ethics* (White paper). Washington, DC: Information Technology Association of America Foundation.

Turiel, E. (1983). *The development of social knowledge: Morality and convention.* New York: Cambridge University Press.

Vincent, A., & Meche, M. (2001). Use of ethical dilemmas to contribute to the knowledge and behavior of high school students. *High School Journal, 84*(4), 50–58.

Wilder, C., & Soat, J. (2001). A question of ethics. *Information Week, 825,* 38–44.

Windsor, J., & Cappel, J. (1999). A comparative study of moral reasoning. *College Student Journal, 33*(2), 281–288.

8

Exploring Dispositions in Teacher Education Through Children's Literature

Daniel T. Holm

These are times of great change in teacher education. The call for more accountability, stricter licensure requirements, and standards-based programs has stimulated national reform for how schools of education prepare teachers. With this national attention on teachers, schools, and teacher preparation programs, understanding what it takes to be a good teacher is paramount. As has already been discussed in previous chapters, teacher education standards developed by the National Council for the Accreditation of Teacher Education (NCATE) and standards for licensure for new teachers developed by the Interstate New Teacher Assessment and Support Consortium (INTASC) have impacted how teachers are preparing to meet the knowledge, skills (performance), and dispositions standards and principles identified by these organizations.

As teacher educators evaluate their programs, they can identify the knowledge of content, diversity, curriculum development, and child development that preservice teachers have acquired. Teacher educators are also able to assess the skills (performances) as preservice teachers lesson plan, organize the classroom for instruction, and assess student learning. In most teacher education programs, evaluating knowledge and skills is routine. However, in many teacher-educator programs, it is less clear how to evaluate or even discuss such dispositional qualities as caring, flexibility, fairness, respect, and tolerance that preservice teachers need to be effective teachers (Williams, Mitchell, & Leibbrand, 2003).

If teacher educators are to assist preservice teachers in developing the dispositional qualities of effective teachers, it is important, then, to provide teacher educators with pedagogical strategies that encourage, develop, and highlight the dispositional values or traits found in effective teachers. This

chapter suggests one such pedagogical strategy utilizing children's literature. For the purposes of this chapter, I will use NCATE's definition of dispositions as:

> The values, commitments and professional ethics that influence behaviors to-
> ward students, families, colleagues, and communities and affect student learn-
> ing, motivation, and development as well as educator's own professional
> growth. (NCATE, 2002)

THE IMPORTANCE OF STORY

Story has been an essential part of humankind. Stories were told to transmit information, to help us remember, to entertain, and to help us make sense of life
and our world (Shannon, 1995). Our own life and the lives of others can be
understood in the context of a narrative or story structure. In the telling of our
story, we have a beginning (birth), middle (life experiences), and end (death).
As we reflect on our lives, we think about our experiential stories as they define and explain who we are. Following this perspective, "the self is given content, is delineated and embodied, primarily in narrative constructions or stories" (Kerby, 1991, p. 1). Stories become an important element to meaning
making (Bruner, 1986, 2002; Polkinghorne, 1988, 1996) and as a means to develop a fuller understanding of actions and feelings (Goodfellow, 2000).

There is a great deal of research on narratives and the use of stories in
teacher education as a way to understand the art and act of teaching. Teacher
stories have been increasing in use in teacher education programs (McEwan
& Egan, 1995). Often, these narratives or stories take the form of teachers
sharing their teaching experiences with others, what Connelly and Clandinin
(1985) refer to as personal practical knowledge. Carter and Doyle (1996), in
their review of teacher narratives and life histories, identify the important
role that stories have in influencing the professional development and understandings of teachers. This influence is identified by Isenberg (1994)
when she writes:

> When, during the courses of my recent musings, these teacher-authors reap-
> peared in my consciousness, I recalled how they validated my affection for my
> students, as well as my horror at the biases and misanthropy of some of my col-
> leagues; how they have shared their mistakes and triumphs in the classroom
> with me, thus helping me cry over the implacability of the system while at the
> same time showing me how to manipulate its constraints; and how they had
> taken me with them on their forays across cultural boundaries. (p. xiv)

As in the reading of teacher narratives, so too, can the reading about teachers, as characters in children's literature offer insights into what it takes to be

a teacher. Dorris (1997) notes that stories influence readers by exposing them to other places and times, sharing in the lives of others, changing who we are by becoming immersed into a character's life, and through the recognition that others share the same hopes, passions, and fears that we all have as people living our lives. Jalongo and Isenberyg (1995) believe that this last concept becomes a critical element of stories as they provide deep insights into the nature of teaching and learning.

Children's literature, that is, literature that is written primarily with children and/or adolescent readers in mind, tells a story. The story might be fictional or actual; believable or fantastic; situated in the past, present, or future. Regardless of the type, literature for children and adolescents tells a story.

Stories that emphasize schools, classrooms, and teacher/student interactions are numerous. These stories, although perhaps primarily written for a reader's enjoyment, are also able to provide insights into teachers and what positive and/or negative teaching looks like within a fictionalized context. These children's stories, sometimes referred to as literature case studies (Griffith, 2002; Griffith & Laframboise, 1998; Laframboise & Griffith, 1997; Laframoise & Klesius, 1993), are especially useful with preservice teachers who do not always have the broad teaching base of more experienced teachers. Griffith and Laframboise (1998) define a literature case study as "a novel that contains school-based events and characters" (p. 365). The benefit of a literature case study, Griffith (2002) argues, is that it "evoke[s] affective responses in students about their aspirations as teachers, their feelings about teaching as a profession, and their identities as teachers" (p. 12).

Why would these types of children's literature be used in an education course? The answer is quite clear; quality children's stories situated in schools or other learning environments provide a rich description of teaching, students, teacher/student interactions and provide a context for discussing dispositional qualities of effective and ineffective teachers. The following section will serve as an example of the elements found in school-based children's literature stories.

A CHILDREN'S LITERATURE EXAMPLE

Frindle (Clements, 1996) is the story of Nick Allen and his interaction with his fifth-grade language arts teacher Mrs. Granger. Through the text we learn that Mrs. Granger loves the dictionary; focusing her students' attention on learning words. A power struggle develops between Nick and Mrs. Granger, when Nicholas decides to coin the word "frindle" to refer to a ballpoint pen. Mrs. Granger tries to keep frindle from becoming a popular word, and even keeps kids after school as a punishment for using the word. Over time, people start to use the word frindle; first locally and than nationally. Many years later, "frindle" is added to the dictionary. It is after the word frindle is added to the dictionary that Nick receives a letter from Mrs. Granger that she had written when his frindle campaign first started. This letter dramatically changes the reader's perception of Mrs. Granger's role in the story. The letter explains that, at first, she was upset with Nick's frindle campaign. But then, she came to understand that trying to stop the use of the word was not a viable option. It was then that she realized how she could encourage an idea that a bright mind gleaned from her class, by taking on the role of villain, that is, to seem as if she were trying to discourage the use of the word while in fact, helping the word to spread through her stance against the word's use.

This surprise ending completely changes how we view Mrs. Granger and offers a rich source of inquiry into teacher and student interactions, and more specifically into teacher dispositions.

Prior to analyzing *Frindle* (Clements, 1996) for INTASC dispositional qualities, it is important to review the elements of the INTASC core principles of: (1) content knowledge, (2) development, (3) individual differences, (4) instruction for diverse learners, (5) learning environment, (6) communication with students, (7) instructional planning, (8) assessment, (9) reflective practice, and (10) communication with community.

Although INTASC's 10 principles focus on knowledge, performance, and dispositions, the focus of this chapter is on the application of only the dispositional standards. The disposition standards associated with each of the 10 INTASC principles are outlined in Appendix A at the end of this chapter. It is suggested that the reader review the dispositional standards prior to reading the next section. After reviewing the dispositional standards, we can now look for links between *Frindle* and the dispositional standards.

Applying Dispositional Standards to *Frindle*

In this section, a one-sentence summary of each of the dispositional standards (found in Appendix A) is provided, followed by applications of the disposition to the book *Frindle*.

Content knowledge dispositions are associated with a teacher's enthusiasm for the discipline and lifelong learning, an understanding to pursue new knowledge, and an appreciation of multiple perspectives. Mrs. Granger demonstrates her understanding that knowledge is ever changing. This is shown through her willingness to support Nick's coined new word. She is also enthusiastic about words and attempts to convey that enthusiasm to her students.

Development dispositions are associated with the respect of a student's strengths and talents as a means to develop competence. Mrs. Granger shows that she appreciates diverse talents by encouraging Nick to carry through with his campaign to coin a new word. She uses his strengths to help him grow as a student.

Individual differences dispositions are associated with a teacher's belief that all children can be successful learners. The teacher believed that Nick could achieve and appreciated his varied talents.

Instruction for diverse learners dispositions are associated with valuing the varied abilities that students bring to the classroom and the willingness to adapt instruction to meet the diverse needs of all students. Throughout the story, Mrs. Granger valued Nick's critical thinking and problem solving and was encouraging of these attributes.

Learning environment dispositions are associated with the teacher organizing the classroom in such a way that all students can be successful in a positive instructional climate. Mrs. Granger valued the role of students in assisting each other in the learning process as well as helping students develop intrinsic motivation for lifelong learning.

Communication with students dispositions are associated with the fostering of a positive classroom environment that values self-expression. Mrs. Granger emphasized the power of language for learning.

Instructional planning dispositions are associated with short- and long-term planning, while realizing that plans are flexible based on the needs of students. The teacher was flexible in coming to realize that Nick needed to explore, in his own way, the content of her class.

Assessment dispositions are associated with the ongoing process of monitoring a student's strengths and areas for improvement. Mrs. Granger informally assessed Nick in her understanding of how he needed to explore to the end a topic of interest to him.

Reflective practice dispositions are associated with a teacher who seeks out help as well as a teacher who is willing to modify his or her instructional plans to better meet the needs of students. Mrs. Granger valued critical thinking and self-directed learning. She also was reflective on her role as teacher in helping Nick to pursue an idea.

Communication with community dispositions are associated with valuing the importance of all aspects of a student's life experiences. Mrs. Granger had the respect of the community. She also met with Nick's parents to share her concerns.

It should be noted that readers might identify other elements related to the INTASC core principles as they read the story. This occurs as a result of what Rosenblatt (1978) refers to as the transactive nature of reading. That is, as a reader reads, the response, the reactions, and the interpretations that the reader carries away from the text will vary. As Rosenblatt (1938) explains:

> There is not necessarily only one "correct" interpretation of the significance of a given work. Not even the author's possible statement of his aims can be

considered definitive, since the drama or poem or novel exists as a separate entity and can possess for us more values that he foresaw. The work must carry its own message to us. (pp. 134–135)

That said, the elements of the story identified here with the aforementioned principles should not in any way be seen as an exhaustive listing of what could be found as the text is discussed with others. Rather, it is a listing of elements readers might identify as they read. It is through exploring dispositional qualities through such activities as discussions with others and through journaling that preservice teachers are able to develop their own dispositional understandings of the story.

EXPLORING DISPOSITIONS

What are some ways in which preservice teachers could develop an understanding of teacher dispositions after reading a children's book? I recommend literature circle discussion and journaling as two means to explore literature-based teacher dispositions. Prior to utilizing a literature circle or journaling as a means to explore dispositions, the preservice teachers should activate their background knowledge concerning dispositions as well as develop an initial understanding of dispositions.

One way in which to activate dispositional background knowledge is by asking the preservice teachers to list key words or phrases that identify a teacher from his or her schooling experience who was a good teacher and one who was a "bad" teacher. Preservice teachers share their lists of words and/or phrases by writing them on the blackboard or chart paper for all to see. Typically, as preservice teachers think about these two types of teachers, the words and/or phrases they generate focus on such issues as: fair or unfair, caring or uncaring, interested or disinterested in students dispositional elements. With this background knowledge activated, the students then compare the compiled lists of words and/or phrases to the INTASC dispositional standards. With these two prereading activities accomplished, the students are now ready to discuss and journal the literature case.

Discussions

Having the preservice teachers engage in a literature circle discussion, what Eeds and Wells (1989) refer to as a "grand conversation" is one way in which they can develop a deeper understanding of the story. Participating in a grand conversation, preservice teachers read and then discuss the story. Elements of the story that the preservice teachers find significant or important are shared within a group of four to six students. Within a grand conversation framework, students respond with their likes and dislikes of the story. Discussions are open-ended, with participants asking one another clarifying questions, while simultaneously making initial connections with the story and their own life experiences. Once this initial discussion occurs, the preservice teachers revisit the story for specific elements the teacher wants to highlight from the story. This more structured analysis of the story could take the form of the preservice teachers looking at the dispositional qualities through the lens of the 10 INTASC principles, or simply to have them identify the positive and/or negative dispositional qualities of the teacher or teachers portrayed in the story.

Journaling

Journaling is another method to engage preservice teachers in thinking about dispositional qualities. The journaling could take numerous forms. The preservice teachers could journal prior to discussing the story with their peers. The teacher educator could leave the journal open-ended, meaning that the preservice teachers could write about their reactions or responses to the story. The prediscussion journal could also be more specific, meaning that the teacher educator could have the preservice teachers respond to specific writing prompts or questions to consider after they have finished the story.

Another form the journal could take is as an after-discussion reflective journal. Again, the teacher educator could leave the journal open-ended, whereby the preservice teachers write about their thoughts, reactions, and responses after having had the discussion with their peers. The after-discussion journal could also be more structured, with the teacher educator asking the preservice teachers to answer specific questions such as: What are the first impressions we have of the teacher? What first impressions do you want students to have of you? Did your first impression of the teacher change over time; if yes, how and why? How are you similar or different from the teacher in the story? How might you work with a challenging, creative, or diverse student? Which of the teacher's characteristics would you want to exhibit in your classroom? Which ones would you disregard? Which dispositional qualities associated with the INTASC core principles does this story highlight?

Using literature discussion circles or journaling provides preservice teachers numerous opportunities to think deeply about the story, the teacher/student interactions, and the positive dispositional characteristics they want to incorporate into their teaching lives.

As preservice teachers use children's literature to develop positive dispositions as teachers, they need to have exposure to a variety of instructional settings, teacher/student interactions, and diversity of students. All books listed in Appendix B to this chapter were selected because they provide a realistic glimpse into schooling in various locations and age groups within the United States.

FURTHER EXPLORATION

Appendix B suggests quality children's books that have stories that lend themselves to exploring dispositional qualities of teachers. Included is a brief summary for each book, which should facilitate selecting literature cases that will meet the needs of the teacher educator. It should be noted that the teachers in these stories are not perfect by any means. In fact, the teachers in these stories often exhibit both positive and negative dispositional qualities, which makes for interesting discussions and analysis.

It is recommended that before using any of these books, the books should be carefully read by the teacher educator so that he or she will know whether the book will engage the preservice teachers in discussing the dispositional issues that are desired. The suggested books are not meant to be exhaustive. However, they do provide a starting point for exploring teacher dispositions through children's literature. Although preservice teachers might want to read books appropriate to a certain developmental level, the books are not organized by school level. The reason for this discussion is that these books contain teacher/student interactions that have a universal quality. That is, they represent realistic examples of teacher/student interactions within various instructional situations and developmental levels that will facilitate engaging discussions of teaching, teachers, and learning.

CONCLUSION

As teacher education programs are challenged to meet accreditation and licensure standards, it is important to understand what it takes to be a quality teacher. With the development of teacher education standards, through such organizations as NCATE and INTASC, it is critical that teacher educators have the tools to prepare teachers to meet the knowledge, skills (performance), and dispositions standards that these and similar organizations have developed.

Throughout the ages, stories have been used to instruct, entertain, and provide a means to pass on social, cultural, and historical knowledge. Stories also provide a rich context for reflection, as Metzger (1979) points out:

Stories go in circles. They don't go in straight lines. So it helps if you listen in circles because there are stories inside of stories and stories between stories and finding your way through them is as easy and as hard as finding your way home. And part of the finding is the getting lost. If you're lost, you really start to look around and to listen. (p. 104)

As argued in this chapter, children's stories, especially literature cases, allow preservice teachers opportunities to discover meaning, enter the minds of characters, and discover deeper understandings about teaching and learning. While preservice teachers are reading, discussing, and journaling about literature cases, they are engaging in, and exploring, explaining, and reflecting on, the dispositional characteristics of effective teachers.

Using children's literature as a means to discuss teacher dispositions is a unique pedagogical strategy in teacher education. As such, these literature case studies, as applied to teacher dispositions, are a rich, untapped area of research. Research questions stemming from scholarly inquiry could include exploring such questions as:

How does studying literature case studies impact a preservice teacher's dispositions?

How could the impact on preservice teachers' dispositions, through analyzing literature cases, be assessed?

Would literature case studies lead developmentally to analyzing traditional case studies?

Are there certain literature case studies that are more appropriate at different stages in a preservice teacher's education sequence?

This last question is especially intriguing, as literature case studies are viewed as beneficial for the development of dispositional qualities. For example, would *Frindle* be an appropriate text for a student just beginning his or her teacher education sequence or later in the sequence?

As interest continues in ways to assist preservice teachers develop the dispositional qualities needed to be effective teachers, it is important to remember that through the use of children's literature, preservice teachers are able to discuss teacher effectiveness, how teachers should relate to students, and the kind of education we want for all children. In this way, literature cases provide a pedagogical strategy to assist teacher educators in helping preservice teachers' understandings of the dispositional characteristics of effective and ineffective teachers.

Appendix A: Dispositional Standards
Principle 1: Content Knowledge
The teacher realizes that subject matter knowledge is not a fixed body of facts but is complex and ever evolving. He seeks to keep abreast of new ideas and understandings in the field.

The teacher appreciates multiple perspectives and conveys to learners how knowledge is developed from the vantage point of the knower.

The teacher has enthusiasm for the discipline(s) she teaches and sees connections to everyday life.

The teacher is committed to continuous learning and engages in professional discourse about subject matter knowledge and children's learning of the discipline.

Principle 2: Development

The teacher appreciates individual variation within each area of development, shows respect for the diverse talents of all learners, and is committed to help them develop self-confidence and competence.

The teacher is disposed to use students' strengths as a basis for growth and errors as an opportunity for learning.

Principle 3: Individual Differences

The teacher believes that all children can learn at high levels and persists in helping all children achieve success.

The teacher appreciates and values human diversity, shows respect for students' varied talents and perspectives, and is committed to the pursuit of "individually configured excellence."

The teacher respects students as individuals with differing personal and family backgrounds and various skills, talents, ant interests.

The teacher is sensitive to community and cultural mores. The teacher makes students feel valued for their potential as people, and helps them to learn to value each other.

Principle 4: Instruction for Diverse Learners

The teacher values the development of students' critical thinking, independent problem solving, and performance capabilities.

The teacher values flexibility and reciprocity in the teaching process as necessary for adapting instruction to student responses, ideas, and needs.

Principle 5: Learning Environment

The teacher takes responsibility for establishing a positive climate in the classroom and participates in maintaining such a climate in the school as a whole.

The teacher understands how participation supports commitment and is committed to the expression and use of democratic values in the classroom.

The teacher values the role of students in promoting one another's learning and recognizes the importance of peer relationships in establishing a climate of learning.

The teacher recognizes the value of intrinsic motivation to students' life-long growth and learning.

The teacher is committed to the continuous development of individual students' abilities and considers how different motivational strategies are likely to encourage this development for each student.

Principle 6: Communication with Students

The teacher recognizes the power of language for fostering self-expression, identity development, and learning.

The teacher values all of the ways in which people communicate and encourages many modes of communication in the classroom.

The teacher is a thoughtful and responsive listener.

The teacher appreciates the cultural dimensions of communication, responds appropriately, and seeks to foster culturally sensitive communication by and among all students in the class.

Principle 7: Instructional Planning

The teacher values both long-term and short-term planning.

The teacher believes that plans must always be open to adjustment and revisions based on student needs and changing circumstances.

The teacher values planning as a collegial activity.

Principle 8: Assessment

The teacher values ongoing assessment as essential to the instructional process and recognizes that many different assessment strategies, accurately and systematically used, are necessary for monitoring and promoting student learning.

The teacher is committed to using assessment to identify student strengths and promote student growth rather than to deny students access to learning opportunities.

Principle 9: Reflective Practice

The teacher values critical thinking and self-directed learning as habits of mind.

The teacher is committed to reflection and assessment as an ongoing process.

The teacher is willing to give and receive help.

The teacher is committed to seeking out, developing, and continually refining practices that address the individual needs of students.

The teacher recognizes his professional responsibility for engaging in and supporting professional practices for self and colleagues.

Principle 10: Communication with Community

The teacher values and appreciates the importance of all aspects of a child's experience.

The teacher is concerned about all aspects of a child's well-being (cognitive, emotional, social, and physical), and is alert to signs of difficulties.

The teacher is willing to consult with other adults regarding the education and well-being of her students.

The teacher respects the privacy of students and confidentiality of information.

The teacher can identify and use community resources to foster student learning. (NCATE 2002)

Appendix B: Titles for Discussion

Avi. (1991). *Nothing but the truth: A documentary novel*. New York: Orchard Books.

Ninth grader Philip Malloy and his English teacher have difficulties in and out of class. Told in a documentary style to enable the reader to make his or her own conclusions about the events.

Caudill, R. (1966). *Did you carry the flag today, Charley?* South Holland, IL: Dell.

An inquisitive kindergarten student with a short attention span is helped to be successful through a variety of nurturing instructional techniques.

Clements, A. (2002). *A week in the woods*. New York: Simon & Schuster.

Mr. Maxwell, a veteran elementary school science teacher takes the students on a weeklong science trip in the woods. He is challenged by Mark, an intelligent, wealthy new boy who was just moved from the big city.

Cleary, B. (1968). *Ramona the pest*. New York: Avon.

Miss Binney is a first-year kindergarten teacher who deals with the literalness, inquisitiveness, and hero worship of young children, especially Ramona.

Codell, E. R. (2003). *Sahara special*. New York: Hyperion.

A fifth-grade teacher in a diverse urban school uses a variety of creative and inspiring instructional strategies to excite students to learn.

Hill, K. (2000). *The year of Miss Agnes*. New York: Simon & Schuster.

Miss Agnes has an alternative style of teaching, which she uses to meet the needs of diverse students in a one-room schoolhouse in rural Alaska.

Hurwitz, J. (1988). *Teacher's pet*. New York: Scholastic.

A fourth grader who has been a teacher's pet since kindergarten must learn to interact with her teacher who shows no favoritism.

Johnson, L. (1992). *My posse don't do homework*. New York: St. Martin's Press.

Ms. Johnson uses her prior military training to initially intimidate a class of unruly high school students who over time respond to her caring and nurturing ways. Based on the author's classroom experiences.

Kleinbaum, N. H. (1989). *Dead poets society.* New York: Bantam.

English teacher John Keating uses creative means to engage the minds of students at an all-boys private college preparatory school.

MacDonald, A. (2001). *No more nasty.* New York: Melanie Kroupa Books.

Simon's Great Aunt Matilda takes over as a long-term substitute teacher in a fifth-grade class. Her unique teaching style challenges students to look at learning from a very different perspective

Sachar, L. (1987). *There's a boy in the girl's bathroom.* New York: Alfred A. Knopf.

Fifth grader Bradley Chaulkers is a disruptive bully who refuses to complete assigned work. Through the efforts of the guidance counselor, Bradley is helped to develop more acceptable behavior.

Shreve, S. (1984). *The flunking of Joshua T. Bates.* New York: Scholastic.

Joshua, who is almost 10 years old, must repeat third grade. Joshua's new third-grade teacher, Mrs. Goodwin, is an experienced, honest, perceptive, and empathetic teacher who spends extra time with him so he can return to his peer group in the fourth grade.

REFERENCES

Bruner, J. (1986). *Actual minds, possible worlds.* Cambridge, MA: Harvard University Press.

Bruner, J. (2002). *Making stories.* New York: Farrar, Strauss, & Giroux.

Carter, K., & Doyle, W. (1996). Personal narrative and life history in learning to teach. In J. Sikula (Ed.), *Handbook of research on teacher education* (2nd ed., pp. 120–142). New York: Macmillan.

Clements, A. (1996). *Frindle.* New York: Simon & Schuster Books for Young Readers.

Connelly, F. M., & Clandinin, D. J. (1985). Personal practical knowledge and the modes of knowing: Relevance for teaching and learning. *NSSE Yearbook, 84*(2), 174–198.

Dorris, M. (1997). Introduction. In M. Dorris & E. Buchwald (Eds.), *The most wonderful books: Writers on discovering the pleasures of reading* (pp. xiii–xv). Minneapolis: Milkweed Editions.

Eeds, M., & Wells, D. (1989). Grand conversations: An exploration of meaning construction in literature study groups. *Research in the Teaching of English, 23,* 4–29.

Goodfellow, J. (2000). Knowing from the inside: Reflective conversations with and through the narratives of one cooperating teacher. *Reflective Practice, 1*(1), 25–42.

Griffith, P. L. (2002). Envisioning teaching: Learning from multiple text types. *Journal of Reading Education, 28*(1), 8–14.

Griffith, P. L., & Laframboise, K. (1998). Literature case studies: Case method and reader response come together in teacher education. *Journal of Adolescent and Adult Literacy, 43*(5), 364–375.

Isenberg, J. (1994). *Going by the book: The role of popular classroom chronicles in the professional development of teachers.* Westport, CT: Bergin & Garvey.

Jalongo, M. R., & Isenberg, J. P. (1995). *Teachers' stories: From personal narratives to professional insight.* San Francisco: Jossey-Bass.

Kerby, A. P. (1991). *Narrative and the self.* Bloomington: Indiana University Press.

Laframboise, K., & Griffith, P. L. (1997). Using literature cases to examine diversity issues with preservice teachers. *Teaching and Teacher Education, 13,* 369–382.

Laframboise, K., & Klesius, J. (1993). Using literature case studies to help preservice teachers develop a knowledge base for decision making. *Teacher Educator, 29*(2), 26–31.

McEwan H., & Egan, K. (Eds.). (1995). *Narrative in teaching, learning, and research.* New York: Teachers College Press.

Metzger, D. (1979). *Circle of stories. Parabola, 4*(4), 104–105.

National Council for the Accreditation of Teacher Education (NCATE). (2002). *Professional standards for the accreditation of schools, colleges, and departments of education.* Retrieved April 15, 2004, from http://www.ncate.org/

Polkinghorne, D. E. (1988). Narrative knowing and the human sciences. Albany, NY: SUNY Press.

Polkinghorne, D. E. (1996). Narrative knowing and the study of lives. In J. E. Birren, G. M. Kenyon, J. Ruth, J. J. F. Schroots, & T. Svenjson (Eds.), *Aging and biography: Explorations in adult development* (pp. 77-99). New York: Springer.

Rosenblatt, L. M. (1938). *Literature as exploration.* New York: Appleton-Century.

Rosenblatt, L. M. (1978). *The reader, the text, the poem.* Carbondale, IL: Southern Illinois University Press.

Shannon, P. (1995). *Text, lies, and videotape: Stories about life, literacy, and learning.* Portsmouth, NH. Heinemann.

Williams, B. C., Mitchell, A., & Leibbrand, J. (2003). *Navigating change: Preparing for a performance-based accreditation review.* Washington, DC: National Council for Accreditation of Teacher Education.

9

Teaching and Evaluating Dispositions in a Preservice Education Course

Gwynn Mettetal and Sara Sage

We believe in a constructivist approach to teaching, so it makes sense that we start any learning experience with the students' core ideas. When we ask students to think about their best and worst teacher, we never get discussion about the teachers' content knowledge and we rarely hear about pedagogical skills. Instead, we get lots of discussion about dispositions—teachers who love to teach, who love children, who are funny, kind, and inspirational versus teachers who are mean, burned out, or uncaring. This is true whether we talk to freshmen, seniors, or in-service teachers, and also extends to conversations with the general public.

The importance of dispositions has also been supported by the professional and research literature. Stronge (2002) says that "many interview and survey responses about effective teaching emphasize the teacher's affective characteristics, or social and emotional behaviors, more than pedagogical practice" (p. 13). He catalogs the research on the importance of caring, fairness and respect, interactions with students, enthusiasm and motivation, attitude toward teaching, and reflective practice (see Stronge for a comprehensive listing of research). The National Council for the Accreditation of Teacher Education (NCATE, 2002) guidelines define and set a target benchmark for teacher dispositions, and the Interstate New Teacher Assessment and Support Consortium (INTASC, 1992) describes a dispositional component for each of the 10 standards. Unfortunately, it can be very difficult to teach and assess dispositions in the traditional classroom format. At Indiana University South Bend (IUSB), we have a variety of ways to assess dispositions at various points in the curriculum. A particular strength of the program is a course titled, F201/202 Personal Demands of Teaching, which focuses primarily on dispositions, allowing us to both teach and assess effective dispositions in our teacher candidates early in their foundations course sequence.

CONTEXT

In the IUSB education curriculum, student dispositions are addressed at several points (see Table 9.1). Freshmen take F100 Introduction to Teaching, which introduces students to the idea of dispositions and encourages them to reflect upon their own dispositions as well as the dispositions evidenced by effective teachers.

During their fourth semester, students must take F201/202 Personal Demands of Teaching. This course, which focuses heavily on dispositions, is described in detail later in this chapter. This is a gateway course that students *must* pass before they are admitted to the teacher education program. Thus, it serves an important dispositions screening function.

Methods courses during the junior and senior years contain a field component, and instructors and supervising teachers give feedback on student knowledge, performance, and dispositions. Finally, student teaching has a heavy focus on dispositions. The evaluation forms require both supervising teachers and university supervisors to rate the student's dispositions for teaching on multiple occasions. Our experience has been that students who struggle or fail student teaching are much more likely to have problems with dispositions than with knowledge or performance.

One method we use to document our concerns about a student's disposition for teaching throughout the program is the Letter of Concern, which al-

Table 9.1.   **IUSB School of Education Model for Student Dispositions**

Timing	Course	Components
Freshmen	F100 Intro to Teaching	Introduction, self-assessment, reflection
Sophomore	F201/202 Personal Demands of Teaching	Instruction, modeling, field-based practice, formal assessment by instructor, field teacher and self. Gateway course.
Junior	Methods courses	Formal assessment by instructor, field teacher, and self.
Senior	Student teaching	Capstone assessment by university supervisor, cooperating teacher, and self.
Any time	Letter of concern	Letter to student and for student file describing concerns about dispositional issues. Two letters can trigger a meeting with the dean to discuss professional development issues.

lows an instructor to document such problems as excessive absences, lack of preparation, or lack of tolerance or respect for diversity. A sample letter is given in the Appendix to this chapter.

F201/202 EXPLORING THE
PERSONAL DEMANDS OF TEACHING

Personal Demands of Teaching is a course with two components, a 2-credit on-campus laboratory course (F201) and a 1-credit field experience (F202). The course is graded satisfactory/fail, and both segments must be passed before a student will be admitted to the teacher education program. Before enrolling in this course, students must pass P250 Educational Psychology and pass all three sections of the Praxis I with the scores required for licensing by the Indiana Professional Standards Board.

This course was created in 1975, when the counseling faculty who taught the Educational Psychology course decided to split the communications/relationship skills aspect of the course and add a robust field experience. They based this new course on a similar skills course from Michigan State University that covered listening, observation, self-disclosure, values-clarification, and feedback. Issues of professionalism, cultural diversity, and classroom management were added. Throughout the years, specific changes have been made, but the general focus on dispositions has remained the same. We currently have a mix of counseling faculty and teacher educators who teach this course. The course enrollment is limited to 14 students, who enroll in linked sections of F201 and F202. Please refer to Table 9.2 for detailed mapping of F201/202 course objectives to the INTASC standards.

F201: On-Campus Laboratory

The on-campus portion of this course is taught as a laboratory—that is, with primarily hands-on activities rather than lecture. Students typically meet 3 to 4 hours per week in class, since most of the course requirements take place in the classroom, rather than as outside studying. We jokingly refer to this course as "Charm School for Teachers," because the emphasis is on creating effective relationships with children, other teachers, administrators, and parents. The content covers a variety of dispositional issues, including:

- Communications skills, including nonverbals, listening, conflict resolution, feedback;
- Diversity, especially urban classrooms and poverty;
- Professional behaviors, such as promptness, professional appearance, and confidentiality;

Table 9.2.   Mapping INTASC Standards for F201/202

Course Objectives	INTASC
IUSB education student will be able to:	
1. Observe and interpret nonverbal cues and situational factors	6
2. Express thoughts, feelings, reactions, needs, and values to others appropriately	6
3. Use active listening and respond appropriately	6
4. Demonstrate giving and receiving appropriate feedback	6
5. Manage conflicts through problem-solving techniques	5, 6
6. Use basic classroom management techniques such as positive communication, encouragement, organization, and assertiveness	5
7. Explain and demonstrate how to work effectively with students/families from different SES backgrounds	3
8. Collaborate with peers to problem solve on educational issues	10
9. Reflect upon personal performance	9
10. Demonstrate professional behavior such as dependability, initiative, and respect for others	9
11. Plan and teach brief lessons to a group of students	5

- Classroom management, which focuses on building a positive classroom climate;
- Reflection, including regular journal entries regarding personal growth and field experiences.

These issues are taught using a variety of strategies, such as discussion, role-play and simulation, case studies, games, and reflections. Books such as Johnson's *Reaching Out* (2003) also contain a number of useful exercises. Of course, individual instructors use a variety of strategies to reach course objectives. Several of these strategies are described below.

One instructor uses a *problem-based learning activity* in which students are assigned to interdisciplinary middle school teams who are asked by the principal to work on increasing parent involvement. They are asked specifically to create a written document that families will receive at the beginning of the upcoming school year. Their school, based on an actual urban middle school where some students do their field experience, is very diverse with low socioeconomic status. "Teachers" must consider these factors when constructing this document and considering how to effectively communicate the document to families. This activity requires students to use their knowledge of diversity (Ruby Payne's [2001] book is a required text for the course), as well as practice their group communication skills, including active listening, effective disclosure, giving feedback, and conflict resolution. It also forces them to address some issues such as how middle school teams function as a unit and how teachers can most effectively communicate with a broad variety of families. At the conclusion of this activity, "teachers" share their draft document with an actual middle school parent.

Many instructors use *short role-plays* to allow students to practice their skills. The role-play situations may come from the instructor, or the students may contribute situations from their own experience. In every situation, a teacher is faced with a difficult interaction with a student, parent, another teacher, or an administrator. For example, a role-play card might read, "8-year-old James frequently falls asleep in class. You have asked his mother to meet with you to discuss the problem," or "Another teacher likes to tell you some juicy gossip about other teachers. You feel uncomfortable knowing this information, but you don't want to hurt her feelings. You're in the lounge, and she is heading for your table." Students form small groups to try out various responses to the situations and then present their best to the class. Lively discussion follows. It can be particularly effective for the instructor to model "bad teacher" and "good teacher" so that students can see the impact.

Art activities can also promote learning and discussion. One instructor puts a large piece of paper on the floor and supplies ample markers for the class. Each student is asked to draw one or more pictures that represent an important concept from Payne's book on poverty. When the paper is filled, it is posted on the wall for all to discuss. It remains there so that students can refer back to it all semester.

The course structure lends itself to *peer feedback activities*. At midterm and final, students are asked to evaluate their own progress toward course goals. They are also asked to prepare feedback for several classmates, usually in a "three strengths and something to work on" format. After discussion of effective ways to give and receive feedback, as well as some role-play practice, students pair off to give one-on-one feedback to one another. Students are usually very apprehensive about this activity, but realize its relevance to effective teaching. Although it never becomes a favorite exercise, they find that it is not scary when they know the correct approach.

Most instructors have students take some sort of a personality test, such as the Myers-Briggs Type Indicator (Myers, McCaulley, Quenk & Hammer, 1998) or the Keirsey Temperament Sorter II (Keirsey, 1998). Then students are assigned to groups of similar types. Each group is assigned a common task, such as planning a party or designing a summer camp. Then groups report out; they discover that their group processes as well as their group products are often very different. Discussion then covers the value of diversity, adapting to diverse learners, and other ways in which people are diverse (see Nelsen, Lott, and Glenn [2000] for a children's version of this exercise).

Resources

Instructors use a number of texts for this course, but there are several core texts. For communication skills, Faber and Mazlish (1996), *How to Talk So Kids Can Learn,* is the standard text. This book is very easy to read and does an excellent job of explaining effective communication skills. Students tend to keep this book to use as a resource. We have had several students tell us how useful this book is once they begin teaching.

For diversity, we use Payne's (2001) *A Framework for Understanding Poverty.* This book speaks directly to the effect of socioeconomic status on children's behavior and communication. We find this book to be particularly effective with our students who are predominately from a middle-class background.

A third text typically focuses on classroom management. Instructor choices include *Positive Discipline in the Classroom* (Nelson at al., 2000), *The First Days of School* (Wong & Wong, 2001), *Teaching with Love and Logic* (Fay & Funk, 1995), *Classroom Management for Elementary Teachers* (Evertson, Emmer, & Worsham, 2003), and *Classroom Management for Secondary Teachers* (Emmer, Evertson, & Worsham, 2003).

Guest speakers are frequently invited to the class to be a resource on real teaching issues as well as to provide a different perspective. These speakers include practicing and retired teachers and administrators, a local NEA president, and special guests such as Indiana Teacher of the Year.

In this course, students use LiveText (2003) to submit their reflective journals. LiveText is a web-based environment designed specifically for educators. Students have access to many teaching resources such as drop-down lists of standards and sample lesson plans and portfolios. LiveText makes it easy for students to submit their work and get feedback from instructors and classmates. It also enhances their technology skills.

F202: Field Experience

F202 is a 1-credit field experience that is taken along with F201. The purpose of this field experience is primarily to help students decide whether they want to pursue a career in teaching before they get too far along in the program. It also helps them understand the importance of effective dispositions in the classroom.

Students spend 30 hours in an urban classroom with significant student diversity. Most of this time is spent in a single classroom, but students spend a few hours visiting other classes. Students begin by observing in the classroom, but quickly move to assisting students one-on-one. They conclude their experience by teaching three lessons to the whole class or to a large group. The purpose of these lessons is not to evaluate their instructional expertise, but simply to allow them to "get their feet wet."

Students write frequent reflections on their experience and discuss it in the F201 class. Their cooperating teacher evaluates them on a number of dimensions, including professional behavior and communication skills.

Assessment

Both the F201 and F202 segments of this course are graded "satisfactory/fail," and students must pass both segments to be admitted to the teacher education program. Their grade is based almost entirely on performance related to dispositions. Students receive frequent feedback during the semester. They do a self-assessment at midterm and final, and instructors provide one-to-one feedback at those times. Students also receive feedback from their classmates (allowing them to practice their feedback skills). We find that this peer feedback is sometimes the most powerful channel in prompting change.

When students do not demonstrate the appropriate dispositions in either segment, we frequently give a grade of "incomplete" rather than "fail." This option allows great flexibility in allowing students to gain and demonstrate skills and dispositions. They might retake part or the entire course the following semester, or other alternatives might be arranged. We have found that most students who receive an incomplete are able to successfully complete the course during the following semester.

Another outcome for students is to receive a Letter of Concern from the instructor (see Appendix, this chapter). This letter describes specific problem behaviors so that students are alerted to areas needing improvement. A copy of the letter is shared with the student, and another copy goes into the student's file. A second letter is usually reason to call a meeting with the student, the dean, and a faculty member to discuss the student's future in the program. Students are required to develop a personal and professional development plan that addresses weaknesses. Upon completion of that plan, they may ask to be reinstated into the program.

Some of the most common reasons that students might not pass the course and/or receive a Letter of Concern include:

- Several absences or late arrivals;
- Frequent lack of preparation;
- Inappropriate self-disclosure;
- Unwillingness or inability to participate fully in class discussions and activities;
- Excessive aggression or passivity;
- Lack of tolerance, flexibility, and respect.

Typical outcomes

Of course, each class has its own unique personality. However, over many years of experience, we have learned to expect that typically out of each class of 14, we will have varied outcomes. The majority of students pass both portions of the course without major concerns. Several students may change or clarify their professional goals. However, typically two to three students receive an incomplete or a letter of concern because of more serious dispositions issues. Most students who retake the course because of an incomplete pass on the second attempt.

Occasionally a student does not pass after two attempts. When this happens, it is usually an indication of deeper problems that make teaching a poor fit. We consider all of these to be satisfactory outcome, since a main objective of the course is to help students determine the appropriate career goal for them, whether within or outside of the teaching profession.

Over the years, we have found a strong anecdotal correlation between success in F201/202 and success in student teaching. Likewise, students who have difficulties in student teaching often have a history of the same problems in the F201/202 course. This reinforces our belief in the importance of this course and in making sure that all instructors stop someone who does not have the appropriate dispositions. Some students merely need some reflection or time to mature—others may need to be counseled to consider a different profession.

TALES FROM THE TRENCHES

Karen and Jennifer (as told by Sara Sage)

Karen and Jennifer were in my F201/F202 class several years ago. I knew that Jennifer, a nontraditional student who had worked in business for many years, and Karen, a traditional student, were both teaching English at a local urban high school where I had been supervising student teachers. I happened to run into Jennifer at an event at a local museum. She made it a point to stop and tell me how much she and Karen still talked about the F201 class and how much they learned, as well as how much they are using the skills now. This past spring, I saw Karen on the very last day of school, after the students had left. She had a big smile and said how much she was enjoying her work. Then she asked, "Remember those 'I messages' we talked about in your class? I am realizing how important they are, and I would like to get the references for that so I can read more about it this summer." I told her that her text, if she still had it, had some good information, and that I had the actual handouts we used on my website. I wrote down the information for her. She said that the F201 class had been one of the most important in preparing her for her work with the teens with whom she was currently working. I felt especially proud that Karen was doing a good job of creating positive relationships with her students, and that she was concerned with her own professional development even in that first moment of summer break!

Steve (as told by Gwynn Mettetal)

Steve was a student in my F201/F202 class several years ago. He was a nontraditional student—an older, married, ex-Marine. Steve was seeking a license in secondary math and let the class know early on that this "touchy-feely stuff" was of no use to him. He participated in F201 activities very begrudgingly. His judgmental attitude alienated most of his classmates. At the midterm feedback session, I told him that he was going to fail the class unless I saw some major changes. A short time later, Steve arrived for class and seemed unusually eager to talk. He told us that he had been invited to sit in on a parent-teacher conference at his field site concerning a troubled middle school student. The parent had arrived eager to collaborate, but had become so angry that security guards were called. Steve felt that the teachers had handled the situation very poorly and had triggered the parent's negative response. "The teachers did everything that you tell us *not* to do!" From that day on, Steve was an enthusiastic participant in class. Classmates gave him very positive feedback. I even received a note from his wife, thanking me for the amazing change that had occurred in her husband! At our final feedback session, Steve told me that he wanted to become a school administrator so that he could be sure that teachers in his school understood the importance of their dispositions and relationship skills to the learning environment.

CONCLUSION

We have a strong strand in our school of education curriculum related to dispositions. The F201/F202 course has been a particularly powerful means of teaching and assessing dispositions. Our students tell us frequently that the skills and dispositions from this course are valuable for their profession, and also for their personal lives. As NCATE focuses on the importance of dispositions, we feel fortunate in having this course as an integral component of our program. We are in the process of collecting and analyzing a broad variety of data from this course, as we prepare to take a leadership role in the teaching and assessment of dispositions with other schools of education.

APPENDIX: SAMPLE LETTER OF CONCERN

MEMO

To: any faculty member who teaches Education students
From: Gwynn Mettetal, Interim Dean of Education
Date: June 10, 2002
Subject: LETTERS OF CONCERN

If you teach Education students, we need your help in assessing student dispositions for teaching.

It is important that teachers have strong content knowledge, as well as strong teaching skills. It is equally important that our students have the personal qualities (dispositions) needed for effective teaching. Dispositions are "the values, commitments, and professional ethics that influence behaviors toward students, families, colleagues, and communities . . . guided by beliefs and attitudes related to values such as caring, fairness, honesty, responsibility, and social justice" (NCATE, Professional Standards, 2002).

Occasionally, an Education student in your class may exhibit dispositions that are inappropriate for a teacher. Behaviors that might cause concern include (but are not limited to) excessive absences or tardiness, rude or aggressive behavior, disrespectful behavior, not taking course content or assignments seriously, lack of tolerance for diversity, strange or inappropriate verbal or nonverbal behaviors, dishonesty, or inappropriate dress.

When a student exhibits these behaviors, I would like to strongly encourage you to write a Letter of Concern. A copy of this letter should be given to the student, and a copy should be placed into the student's advising file. If a second Letter is filed, the student will meet with an advisor, the area coordinator, and the Dean to discuss a plan for improvement or other actions.

When a student applies to student teach, faculty sometimes voice strong concerns about their dispositions. It is very difficult to explain to a student that faculty members have strong reservations about placing them in student teaching when they have had no advance warning of any problems. It is also poor teaching practice to wait until the end of coursework to let a student know that improvement is needed. Because many of these behaviors are not reflected in grading practices, a student might have no idea that teachers are concerned about his or her behavior. This is not just for F201/202 instructors! Instructors of any course as well as professional staff are urged to file a letter if they have any concerns about dispositions.

I am attaching a prototype of a Letter of Concern. You do not need a special form. You are encouraged to discuss the letter with the student, but you may simply mail it to him or her instead. A second copy should be given to the Advising office, with instructions to place it into the student's file. If you are in doubt as to procedure, you could simply send a letter to the Dean's office, noting whether or not a copy has been given to the student. We will be sure that it is filed appropriately.

Our university lawyers have advised us that the use of these letters is entirely legal, and even advisable. Previous problems occurred because the student was not given a copy of the letter, not because of the letter itself.

December 6, 2002

(Start with some background info about the course and context)
I am writing this letter for the file of Susan Student, who was a student in my M310/R301 course this past fall semester. This is a required course that occurs early in the Teacher Education Program. The focus of the course is on basic techniques such as writing a lesson plan.

(Try to say something about the student's strengths and any mitigating circumstances)
Susan is a nontraditional student who brings maturity, teaching experience, and generally strong communication skills to our class. She is active in discussions and takes the initiative in conversations. She is very intelligent, very motivated, and has a very sincere desire to improve her skills.

I have had Susan in class before, and I have talked to her from time to time over the past year. I know that she has taken a job to bring in some much needed income. She is also a single mother. All in all, this has been an extremely stressful year for Susan, and I think that most (if not all) of the behaviors that concern me are due to the high stress and busy schedule that she has had. I am putting this letter in her file in case I am wrong and these behaviors are a continuing pattern.

(Describe your concerns. Be detailed if possible.)
My first concern about Susan has to do with reliability. Our class met twice a week, for 30 class meetings. Of those 30 meetings, Susan was absent five times (twice without calling) and she was late 11 times. Assignments were late 7 out of 12 times.

My second concern is about some of Susan's behaviors in our classroom. She frequently dominated class discussions, despite my efforts to keep her contributions short. When I talked to her about this after class, she improved for a short time, but quickly slipped back into the same pattern. Even in small groups, she often forgot to listen to others' viewpoints. Nervous habits, such as tapping her pencil or snapping her gum were distracting to most of the other students. By the middle of the semester, other students were actively avoiding sitting near her or being placed into a group with her.

Finally (and most seriously) Susan was absent during our last meeting as a class and did not participate in the final group presentation. She never did call to explain her absence. Her final grade was greatly affected by this negligence.

I am very disappointed in Susan's behavior in this course, particularly at the end. Although I still feel that she has many of the qualities expected in a teacher, I would be reluctant to recommend her at this time.

(Explanation of process)
I understand that if this is the only expression of concern in Susan's file, this will not hinder student teaching placement. However if others express concerns, Susan will be called in to discuss these issues, and it may affect her progress in the program.

Gwynn Mettetal, Ph.D.
Associate Professor

ACKNOWLEDGMENT

We acknowledge the contributions of Counseling/Education Psychology faculty members Randall Isaacson and J. Vincent Peterson in the original development of the F201/F202 course at Indiana University South Bend. Their vision for the course has rung true for nearly 30 years.

REFERENCES

Emmer, E. T., Evertson, C. M., & Worsham, M. E. (2003). *Classroom management for secondary teachers* (6th ed.). Boston: Allyn & Bacon.

Evertson, C. M., Emmer, E. T., & Worsham, M. E. (2003). *Classroom management for elementary teachers* (6th ed.) Boston: Allyn & Bacon.

Faber, A., & Mazlish, E. (1996). *How to talk so kids can learn.* New York: Fireside/ Simon & Schuster.

Fay, J., & Funk, D. (1995). *Teaching with love and logic.* Golden, CO: Love and Logic Press.

Interstate New Teacher Assessment and Support Consortium (INTASC). (1992). *Model standards for beginning teacher licensing and development: A resource for state dialogue.* Retrieved June 13, 2003, from http://www.ccsso.org/intascst.html

Johnson, D. (2003). *Reaching out: Interpersonal effectiveness and self-actualization* (8th ed.). Boston: Allyn & Bacon.

Keirsey, D. (1998). *Please understand me II: Temperament, character, intelligence.* Del Mar, CA: Prometheus.

LiveText. (2003). *College LiveText: Edu solutions.* Retrieved August 5, 2003, from http://college.livetext.com/college/index.html

Myers, I. B., McCaulley, M. H., Quenk, N. L., & Hammer, A. L. (1998). *MBTI manual* (3rd ed.). Palo Alto, CA: Consulting Psychologists Press.

National Council for Accreditation of Teacher Education (NCATE). (2002). *Professional standards for the accreditation of schools, colleges and departments of education.* Washington, DC: Author.

Nelsen, J., Lott, L., & Glenn, H. S. (2000). *Positive discipline in the classroom* (3rd ed.). Roseville, CA: Prima Publishing.

Payne, R. (2001). *A framework for understanding poverty* (rev. ed.). Highlands, TX: Aha! Process.

Stronge, J. H. (2002). *Qualities of effective teachers.* Alexandria, VA: Association for Supervision and Curriculum Development.

Wong, H. K., & Wong, R. T. (2001). *The first days of school* (2nd ed.). Mountainview, CA: Harry K. Wong Publications.

10

Exploring Dispositions in Student Teaching and Field Experience

Linda J. Young and Diane C. Youngs

Accountability in teacher education is not new. U.S. schools and teachers have long been scrutinized in their efforts to educate all children who come through their doors. Often schools and teachers are blamed when student achievement does not measure up to the community's expectations. The federal No Child Left Behind Act (2002) requires that all children in U.S. schools be taught by highly qualified teachers.

Teacher education programs also shoulder the blame for the lack of student achievement when critics claim that teacher education programs do not adequately prepare new teachers to meet the demands of teaching children in the 21st century (National Commission on Teaching and America's Future, 1996). The community, teachers, teacher educators, and researchers all agree that effective teaching happens when teachers know their subject matter thoroughly, use research-based best teaching practices, and display the dispositions that foster student learning and growth (Taylor & Wasicsko, 2000).

Our research base from a preservice teacher education perspective is primarily grounded in work by Carter (1990), LaBoskey (1994), and Clandinin, Davis, Hogan, and Kennard (1993), who have noted the great importance of helping future teachers develop practical and procedural knowledge within the context of real classrooms. Our goal is to place students in classrooms with teachers who model appropriate and desirable dispositions. Often students are confronted with cultural experiences vastly different from their own. They are forced to examine their own biases, attitudes, beliefs, and behaviors. We try to help students translate this new awareness into actions that improve teaching, the learning environment, and positive interpersonal relationships.

Assessing dispositions of student teachers and field experience students in the field is no easy matter. Although dispositions are attitudes and beliefs that are held internally, they do manifest themselves in the form of observable behavior. Often the assessment of dispositions involves a series of checklists, observations, self-evaluations, and an assortment of artifacts. Using a variety of techniques and artifacts provides a more accurate assessment of a student's dispositions related to teaching. Challenges are a constant dynamic in the classroom. The manner in which a student teacher or field experience student responds to these challenges over time provides an indication of probable future classroom effectiveness. By requiring an ongoing performance assessment opportunity in both field experiences and student teaching, teacher educators can be more certain that successful student teachers and field experience students hold the promise of being successful classroom teachers. By assessing dispositions in the field, teacher educators can also be more certain that their graduates will carry dispositions to their classrooms that are appropriate for beginning teachers.

To meet the challenges of the new standards, accreditation, licensing requirements, and public demand for effective teachers, the faculty and staff of the School of Education at Indiana University South Bend (IUSB) have restructured and redesigned the undergraduate teacher education programs (TEPs). Elementary education majors who will be licensed in both Early Childhood (primary grades) and Middle Childhood (intermediate grades) spend approximately 180 hours in a variety of schools completing field experiences prior to student teaching. Secondary Education majors who will be licensed in Early Adolescent (middle/junior high school) and Young Adult (high school) spend approximately 80 hours in a variety of schools completing field experiences prior to student teaching. Special education carries an additional 80 hours of field experience prior to student teaching when added on to an elementary or secondary program. Student teaching is a semester-long experience in elementary education, secondary education, and special education.

In this chapter, the term dispositions describes a set of values, attitudes, beliefs, and professional ethics that are demonstrated by various behaviors. Dispositions affect P–12 student learning, motivation, and development. Dispositions also affect overall classroom climate. A teacher's perceptions and attitudes about students and their families, about planning and teaching, and about themselves can have a profound effect on their students. These dispositions influence the teacher's overall success in the classroom and their ongoing professional development. Effective teachers are warm and caring; they enjoy life and are enthusiastic about helping other people grow and develop. They possess the requisite dispositions.

What do the IUSB students' dispositions "look like"? How do we assess those dispositions? What artifact evidence do our students compile to demonstrate they have the desired dispositions? How do our university faculty and staff mentor students during their teacher education program so that the requisite dispositions' standards are met? How do we help our students grow and develop into effective teachers? This chapter presents the IUSB clusters of dispositions along with discussion of how we address the aforementioned questions.

THE IUSB CLUSTERS OF DISPOSITIONS

Our faculty and supervisors expect IUSB students to know and be enthusiastic about their subject matter in the field experience setting. When we formally observe our students teaching lessons in the field, we look at their performance for clues as to their dispositions. Specifically, we look at these areas:

- Student appears warm, caring, and enthusiastic in interacting with children;
- Lesson introduction captures the children's interest;
- Activities are developmentally appropriate and linked to Indiana's academic standards;
- Lessons are relevant to children's diverse needs and experiences;
- Materials selected are appropriate and interesting;
- Technology is interwoven into the lesson appropriately;
- Children are actively involved in learning.

A student teacher's dispositions related to the content they are teaching colors their students' perceptions of the content and greatly influences their ability to effectively teach that content. The student teacher who appreciates multiple perspectives, teaches with enthusiasm, and projects the attitude that the content is not a fixed body of facts, but rather an ever expanding field requiring continuous learning will instill many of those perceptions in her students. A student teacher might document these dispositions with various artifacts. One example might be a rubric such as the one shown in Table 10.1 that would be used to assess a student project:

Dispositions Related to Diverse Learners

In our methods courses, accompanied by field experiences, IUSB students write lesson plans that are developmentally appropriate for the children they are teaching in their field placement. Lessons are planned with explicit adaptations for meeting the individual needs of those children. These needs include children with disabilities, language or dialectical

Table 10.1. Student Project Assessment Rubric

Christopher Columbus Project and Presentation Rubric

	Target	Acceptable	Unacceptable
Content	Targeted performance is evidenced by . . . Incorporation of accurate information about Christopher Columbus. Although the Eurocentric perspective should be included, the information should reflect other perspectives equally.	Acceptable performance is evidenced by . . . Incorporation of accurate information about Christopher Columbus. Although more than one perspective in included, the information is biased to the Eurocentric perspective.	Unacceptable performance is evidenced by . . . Information about Christopher Columbus is presented from a single perspective only.
Presentation	Targeted performance is evidenced by . . . Use of appropriate presentation skills including clear voice tones and appropriate volume and interacting with the audience continually.	Acceptable performance is evidenced by . . . Appropriate voice tones and volume. Speaker interacts with audience frequently.	Unacceptable performance is evidenced by . . . Poor voice quality and/or volume, lack of interaction with the audience.
Technical merit	Targeted performance is evidenced by . . . No spelling or grammatical errors.	Acceptable performance is evidenced by . . . Few grammatical or spelling errors.	Unacceptable performance is evidenced by . . . Many spelling and/or grammatical errors.

differences, cultural differences, various learning styles, and children who learn at varying rates. The No Child Left Behind Act (2002) has reinforced the concept that all children can learn at high levels; they just do so in different ways. Successful teachers tailor their lessons to meet the learning needs of the students.

As faculty, we emphasize the importance of knowing the children's strengths and using those strengths as the foundation for new learning. We present a wide variety of research-based teaching strategies in our methods classes. IUSB students engage in simulated learning activities using the strategies. They experience how the strategies work and how the strategies can be used in teaching lessons in their field experience placements. Many of the IUSB students then use those strategies when they teach lessons in their field experience classrooms.

Faculty members also formally observe IUSB students teaching and interacting with children in the field experience classrooms. We also use written observation feedback from the field experience host teachers. Formal observation notes provide written documentation and feedback to the student for these performance areas that reflect their dispositions:

- Student is dressed professionally;
- Student uses correct oral and written language;
- Classroom management techniques are used;
- Student responds to children's questions;
- Student has good rapport with children;
- Student models that errors are okay and can be used as a learning tool;
- Student knows and calls on children by name.

The lesson plans IUSB students write and the strategies they select to use indicate what they believe about learning. Explicit planning that documents specific adaptations for diverse learners provides insights into the students' dispositions. The lesson analysis narratives accompanying each lesson plan address what did and did not go well in the lesson, and what the student would do differently the next time. These narratives often touch upon the need to plan and implement additional and/or different adaptations for specific children. Often students' growth is seen in this area as they teach more lessons and gain the confidence that comes with experience. During class time, discussion of field experiences occurs. What the students say about the school, the teacher, and the children reveals information about the students' dispositions. Their reflective journals are also valuable dispositions artifacts.

Student teachers must be concerned with learners and their differences. The student teacher who appreciates the individual differences in students uses these variations to help students learn. A student teacher who values student differences uses student strengths as well as student errors as an opportunity for growth. This student teacher will take advantage of opportunities to help students who are not meeting objectives. The student teacher will value the experience and insights gained from that interaction. These interactions may provide valuable insights that could not be gained otherwise. A student teacher's documentation related to this disposition might include a tutoring log that lists the skills that the student teacher worked on with students. Student work samples from before and after the help sessions on the specific skill would further document the impact of this interaction on student learning.

Dispositions Related to Instruction

We document these dispositions by the lesson plans the IUSB students prepare and by observations of the students teaching their lessons. Observation is guided by these performances:

- Student appears confident while teaching;
- Student is prepared to teach the lesson as formally planned;
- Student "thinks on his (or her) feet" and changes the plan when it isn't working;
- Student handles interruptions such as a visitor, unexpected announcements, or a fire drill;
- Objectives chosen for the lesson focus on higher order thinking;
- Student uses a variety of questions while teaching;
- Student responds appropriately to children's creative or divergent responses;
- Student engages children in active learning experiences;
- A variety of assessments are used;
- The student facilitates transitions between activities.

Student teachers should value the development of critical thinking, problem solving, and performance skills in their students. These skills can and should be developed by the manner in which the student teacher plans and carries out instruction. Student teachers should be flexible in their teaching styles and value the learning that they themselves gain from the exchange as well. Lessons that a student teacher learns in the classroom should inform their classroom practice from that point forward. Lesson plans should reflect a variety of instructional strategies and can be used to document the flexibility and variety of instruction implemented in the classroom. The ongoing nature of lesson planning and implementation provides abundant opportunities to increase skill in this area.

Dispositions Related to Motivation

In most of their field experiences, IUSB students have no say as to the physical arrangement of the classroom or the classroom management system used. Since they are guests in the classroom, they must adapt to the system in place. What they can control is their own demeanor and how they interact with children. They can sit back and observe or they can actively interact with the children and host teacher. They can take initiative and work with individual students or groups. They can offer to create learning centers or materials that complement the classroom teacher's instruction.

Focused reflective journals are required for most of our field experience courses. One journal requirement focuses on classroom organization. Using a series of questions to guide their observations, IUSB students write about how the field classroom is physically organized, what procedures are in place, what rules are posted, and how discipline is handled. Students are encouraged to describe what they like and what they would change. Their comments are often good indicators of their dispositions. Some students describe how they would arrange the desks differently. Some write about using cooperative learning groups. Some mention how student work is displayed and how grading is done. Some mention how the classroom "feels" to them. They describe their vision of the climate of their own future classrooms.

Lesson plans also provide a wealth of information. We look for plans that address the following:

- *Lesson introduction*—student engages the children. Student ties new learning to what is already known.
- *Type of instruction selected*—large group, small group, or individual activities.
- *Method of instruction selected*—Lecture, discussion, hands-on activities, or demonstrations.
- *Audio-visual aids or technology used.*
- *Method of assessment*—Do the children read, write, talk, draw, or make something? Assessment is authentic.
- *Specific adaptations are planned for diverse learners.*

Effective teachers take all of the above into account as they plan their lessons. IUSB students' lesson plans and reflective journals provide insight into their dispositions related to motivation.

Motivating students is perhaps one of the most difficult aspects of the learning experience that student teachers encounter. As novices, student teachers may have little experience with the process of developing intrinsic motivation in their students. Motivation also includes assisting students in recognizing their role in promoting one another's learning. Student teachers who are successful in motivating students are committed to the ongoing development of individual student abilities. When students' abilities are recognized and nourished in the classroom, they will be more motivated to learn. Motivation cannot occur without communication. The manner in which a student teacher communicates expectations will influence the amount of motivation they are able to inspire in their students. Student teachers who utilize a variety of effective communication styles as well as thoughtful and responsive listening techniques will likely be more "motivating" to their students than a student teacher who does not. A video- or audiotape of the discussion between the student teacher and their students about expectations, where these skills are demonstrated, would provide documentation for this set of skills. A summary or transcript of this discussion might serve this purpose as well.

Dispositions Related to Communication

IUSB students complete many written reflective assignments and participate in class discussions. Faculty members model and reinforce the importance of talking and writing in learning. One assignment per course is submitted to the instructor via LiveText, an Internet-based archival system used by the IUSB School of Education. When students submit an assignment on LiveText, they also write a reflection on one or more of the IUSB knowledge, performance, or dispositions standards and why the artifact demonstrates mastery of the selected standard(s). In IUSB courses, faculty members observe the students during discussions and activities. We look for:

- Students are engaged in the discussion;
- Their nonverbal signals (posture, gestures, overall responsiveness, eye contact);
- Students show respect for each other and the instructor;
- Students are aware of cultural differences in communication styles;
- Students are tolerant of opinions different from their own.

We also look to gain information while reading the students' reflections. Biases and opinions appear in the reactions students have to what they encounter in their field experiences. A great deal can be learned about a student's beliefs when they are critical of a teacher or class they have observed during field experience.

Finally, formal observation of IUSB students teaching lessons in field experience provides information as to their dispositions related to communication. Dispositions of a student teacher relating to communication can have a profound effect on both their effectiveness in the classroom and their ability to connect in a meaningful way with their students, parents, and community members. Student teachers who utilize the power of language to promote learning in their classrooms can document this aspect of their teaching by providing examples of newsletters, progress reports, and other written communication with students and parents. Another example might be labels throughout the classroom reflecting not only English but various native languages of the students in the classroom. Beyond the instructional considerations of communication, student teachers must be aware of communication styles that may be specific to certain cultural groups. For example, a student or parent reluctant to look the teacher in the eye may be displaying a culturally appropriate form of respect. Educators who are unaware of cultural differences in communication styles may mistake this behavior for inattentiveness or evasiveness. Teaching by its very nature depends on effective communication. A student teacher must utilize effective and culturally responsive communication techniques both in verbal and written forms and display dispositions that enhance the effectiveness of that communication for the benefit of all learners.

Dispositions Related to Planning

Although IUSB students develop units of instruction in several courses, they do not usually have the opportunity to teach the whole unit in field experience. They must fit the lessons they teach into the existing curriculum of the host teacher, who may or may not have a choice as to what to teach or when to teach it. Some area schools adhere to a curriculum prescribed by their school corporation based on Indiana's K–12 academic standards (Indiana Department of Education, 2003a). Other schools allow teachers more freedom in deciding how to meet the academic standards.

Sometimes IUSB students are paired for a field experience placement and have the opportunity to plan their lessons together and team-teach. Some students work closely with their host teacher in planning lessons, while others are given free rein as to the lessons they teach. Their lesson analysis reflections often state that they learn, sometimes the hard way, that teaching requires them to be flexible and deviate from their lesson plan. This is especially true of lessons that go poorly.

As field experience observers, sometimes we see those lessons that go poorly. Sometimes the student knows the lesson is not working, but she does not know what to do to change direction or when to stop the lesson and regroup. Sometimes the host teacher steps in or makes a suggestion, but often the student learns more from the experience if allowed to fail. Then as a team we work with the student on what she could have done differently. This type of one-on-one coaching and mentoring has been effective for many IUSB students.

Student teachers are placed in situations where they are both learning to teach and teaching to learn. An integral part of this process is the mentoring and support they receive from both the teacher in their assigned classroom and their assigned supervisor. These key individuals provide support, encouragement, suggestions for improvement, and pats on the back to student teachers throughout their experience. When a student teacher falls short of expectations in a given area, these individuals guide them toward their target and continue to monitor their progress.

Dispositions Related to Assessment

Assessment and instruction should be seamlessly interwoven. IUSB students hear the mantra "The purpose of assessment is to plan instruction." In methods classes, students learn to write a lesson plan. First, the instructional objectives ("Students will be able to . . .") are written. Then an assessment is generated to match each objective. Finally, mastery level criteria are determined. Students must also develop extension activities for each lesson plan. Reinforcement or supplementary extension activities must be listed for those children who master the objectives. Reteaching ideas are generated for those children who do not achieve mastery.

Unfortunately, with the prevalence of high-stakes assessment, IUSB students do not receive the same assessment message in field experiences. Many teachers in the field are given assessments to use as part of the prescribed curriculum. If teacher-generated assessments are used, the format is usually a pencil and paper activity that is useful mainly for accountability purposes. Assessment is often a difficult area for IUSB students because what they learn in coursework frequently is not what they observe in the field.

Another problematic area for student teachers is assessment. Although expertise in this area is gained with experience, initial positive attitudes toward assessment will serve student teachers well. It is crucial that student teachers value ongoing assessment and recognize the vital role it plays in the instructional process. Assessment is both that of student achievement in light of instructional goals, but also assessment of their own performance in the form of reflective teaching practice. Ongoing assessment should be used to identify areas of weakness and strength in both learner and student teacher. Ongoing assessment can be documented by student teachers supplying samples of assessments used with students. An artifact that would provide documentation of a student teacher reflective practice could include:

- A first draft of a lesson plan;
- A reflective piece on how this lesson could be improved;
- A revised lesson plan that indicates the changes the student teacher made to the initial plan in light of reflecting on the first draft of the plan.

Assessment of all aspects of the learning experience is crucial if learning is to be an ongoing process.

Dispositions Related to Reflection

One of the biggest complaints we hear from field experience students concerns the amount of time they spend writing reflective papers or journals. A typical complaint is that real teachers do not have time to spend writing reflections about everything they teach. Although that may literally be true, many teachers do keep a journal in which they write about their teaching, their students' learning, their successes and failures, and other concerns. Many more reflect on their teaching in conversations with colleagues, family, and friends. With experience, reflecting on teaching becomes automatic. Growth as a teacher comes with change, and change happens when reflection takes place. Teachers become better teachers by teaching and by reflecting on what works and what does not work. IUSB students use the lesson plan analysis portion of the lesson plan to demonstrate the appropriate reflection dispositions. They are required to articulate their teaching strengths and weaknesses as well as what they would do differently in writing their reflections.

Student teachers are expected to be reflective practitioners. As discussed with assessment, evaluation of one's own performance is essential if learning is to be an ongoing process. Student teachers at IUSB are required to complete reflective journal entries throughout their experience at regular intervals. These reflections can be statements of general feelings of the student teacher, relating to specific classroom incidents, or about concerns related to the student teaching experience. Typically a given student teacher's reflections as a whole will contain all of these components by the end of their experience. These written reflections, as well as reflective statements on lesson plans, can provide documentation of this important area of teacher competence.

Dispositions Related to Community

During our current field experiences IUSB students have limited opportunities to experience the various aspects of the children's lives outside of school. Although students observe in a variety of classrooms prior to student teaching, they do not get the in-depth exposure to the school and greater communities until they student teach.

Thus, faculty members who observe IUSB students teaching during field experiences become an integral connection between the campus and the community. When discussion of field experiences takes place on campus, faculty members provide information about the schools and teaching. We make students aware of trends in education and legislation that impact schools. We explain teacher roles and how to work with support staff. Finally, we mentor the IUSB students as they progress through their various field experiences.

In addition to classroom concerns, student teachers must concern themselves with individuals and experiences beyond the classroom. Children bring a wealth of experiences to the classroom; these can be from home and family, church, and community as well as from interactions with their peers. Student teachers should recognize the importance of all aspects of their students' lives. The lives of students can be complex, with many unseen factors influencing classroom performance. Student teachers must be willing to confer with other adults regarding the performance of their students. Parents, teachers, administrators, other educational professionals, and community members can provide valuable insights into factors that may influence the manner in which students interact and perform in the classroom. That said, it is critical that student teachers respect and uphold the confidential nature of information that relates to their students. When student teachers consult with others to gain insight about their students, they should document this in a manner that maintains the confidentiality of students.

CONCLUSION

Assessing Dispositions in the Field

At IUSB we use observation, reflective journals, and lesson plan analysis reflections as the main methods of assessing student dispositions for field experience courses. Reflection papers are required assignments for IUSB students, beginning with foundations level courses and continuing through the methods courses taken prior to student teaching. In addition, in the upper levels methods courses students teach at least four lessons in the field experience classroom and reflect on their teaching and planning. IUSB faculty members formally observe the students teaching lessons during the field experience. Classroom host teachers provide written lesson feedback to the students. A final written evaluation of each IUSB student is completed by the classroom host teacher at the end of each field experience.

When a faculty member has reservations about a student's performance or dispositions, a Letter of Concern is written and placed in the student's advising file. The Letter of Concern outlines background information about the course, the student's strengths, a detailed description of concerns, mitigating factors, and an explanation of the Letter of Concern process. A copy of the letter is given to the student as well. Often the faculty member will meet with the student and offer suggestions for improvement. If more than one faculty member expresses concern about a student, action is taken at the administrative level. The Letters of Concern have been effective in providing concrete documentation of students who struggle and either do or do not make improvements.

Student teachers are placed in situations where they are both learning to teach and teaching to learn. An integral part of this process is the mentoring and support they receive from both the teacher in their assigned classroom and their assigned supervisor. These key individuals provide support, encouragement, suggestions for improvement, and pats on the back to student teachers throughout their experience. When student teachers fall short of expectations in a given area, these individuals guide them toward their target and continue to monitor their progress.

Effective Strategies

IUSB faculty members model excellence in teaching in their courses. We explicitly show our students what good teaching "looks like" related to knowledge, performances, and dispositions. IUSB students are formally and informally observed in class as well as in the field. Narrative documents such as reflective journals or reflection papers are required assignments. Lesson plans demonstrate the students' ability to plan for and teach diverse students.

Students complete dispositions surveys at various checkpoints during the TEP as delineated in our Unit Assessment System, which is required by the Indiana Professional Standards Board (IPSB). Faculty members complete a disposition survey for each student immediately prior to student teaching. Letters of Concern are another way of documenting a student's dispositions.

LiveText offers a way for students to accumulate and store their artifacts and for faculty to evaluate artifacts and provide feedback. The student teaching notebook provides students with ways to document their proficiencies in regard to the IUSB knowledge, performances, and dispositions. In addition, our student teachers complete and submit a modified portfolio based on the Beginning Teacher Assessment Program (Indiana Department of Education, 2003b) requirements. This portfolio consists of a classroom learning community commentary, five lesson plans in literacy or numeracy, analysis of student learning for two students, and final reflections. Table 10.2 is the form we are currently using to assess student teacher dispositions.

Future Directions

Faculty members are looking at several different ways to better assess dispositions in our field experience students and student teachers. Beginning teachers in Indiana are required to submit a portfolio for license renewal under the Beginning Teacher Assessment Program (BTAP). "BTAP is organized

Table 10.2.   Indiana University South Bend–School of Education Student Teaching Form E

Area 1: Knowledge of Subject Matter

1.1   When presenting information to the class, the student teacher:

1.11   Consistently conveys accurate and complete information to students (INTASC 1)

1.12   Answers student questions accurately (INTASC 1)

1.13   Provides examples and nonexamples to illustrate principles or concepts (INTASC 1)

1.14   Avoids making content unnecessarily confusing to students (INTASC 1)

1.15   Takes advantage of opportunities to extend student thinking (INTASC 1)

1.2   When planning lessons or units of instruction, the student teacher:

1.21   Does not conform exclusively to the textbook in making curriculum decisions, utilizes supplemental materials (INTASC 4)

1.22   Assigns tasks with a varying levels of cognitive challenge (INTASC 4)

1.23   Incorporates difficult but appropriate concept and ideas (INTASC 4, 5)

1.24   Develops curriculum that is culturally responsive to diversity (INTASC 3, 4)

1.25   Conforms to the IUSB Student Teaching Template or an approved alternate format

1.26   Uses technology to enhance planning, instruction, productivity, professional practice, and to enhance student learning (INTASC 1, 4, 7)

1.3   When planning and/or implementing assessment of student learning, the student teacher:

1.31   Aligns assessment with instructional objectives (INTASC 7, 8)

1.32   Accurately computes scores and grades (INTASC 8)

1.33   Makes reasonable interpretations of assessments (INTASC 8)

1.34   Focuses feedback on accomplishments rather than mistakes (INTASC 5, 8)

1.35   Acknowledges levels of effort and rewards excellent work (INTASC 5, 8)

1.4   When planning and/or implementing instruction, the student teacher:

1.41   Uses proper grammar in writing and verbally, avoids spelling and mathematical errors (INTASC 1)

1.42   Speaks clearly and with appropriate voice tones and volume (INTASC 6)

Area 2: Instructional Problem Solving

2.1   When diagnosing learning difficulties experienced by a student or a group of students, the student teacher:

2.11   Considers the "instruction" or the "teacher" as a potential source of student difficulty (INTASC 4, 7, 8, 9)

2.12   Shows appropriate concern when it is evident that the goals of the lesson were not attained (INTASC 6, 8)

2.13   Takes advantage of opportunities to help students who are not meeting objectives (INTASC 4, 5)

2.14   Avoids focusing on the past (last years teacher) or in the learners traits (laziness or low ability) to find causal factors for student difficulties (INTASC 2, 6, 8)

2.2   When planning or implementing a lesson after receiving feedback about previous lessons, the student teacher:

2.21   Makes an effort to incorporate prior feedback (INTASC 7, 9)

2.22   Avoids making previously identified mistakes (INTASC 9)

Table 10.2. (*continued*)

Area 3: Relationships with Students

3.1 When speaking informally with students outside of a "lesson" context, the student teacher,

3.11 Makes appropriate personal connections and exchanges with students (INTASC 2, 6, 9)

3.12 Listens to what students are saying (INTASC 6)

3.13 Communicates interest in student's areas of interest (INTASC 6)

3.14 Uses student names in the classroom and hallways (INTASC 6)

3.2 When given appropriate opportunities to learn about the lives of students outside of the classroom, the student teacher:

3.21 Makes an effort to learn about student's lives outside the classroom (INTASC 2, 6)

3.22 Links lesson topics and activities to the lives of students (INTASC 2, 5, 6, 7)

Area 4: Engaging Students in Active Learning

4.1 When planning and implementing lessons, the student teacher:

4.11 Engages students in meaningful group projects (INTASC 4, 5)

4.12 Provides opportunities for students to make choices about how to respond to classroom tasks (INTASC 4, 5)

4.13 Provides opportunities for students to share their own personal ideas, and responds appropriately to student input (INTASC 6)

4.14 Encourages independent thinking on the part of students (INTASC 3, 4, 6)

4.2 When leading discussions in a small group or with the whole group, the student teacher:

4.21 Accepts responses from volunteer students and elicits responses from nonvolunteers as well (INTASC 4, 5, 6)

4.22 Avoids talking for long periods of time (does not monopolize the talk time) (INTASC 6)

4.23 Attends to students who go "off-task" (INTASC 2, 5, 6)

4.24 Provides time for students to reflect before responding to questions or tasks (INTASC 5, 6)

Area 5: Managing Student Behavior and Classroom Activities

5.1 When conveying expectations for student roles in a lesson or activity, the student teacher:

5.11 Clearly conveys expectations for student tasks (INTASC 6)

5.12 Conveys to students a sense of urgency to learn, to participate and to achieve, motivates students to learn (INTASC 5, 6)

5.13 Connects teacher expectations to what the students may view as important or valuable (INTASC 5, 6)

5.2 When responding to disruptions in the class routine, the student teacher:

5.21 Maintains control of emotions and/or expresses them appropriately (INTASC 6, 9)

5.22 Makes use of alternative strategies to address the problem (INTASC 5, 6)

5.23 Responds in ways that are consistent and fair (INTASC 5, 6)

5.24 Avoids viewing classroom incidents as a "power struggle," and avoids taking these incidents personally (INTASC 6, 9)

(*continued*)

Table 10.2. (*continued*)

5.25 Establishes a system of consequences for antisocial, unproductive student behaviors (INTASC 5)

5.26 Uses a system to cue students before during and after transitions (INTASC 6)

5.3 When involving students in instructional activity, the student teacher:

5.31 Provides an environment where students are at minimal risk from harm (INTASC 2, 7)

5.32 Uses efficient procedures to avoid wasting student's instructional time and opportunities (INTASC 4, 7)

Area 6: Conscientiousness as a Teacher

6.1 When making promises to students, cooperating teachers, and/or university supervisors, the student teacher:

6.11 Follows through (INTASC 6, 9)

6.12 Takes responsibility and does not make excuses (INTASC 6, 9)

6.2 When committing time to student teaching assignments, the student teacher:

6.21 Avoids outside commitments (full-time employment, extra-curricular activities etc.) that would interfere with the quality of the student teaching effort. If these commitments are unavoidable, they do not diminish the quality of the student teaching effort (INTASC 9)

6.22 Expects of his/herself the level of performance expected by the university and classroom teacher, does not settle for a weak approximation of what is expected (INTASC 9)

6.23 Avoids appearing disorganized by not being late to class, late in correcting papers, late in handing in grades and or late in meeting deadlines (INTASC 9)

6.24 Completes university assignments according to the guidelines provided (INTASC 9)

6.3 When teaching a lesson, the student teacher:

6.31 Teaches in a manner characterized by energy enthusiasm and/or conviction (INTASC 5, 9,10)

6.32 Teaches in a manner that demonstrates adequate preparation (INTASC 7, 9, 10)

6.33 Behaves in a proactive, rather than a reactive manner (INTASC 9)

Area 7: Quality of Professional Judgments

7.1 When relating to other professionals in the classroom or building, the student teacher:

7.11 Conveys respect for and encourages the views, opinions, and responsibilities of diverse others (INTASC 3, 6)

7.12 Maintains confidentiality and is discreet in conveying information to others when appropriate (INTASC 6, 9)

7.2 When conversing with class or individuals in a lesson or outside of a formal classroom situation, the student teacher:

7.21 Uses appropriate language and examples (INTASC 4, 6)

7.22 Avoids making comments or statements that convey disrespect for individuals or groups of individuals (INTASC 3, 6, 9)

7.23 Establishes appropriate relationships with individuals and groups of students (INTASC 5, 6, 9)

7.3 When preparing to come to school, the student teacher:

7.31 Wears only appropriate clothing and jewelry, body is adequately covered (INTASC 9, 10)

Table 10.2. *(continued)*

7.32	Displays good grooming and hygiene (INTASC 9, 10)
7.4	When selecting topics and/or assessment for the class, the student teacher:
7.41	Chooses topics that are appropriate for students (INTASC 2, 7)
7.42	Chooses assessment tasks that are appropriate for students (INTASC 2, 8)
7.43	Applies appropriate standards to student work (INTASC 2, 7)

Source: Raths and Lyman (2003)
Note: Evaluation of Competence in Student Teaching—Midterm and Final
Unlike the formative evaluation forms for student teaching, the purpose of this form is to make an assessment of student teacher competence which will determine the overall competence of the student teacher which will impact the final student teaching grade. This form is divided into 7 areas of student teacher competence. Please familiarize yourself with the rating scale and rate the student teacher in each area accordingly.

1 = Unsatisfactory—performance is well below the level expected. This is an area of weakness, requiring a plan for improvement.
2 = Basic—performance slightly below the expected level
3 = Proficient—student teacher performs at the expected level.
4 = Skilled—student teacher performs above the expected level.

around IPSB standards-based portfolio assessments with related building- and district level support, and it is linked to the standards and recently adopted staged licensure framework" (Indiana Department of Education, 2003b). In order to prepare our students for this process, we are using a modified portfolio based on the BTAP guidelines with student teachers. In addition to preparing students for BTAP, the modified portfolio also shows promise for assessing and documenting our students' dispositions as well.

REFERENCES

Carter, K. (1990). Teachers' knowledge and learning to teach. In W. R. Houston (Ed.), *Handbook of research on teacher education* (pp. 291–310). New York: Macmillan.
Clandinin, D. J., Davis, A., Hogan, P., & Kennard, B. (1993). *Learning to teach, teaching to learn: Stories of collaboration in teacher education.* New York: Teachers College Press.
Indiana Department of Education. (1999, September). *Comprehensive standards document.* Retrieved June 13, 2003, from http://www.IN.gov/psb/standards/teacher index.html. Indianapolis, IN: Indiana Professional Standards Board.
Indiana Department of Education. (2003a, February). *Indiana K–12 academic standards.* Retrieved August 26, 2003, from http://www.indianastandards.org. Indianapolis, IN: Indiana Professional Standards Board.
Indiana Department of Education. (2003b, June). *Beginning teacher assessment program: A guide for beginning teachers. 2003–2004 School year.* Retrieved August 25, 2003, from http://www.state.in.us/psb/beginningteachers/GuidetoBTAP_summer2003.pdf. Indianapolis: Indiana Professional Standards Board.

Interstate New Teacher Assessment and Support Consortium (INTASC). (1992). *Model standards for beginning teacher licensing and development: A resource for state dialogue.* Retrieved June 13, 2003, from http://www.ccsso.org/intascst.html

LaBoskey, V. K. (1994). *Development of reflective practice: A study of preservice teachers.* New York: Teachers College Press.

LiveText, Inc. (1997). *College LiveText edu solutions.* Retrieved June 17, 2003, from http://college.livetext.com/college/index.html

National Commission on Teaching and America's Future. (1996). *What matters most: Teaching for America's future.* New York: Author.

National Council for Accreditation of Teacher Education (NCATE). (2000). *Professional standards for the accreditation of schools, colleges, and departments of education.* Washington, DC: Author.

No Child Left Behind Act, P.L. 107-110 (H.R. 1), 115 STAT. 1425 (2002).

Raths, J., & Lyman, F. (2003). Summative evaluation of student teachers: An enduring problem. *Journal of Teacher Education, 54,* 206–216.

Taylor, R. L., & Wasicsko, M. M. (2000, November 4). *The dispositions to teach.* Retrieved June 13, 2003, from Eastern Kentucky University, College of Education website: http://www.education.eku.edu

Wasicsko, M. M. (2002, April). *Assessing educator dispositions: A perceptual psychological approach.* Retrieved June 13, 2003, from Eastern Kentucky University, College of Education website: http://www.education.eku.edu

11

Teaching Critical Thinking Skills and Dispositions: A Graduate Case Study

E. Marcia Sheridan

In order for schools and colleges of education to obtain accreditation from the National Council for the Accreditation of Teacher Education (NCATE, 2002) they must be able to demonstrate that their graduates have the knowledge, skills, and dispositions for teaching. In addition, the Interstate New Teacher Assessment and Support Consortium (INTASC, 1992) has 10 standards for new teachers, including specific objectives for knowledge, performance, and dispositions. Although educators have long been familiar with the concepts of knowledge and skills or performance, the notion of dispositions is the newest requirement of teacher educators. Dispositions are defined as:

> . . . the values, commitments, and professional ethics that influence behaviors toward students, families, colleagues, and communities and affect student learning, motivation, and development as well as the educator's own professional growth. Dispositions are guided by beliefs and attitudes related to values such as caring, fairness, honesty, responsibility and social justice. For example, they might include a belief that all students can learn, a vision of high and challenging standards, or a commitment to a safe and supportive learning environment. (NCATE, 2002, p. 53)

In particular, there are two standards in INTASC (1992) that directly address the development of critical thinking knowledge, performance, and dispositions. First, Standard 4 requires teachers to understand and use a variety of instructional strategies to encourage critical thinking, problem solving, and performance skills and value the development of these in their students. Second, Standard 9 requires that teachers be reflective practitioners, with dispositions valuing critical thinking and self-directed habits of mind and be committed to reflection and ongoing learning.

The Delphi Report is the summary of findings from scholars around the nation convened to define critical thinking and its elements. Their consensus statement on the ideal critical thinker embodies many dispositional traits they considered the basis for a democratic society:

> The ideal critical thinker is habitually inquisitive, well-informed, trustful of reason, open-minded, flexible, fair-minded in evaluation, honest in facing personal biases, prudent in making judgments, willing to reconsider, clear about issues, orderly in complex matters, diligent in seeking relevant information, reasonable in the selection of criteria, focused in inquiry, and persistent in seeking results which are as precise as the subject and the circumstances of inquiry permit. (Facione, 1990, p. 2)

The currently existing National Standards for Civics and Government (NSCG) for K–12 (Center for Civic Education, 1994) are supported by the Office of Educational Research and Improvement (OERI) of the U.S. Department of Education and have been heavily used in the construction and assessment of these subjects by the National Assessment of Education Progress (National Center for Education Statistics, 1999). According to the Center for Civic Education, the NSCG standards include the civic dispositions or character traits important to the preservation and improvement of U.S. democracy and require that students should voluntarily adhere to self-imposed standards of behavior rather than be required by the imposition of external controls. These civic dispositions, called civic virtues by the founding fathers, include both public and private character traits. These include moral responsibility, self-discipline, respect for individual worth and human dignity, public spiritedness, civility, respect for the rights of other individuals, respect for law, honesty, open-mindedness, critical mindedness, a willingness to negotiation and compromise, persistence, civic mindedness, compassion for the well-being of others, especially for the less fortunate; patriotism, courage and tolerance of ambiguity (Center for Civic Education, 1994).

Based on accreditation requirements to ensure that teachers have the knowledge, skills, and dispositions themselves, as well as promote these in their students, teacher educators must provide the kinds of learning opportunities for their students to acquire the critical thinking knowledge, skills, and dispositions in order to teach these to K–12 students. The purpose of this chapter is to describe a study involving the development of critical thinking knowledge, skills, and dispositions of graduate education students over a series of years in a class that analyzes the major problems set for education by the pluralistic culture of U.S. society.

CRITICAL THINKING: COGNITIVE, METACOGNITIVE, AND DISPOSITIONAL

The Delphi Report consensus statement on critical thinking incorporated the disposition virtues or habits of mind mentioned previously as well as defined critical thinking as "purposeful, self-regulatory judgment which results in interpretation, analysis, evaluation, and inference" (Facione, 1990, p. 2). In other words, critical thinking has three essential components: a cognitive, a metacognitive, and a dispositional, and all three must be present for effective critical thinking to occur (see Figure 11.1).

First, cognitively, constructivist theory emphasizes that learners must take an active role in their construction of knowledge and that this is

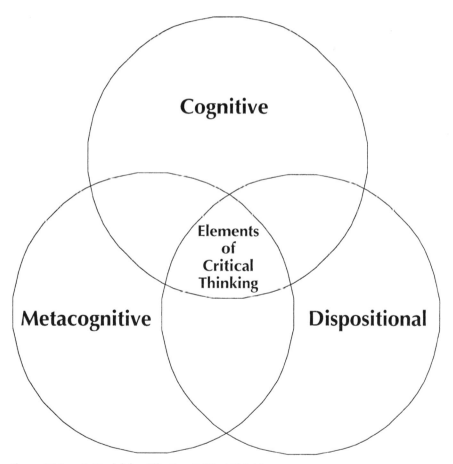

Figure 11.1.   A Model for Effective Critical Thinking

socially constructed (Vygotsky, 1978). In Piaget's (1977) terms, learners develop either through assimilation or accommodation in a process of equilibrium and disequilibrium. When preexisting cognitive structures are inconsistent with new information, learners experience disequilibrium and act to reduce cognitive dissonance (Festinger, 1957). Reactions to experiences of cognitive dissonance can range from outright denial and resistance to the discrepant information, to anxiety and uncertainty, or optimally to the reorganizing, construction, reconceptualizing, or transforming of major cognitive schema.

Disequilibrium occurs prior to major cognitive growth and development. The mental state needs to remain open to the tensions between the desire for order and stability or even stagnation on the one hand, and for disorder and dissonance. So Phelps (1990) says that "change is inevitable" given the experiences of one's life, "development is not" (p. 392) depending on the willingness to act on and integrate the dissonant information.

Within the conceptual framework of metacognition, there are two dimensions: the knowledge that human thinkers have about their own cognition and its regulation (Lawson, 1984). Metacognitively, students must be able to manage their cognitive processes or self-regulate and monitor their own learning. This includes the students' ability to converse, describe, explain, and criticize their own cognitive strategies (Romainville, 1994). According to Oxman-Michelli (1992), metacognition includes having awareness for reflective thinking as well as having a strong sense of self-efficacy.

The third aspect of critical thinking—disposition—can be viewed as the tendency or inclination to behave a certain way. Dispositions are defined as "the personal qualities or characteristics that are possessed by individuals, including attitudes, beliefs, interests, appreciations, values, and modes of adjustment" (Taylor & Wasicsko, 2000). In addition Oxman-Michelli (1992) defines the dispositions of critical thinkers as having critical spirits or states of mind signifying an inclination, as opposed to the ability, to think critically. She also uses several synonyms interchangeably to express the meaning of critical thinking dispositions. Those include personality attributes, intellectual virtues, character traits, and motivating values. She emphasizes specific dispositions of critical thinking such as wholeheartedness, open-mindedness, intellectual autonomy, self-understanding, independence of mind, self-confidence, integrity and humility, sense of objectivity, and intellectual courage.

Furthermore, what sets good thinkers apart from others is not their depth of profound knowledge or superior skills, but their pervasive tendency to explore, inquire, gain understanding, take cerebral risks, and think critically and imaginatively. These tendencies can be identified as "thinking dispositions" and can be productive or counterproductive (Tishman, Jay, & Perkins, 1993).

TEACHING CRITICAL THINKING KNOWLEDGE, PERFORMANCE, AND DISPOSITIONS

If teachers are to acquire the knowledge, performance, and dispositions of critical thinking themselves to teach it to their students, effective research in this area is needed. Nonetheless, after reviewing empirical data, there are very few studies with results on how to teach critical thinking dispositions.

Tishman, Jay, and Perkins (1993) advocate using an approach of creating a classroom culture that nurtures good thinking dispositions. This enculturation approach focuses on modeling critical thinking skills, utilizing interaction among peers to facilitate the meaning of critical thinking, and classroom instruction that directly explains culturally important skills and concepts.

Oxman-Michelli (1992) suggests coaching students through critical thinking tasks to explicitly teach the nature of critical thinking processes, develop metacognitive strategies, and reinforce behaviors that evidence critical thinking dispositions. She supports the idea that critical thinking dispositions can be taught both directly and indirectly, and stresses the usefulness of teachers using coaching strategies that promote their dispositions. In particular, she suggests rewarding students for evidence in growth of tolerance and acceptance for ambiguity in critical thinking tasks when they encounter risk and anxiety, which must be overcome. Although acknowledging the importance of developing critical spirit in students, Oxman-Michelli warns the teacher to expect resistance and to be prepared for it, as it is often a major obstacle when introducing critical thinking tasks to students.

Perkins and others (2000) conducted an extensive review of the research related to thinking dispositions, which they define as how people are disposed to use and invest their abilities. In their attempt to answer the question as to whether thinking dispositions could be learned, their review provided very little research that examined thinking dispositions apart from measuring intellectual ability. However, they strongly recommended an environment that encourages risk-taking.

SOCRATIC SEMINARS

Interest in Socratic seminars as a method for teaching critical thinking emerged from Adler (1982), whose Paideia Principles state that good teaching consists of the didactic teaching of organized knowledge, coaching in the habits and skills of learning, and Socratic seminars for enlarged understanding of ideas, values, and issues. As opposed to the Socratic method in the legal profession, Socratic seminars are not confrontational, but seek to develop a shared understanding among participants through the discussion of texts and artifacts from the arts. Socratic seminars consist of four elements: the text, the participants, the facilitator, and the questions.

The Text

The text may be chosen from a variety of disciplines but should contain some ambiguity and important ideas for which there is no right or wrong answer. Students are required to carefully read in order to participate in discussion of the text, ask questions if they do not understand either the text or comments made about it, and listen carefully as well as talk. Participants are required to read the text in advance of the seminar and engage in thoughtful and effective interpersonal communication skills.

The Questions and the Facilitator

The opening question proposed by the facilitator should focus on the text, requiring the participations to refer back to it as they discuss the questions. Student responses can generate new questions, and participants may even ask their own questions of one another.

The Participants

Talk, as well as "think time," is valued, and allowing others to participate should be stressed with the rule to "take turns." In addition, students are encouraged "to pass" if they do not have an idea they wish to share at that point or because their ideas are not yet formulated. Because one of the rules of Socratic seminars is that participants "take turns," students do not raise hands to be called on in order to participate. So they must become more aware of the different styles of participation, the need to be fair to allow others to express their ideas, and to become more sensitive to nonverbal cues. Both loud and soft voices are given an opportunity to participate fully in a discussion of ideas without digressions into subjective opinion that cannot be subject to reasoned judgment.

Gradually students should learn that the teacher is not the source of the "right answer" and begin looking at and addressing their ideas to the other participants, not just the teacher, as in the typical classroom situation. They learn to take responsibility for their comments, with the understanding that the seminar's purpose is a shared understanding of ideas, and that does not necessarily mean agreement (Gray, 1988).

One of the primary benefits of the seminar is learning to understand another's point of view that is supported by evidence and subject to logic. Although the values underlying points of view may differ, students learn to agree to disagree, agreeably, on this basis of value conflict. As students become more familiar with the procedures in the seminars, they gradually begin to assume more responsibility for their own behavior and the "flow" of the seminar. As a result, students become more adept at participating in civil discourse on issues for which there are no easy or even right answers (Los Angeles County Office of Education Professional Development Consortia, n.d.).

Although Socratic seminars require students to refer their comments back to the text in order to relate the reasons for their particular inference or conclusion, they often relate different experiences that have brought them to their interpretation or judgment. This sharing of experiences and the diversity of these experiences is a major benefit of seminars. Because an atmosphere of trust develops over time, students feel comfortable in relating experiences reflecting different socioeconomic, ethnic, racial, gender, and educational differences.

Since students, as well as the teacher, are not expected to have all the answers, participants gradually feel freer to ask questions they may have been embarrassed or not have thought to ask in more traditional situations. Since civil discourse requires civil behavior, students are more likely to share ideas when they know the rules require them to contribute to the feeling of group trust and to a nonthreatening atmosphere where others will risk saying what they actually think. Although sometimes participants are surprised to hear what some others may really think, tolerance and respect for other views are the major goals in Socratic seminars.

Socratic seminars incorporate values that are consistent with good character development as well as good critical thinking. Students are told that humility might be the most valuable trait developed in Socratic seminar. In a good sense, neither the teacher nor the students are expected to "know it all," and seminars do not have to come to closure. The participants know they sometimes leave the seminar with more questions than when they arrived.

Reflection After Seminars

At the conclusion of the seminar, participants engage in metacognitive reflection on the seminar process, including ways in which future seminars could be improved. Typically, following the seminar, students are asked to write on how their thoughts have been affected by the seminar itself.

METHODS AND PROCEDURES

Over a 5-year period, the subjects in the study were graduate students enrolled in a master's degree program in elementary, secondary, or special education. Although most were practicing teachers, there were a small number of preservice teachers enrolled in a master's degree with licensure. All subjects were enrolled in a course called Education and Social Issues, a social and philosophical foundations course that identified and analyzed major problems in the field of education due to the pluralistic culture of U.S. society. Major concepts and issues in the course dealt with democracy, pluralism, and change.

Objectives of the course expected the students to be able to demonstrate active listening, pro-social behavior, and good interpersonal communication and cooperative/collaborative learning skills. They were also expected to demonstrate growth in critical thinking, dialogue, and process writing skills and reflective, metacognitive thinking. Methods used in teaching the course included Socratic seminars, large and small group dialogues on course issues, process writing of reflective journals and collaborative group papers, and practice and self-assessment on dialogue skills.

Students were taught about critical thinking skills and dispositions and how to write research papers consistent with the elements of critical thinking. In addition, the concepts of assimilation, accommodation, and cognitive dissonance were taught with respect to open- and close-mindedness and understanding others' points of view. Students were trained to apply intellectual standards (Elder & Paul, n.d.) of clarity, accuracy, precision, relevance, depth, breadth and logic, and intellectual traits (Paul & Elder, n.d.) in peer-editing sessions of one another's writings. The intellectual traits included humility, courage, empathy, integrity, perseverance, faith in reason, and fair-mindedness. Students' written work was also evaluated using these criteria. These standards and traits were the operational basis to assess critical thinking, seminar conduct, and writing by the instructor.

Conscious work on improvement in dialogue skills occurred throughout the semester and was related to all group discussions in class. Students participated in both large and small group discussions related to all class topics. Assessment of dialogue skills occurred in these discussions, as well as following the Socratic seminars. Over time, students engaged in self-assessment and peer coaching on a total of 20 dialogue skills. Self-assessment and teacher assessment of these skills occurred as end of course assessment as well.

Portfolio Assessment

Over the course of a semester, students wrote a series of reflective journals on both Socratic seminars and other class discussions. At the conclusion of the course, students collected their journals, including any they chose to revise, and assembled them into a portfolio. They were instructed to arrange their journals in decreasing order of effectiveness from best to least effective. In a final journal placed on top of the other journals, they reflected why the top three works were their best as compared to the others. They also included an evaluation of their development process and how these met the course goals and their own goals. They were asked to share any problems, solutions, and accomplishments they would include on their development process (North Central Regional Education Laboratory, n.d.).

They were then asked to complete and include a portfolio self-assessment that included three major categories of criteria. The first category was presentation of the portfolio and included ease of locating information, visual appeal, completeness of requirements, and following directions. The second category of portfolio assessment dealt with writing ability and included style, mechanics, and some of the intellectual standards such as logic and relevance, and clarity, accuracy, and precision. The third category was the most important in terms of assessment and dealt with evidence of understanding. Some of the intellectual standards were also evaluated here, such as accuracy, depth, and breadth. Many of the intellectual traits were also included such as humility, courage, empathy, integrity, perseverance, faith in reason, and fair-mindedness. Knowledge of content as well as growth and development of understanding were also assessed. Growth and development of understanding over time was the single most important criteria, and the portfolio was scored holistically.

RESULTS AND CONCLUSION

Although students engaged in both self- and peer evaluation, as well as received teacher evaluation on both oral and written activities, students came to appreciate they were involved in their own personal development as thinkers and teachers. As they came to know one another through dialogues on various topics, they came to appreciate both their own strengths and those of others in a way very different from traditional classroom activities. They begin to value those who easily contributed their ideas as well as those who gave careful thought to each word before speaking (Sheridan, 1999, 2000).

An essential part of every Socratic seminar was a reflection after the seminar of whether it was effective and how participants could set goals for improvement in subsequent seminars. In this way, participants took responsibility for what they did and did not say during the seminar and recognized that they need to become more aware of the need for others to become engaged. Often, there was discussion regarding the different amount of time some people need to respond, with some jumping right in and "talking off the top of their heads," and others needing to "organize their thoughts" before they would say what they thought.

Following each seminar, students wrote metacognitive reflective journals about the topic of the text and the seminar. There is a substantial body of research from the National Paideia Center (2001) among elementary and secondary level students that Socratic seminars significantly improve student writing.

Based on many self-reports, students wrote about how their thoughts on an issue changed as a result of seminars. Having been exposed to others' points of view enlarged their understanding, and as a result they were able to write with greater clarity and depth.

Metaphors for Thinking and Understanding

Over the years of the study, metaphors used in speaking and writing were observed and collected that described the evolution of student thinking and understanding of major course issues. These critical thinking metaphors were used to describe how participants changed their minds on issues, began to understand other points of view, or still had not made up their minds on some of the unsolvable problems in the education field. As the data were analyzed, certain categories of metaphor emerged as ways in which students talked and wrote about their thinking.

Several of these categories were sensory. The first was visual and had two subcategories. The first dealt with not seeing and seeing (see Table 11.1). Lack or difficulty of understanding was referred to as being blind to something or seeing through a tunnel or with blinders on. Ideas were fuzzy or clouded. References to eyes were made as in a mind's eye, a critical eye, and opening one's eye to ideas. Many references to seeing were made, as in seeing meaning, seeing different points of view, the other side, and things in different ways. Sight was another way of portraying understanding in words such as hindsight, foresight, and outlook and shared vision.

The other visual category included references dealing with light and insight. Metaphors that used references to light included shedding light on something, enlightening, and seeing things in a new or different light. When students had a cognitive breakthrough and finally came to understand something that had been difficult for them, an insight, they used phrases such as I got it, had an epiphany, or talked of the lights going on for them.

The second sensory category was auditory, and students used metaphors dealing with hearing, speaking, and voice. Metaphors using hearing included hear what you are saying, hearing right, being all ears, being heard out, and something being music to one's ears. Using metaphors for speaking, students talked off the top of their heads, and chose their words. References to voice were made as in voicing one's opinion and having a voice in writing to the teacher.

A third category used language dealing with perspectives and frameworks. Students talked of focusing on details or stepping back to examine thinking or for the bigger picture. Metaphors dealing with frames of reference,

Table 11.1.   Categories of Metaphor

Category 1a—Visual (Not Seeing, Seeing, and Sight)

Descriptors	Examples
Are blind to . . .	I see what you mean
Unable to see another point of view	Seeing different points of view
Seeing things with blinders on	Different people see things different ways
Fuzzy concepts	Seeing is believing
Clouds thinking	Seeing the big picture
Tunnel vision	See the other side
In your mind's eye	Hindsight
A critical eye	Foresight
My eyes were opened/Opened my eyes/Eye opener	Outlook
A new way of seeing things	Shared vision

Category 1b—Visual (Light and Insight)

Shedding light on the topic	Aha!
See things from a new or different light	An epiphany!
Enlightening or illuminating	I got it!
Like a surge of bright light in a cave	The light went on!
Insight/reflection	Color/lens

Category 2—Auditory
Hearing, Speaking, and Voice

I hear what you're saying	Talk off the top of your head
Am I hearing right?	Choose your words
I'm all ears	Think before speaking
I can't bear hearing about it	Put thoughts into words
Hear me out	Voice your opinion
Music to my ears	Voice your view through writing so that at least the teacher is listening

Category 3—Perspectives and Conceptual Frameworks
Perspective and Frameworks

Not on the same page	Put things in perspective
Focus on the details	Step back and get the big picture
Examine the context of the information	Point of view
Step back and examine your thinking	My paradigm shifted
Frame of reference	

Category 4—Thinking
Thinking

Grasp the information or meaning	Jump to conclusions
Covering the information	Broaden understanding
Trigger your thoughts	Thinking and rethinking
Draw conclusions	Thinking patterns
Ponder the matter	Above thought

(continued)

Table 11.1.   (continued)

Think about thinking	Reflect on your thoughts
School of thought	Organize your thoughts
Digging deeper, delving, and making an impression	Stretch your thoughts

Category 5—Metaphors of the Mind

Category 5a—Mind

Open, broad, narrow, or close-minded	Train the mind
Have things on your mind	Quiet mind
Speak your mind	Stillness of mind
My mind was opened/Open your mind	State of mind
An open mind	Clear mind
Broaden understanding	Clarity of mind
What's on your mind?	Mirror of your mind
Change your mind	Mindfulness
On my mind	Make up your mind
Jog your mind	
Category 5b—*Mind as Body*	
A taste of knowledge	Thinking cap
A body of knowledge	Absorb and digest the matter
Getting to the heart of the matter	Swallow your pride
The matter at hand	Regurgitate information
I catch your drift.	Spit it out
Handed the reins	Stir the pot
Inhale . . . exhale	Food for thought
Bumping up against the wall of reality	

perspective, and points of view were used as well as one student expressing a paradigm shift.

A fourth category of metaphor described the mental operations of thinking. Metaphors abounded with respect to thinking. Students grasped meaning, drew or jumped to conclusions, pondered. They dug deeper and made impressions. Their thinking had patterns, was broadened, rethought, organized, and reflected upon.

And last, there was a fifth category of metaphors of the mind. One subcategory had many references to things that happened to their minds. They talked of open, broad, narrow, or close-mindedness. Their minds were trained, quiet, stilled, clear, and made up. The next subcategory of mind used metaphors for thinking with references to the mind as body. Knowledge had a taste and a body. They got to the heart or hand of the matter. They caught one's drift. They absorbed, swallowed, digested, and referred to regurgitation. The language of the metaphors was used to portray the dissonance students experienced when they realized that their own thinking on an issue was incomplete or inconsistent with others' points of view. There were also metaphors that were used to show clarity of understanding, when things made sense, came together, and breakthroughs in comprehension occurred.

CONCLUSION

Teachers can use the power of all the interpersonal communication skills to enhance and assess students' critical thinking since Socratic seminars integrate both the receptive language skills—reading and listening—and the expressive language skills—writing and speaking. In assessing these expressive skills, writing and speaking, one is able to evaluate critical thinking growth over time in disposition, dialogue skills, and in reflective writing.

Self-esteem comes from contributing to the intellectual life of the community of participants with the knowledge that each person is listened to and respected. Based on Socratic dialogue on significant topics such as democracy, change, and pluralism, students took pride in their own growth of understanding and their ability to benefit from the knowledge and experiences of others. Self-esteem developed from a sense that one's contributions were respected and valued by one's active involvement in a community of learners (Kohn, 1994).

Using a combination of Socratic seminars, reflective journals, emphasis on interpersonal dialogue skills, and portfolio assessment, graduate education majors showed increased incidences of use of metaphorical language to describe the internal development of both their perceptual and conceptual worlds related to critical thinking knowledge, skills, and dispositions. Although many of these metaphors were easily recognizable, some were quite original. There is a language of conveying one's internal understanding that is a part of the everyday life of teaching and learning that helps teachers communicate to others how we would like them to think, as well as what we would like them to understand. It is also a way for students to convey to us that they are experiencing growth of understanding in how they construct their own internal reality.

ACKNOWLEDGMENT

I thank Leslie Stockdale for her assistance in the preparation of this chapter.

REFERENCES

Adler, M. (1982). Democracy and education. In *The Paideia proposal: An educational manifesto* (pp. 3–8). New York: Collier Macmillan.

Center for Civic Education. (1994). *National standards for civics and government 9–12 content standards.* Retrieved June 6, 2003, from http://www.civiced.org/912erica.htm

Elder, L., & Paul, R. (n.d.). Universal intellectual standards. Retrieved March 1, 2001, from http://www.criticalthinking.org/University/unistan.html

Facione, P. (1990). *Critical thinking: A statement of expert consensus for purposes of educational assessment and instruction.* Executive Summary, The Delphi Report. Retrieved March 2003, from: www.insightassessment.com/pdf_files/DEXadobe.PDF

Festinger, L. A. (1957). *A theory of cognitive dissonance.* Evanston, IL: Row, Peterson.

Gray, D. (1988). Socratic seminars: Basic education and reform. *Basic Education, 3*(4), 4–8.

Interstate New Teacher Assessment and Support Consortium (INTASC). (1992). *Model standards for beginning teacher licensing and development.* Retrieved April 26, 2003, from Council of Chief State School Officers website: http://www.ccsso.org/intascst.html#draft

Kohn, A. (1994). The truth about self-esteem. *Phi Delta Kappan, 76*(4), 272–283.

Lawson, M. J. (1984). Being executive about metacognition, In J. R. Kirby (Ed.), *Cognitive strategies and educational performance.* Orlando, FL, Academic Press.

Los Angeles County Office of Education Professional Development Consortia. (n.d.). *Professional development Socratic seminars.* Retrieved January 13, 1999, from http://www.lacoe.edu/pdc/professional/socratic.html

National Center for Education Statistics, Institute of Education Sciences, U.S. Department of Education. (1999). *NAEP 1998 civics report card for the nation.* Retrieved June 6, 2003, from http://nces.ed.gov/nationsreportcard/pdf/main1998/2000457.pdf

National Council for the Accreditation of Teacher Educators (NCATE). (2002). *The standard of excellence in teacher education.* Retrieved March 12, 2003, from http://www.ncate.org/2000/unit_stnds_2002.pdf

National Paideia Center. (2001). *National Paideia Center research evaluation.* Retrieved March 12, 2001, from http://www.paideia.org/html/research.html

North Central Regional Education Laboratory. (n.d.). *Self-assessment in portfolios.* Retrieved March 3, 2004, from http://www.ncrel.org/sdrs/areas/issues/students/learning/lr2port.htm

Oxman-Michelli, W. (1992). Critical thinking as "critical spirit." *Institute for Critical Thinking Resource Publication Series, Montclair State College, 4,* 7.

Paul, R., & Elder, L. (n.d.). Valuable intellectual traits. Retrieved March 1, 2001, from http://www.criticalthinking.org/University/intraits.html

Perkins, D., Tishman, S., Ritchhart, R., Donis, K., & Andrade, A. (2000, September). Intelligence in the wild: A dispositional view of intellectual traits. *Educational Psychology Review, 12*(3), 269–293.

Phelps, L. (1990). Developmental challenges, developmental tensions: A heuristic for curricular thinking. In R. Beach & S. Hynds (Eds.), *Developing discourse practices in adolescence and adulthood* (pp. 76–116). San Francisco: Jossey-Bass.

Piaget, J. (1977). *The essential Piaget: An interpretive reference and guide* (H. Gruber & J. Voneche, Eds.). New York: Basic Books.

Romainville, M. (1994). Awareness of cognitive strategies: The relationship between university students' metacognition and their performance. *Studies in Higher Education, 19*(3), 1–9.

Sheridan, E. (1999, November). *Socratic seminars: Assessing growth of understanding through oral and written discourse.* Symposium conducted at the Assessment Institute, Indianapolis.

Sheridan, E. (2000, November). Performance assessment: Portfolios, rubrics and tools for meeting the needs of diverse learners. Symposium conducted at the Assessment Institute, Indianapolis.

Taylor, R., & Wasicsko, M. (2000, November). . *The dispositions to teach.* Retrieved February 3, 2003, from http.//www.educatin.eku.edu/Dean/The%20Dispositions%20to%20Teach.pdf

Tishman, S., Jay, E., & Perkins, D. (1993, Summer). Teaching thinking dispositions: From transmission to enculturation. *Theory Into Practice, 32,* 147–153.

Vygotsky, L. (1978). *Mind in society* (M. Cole, V John-Steiner, S. Scribner, & E. Souberman, Eds.). Cambridge, MA: Harvard University Press.

12

Unleashing the Dispositional Imperative: Legal and Policy Implications

David Freitas, Denise Skarbek, Ella Taylor, and Hilda Rosselli

Improving the quality of our schools continues to receive unprecedented attention in our nation. A plethora of national reports espouse reform proposals, while others, such as the No Child Left Behind Act, mandate interventions through federal legislation. One underlying theme is present in virtually all—the quality of teachers in the classroom is pivotal to long-term, systemic, and continuous school renewal.

This emphasis places teacher educators, as preparers of aspiring teachers and as one of the primary gatekeepers to the profession, in a critical position. As such, an overarching question logically flows. What can teacher educators do to enhance the quality of future teachers?

Content knowledge coupled with appropriate pedagogy has historically been viewed by many as the two core ingredients essential to teaching. A more enlightened approach, occurring over a decade ago, recognized and overtly fused dispositions into a renewed foundational triad for quality teachers.

Few teacher educators now debate the merits of requiring aspiring teachers to develop, model, and demonstrate acceptable dispositions. Since aspiring teachers' dispositional attitudes, beliefs, and core values undergird the learning environment and culture created within their classrooms, assessing the dispositions of aspiring teachers remains a priority.

The National Council for Accreditation of Teacher Education (NCATE), for example, requires teacher education programs to "systematically assesses the development of appropriate professional dispositions" by aspiring teachers. Additionally, graduates of these programs must "know and demonstrate . . . dispositions necessary to help all students learn" (NCATE, 2002).

NCATE (2002) defines dispositions as "the values, commitments, and professional ethics that influence behaviors toward students, families, colleagues, and communities and affect student learning, motivation, and development as well as the educator's own professional growth" (p. 63). This broad definition integrates dispositional expectations into every professional experience and interaction.

The Interstate New Teacher Assessment and Support Consortium (INTASC) also places primacy on the dispositions of aspiring teachers. They conceptually believe that the "the glue that holds members of a profession together . . . is a common commitment to ethical practice" (Council of Chief State School Officers, 1992, p. 6).

This value permeates their *Model Standards for Beginning Teacher Licensing, Assessment and Development: A Resource for State Dialogue* (Chief State Schools Officers, 1992). In fact, multiple dispositional statements are contained in each of their 10 principles—teachers appreciate multiple perspectives (Principle 1); teachers believe that all children can learn at high levels and persist in helping all children achieve success (Principle 3); teachers are thoughtful and responsive listeners (Principle 6); teachers are committed to reflection, assessment, and learning as an ongoing process (Principle 9); teachers recognize their professional responsibility for engaging in and supporting appropriate professional practices for self and colleagues (Principle 9) (Chief State Schools Officers, 1992). These INTASC principles are now incorporated into frameworks in many states.

Assessing the dispositions of aspiring teachers is not only externally mandated for most accredited teacher education institutions, it is sound professional and responsible practice. Implementation, however, is rife with legal and policy implications. Anecdotes, speculation, myths, and hearsay must be avoided and replaced with data-driven, informed judgments resulting in finely crafted policies and procedures. When properly implemented, institutions are generally inoculated from substantial interference by the legal system.

Although most challenges to academic decisions usually occur because of an adverse effect on a student, a perceived procedural defect is often the reason cited. (If the process to make the decision is flawed, the decision is flawed according to this logic.) Formulating policies and procedures consistent with relevant legal principles, therefore, will significantly lower the risk of litigation.

Infusing dispositional expectations for aspiring teachers into preparation programs creates unique legal and policy challenges in specific areas—admission to a teacher education program, retention in the program, and recommendation for licensure. The implications are crystallized when contemplating answers to the following questions: What qualities and behaviors are sought in candidates for entry into a teacher preparation program? What qualities and behaviors should aspiring teachers demonstrate to continue in the program? What qualities and behaviors should aspiring teachers demonstrate in student teaching? What qualities and behaviors are necessary to be recommended for licensure by an institution? Although some dispositions will be common across the entire preparation program, some may be discrete or emphasized more at a specific milestone.

Answers to these questions should be determined first by teacher educators and others in the educational community, not by lawyers. The set of core dispositional values should evolve from the academy. Once delineated and accepted, procedural guidance and review by legal counsel is then timely and appropriate.

ADMISSION

Admission to a professional school, such as a college of education, is a privilege, not a right. There is no constitutional or accepted legal theory guaranteeing admission to all who apply regardless of qualifications. Applicants are entitled, however, to certain procedural safeguards.

Three overarching legal principles apply. Decisions must not be made in an arbitrary or capricious manner, published policies and criteria must be followed, and institutions may not unjustifiably discriminate on the basis of race, age, gender, disability, or citizenship. The admissions selection process must be thoughtful and deliberate. All documentation submitted should be thoroughly reviewed and considered by professionals through an established process. Irrelevant factors should be dismissed. Published admission policies and criteria hold the legal standing of a contract between the institution and applicants. Yet, failing to follow prescribed policies is one of the most common reasons for courts to overturn institutional admission decisions. Institutions need to resist cavalier practices by closely following established policies. Although exceptions may be tempting on occasion, they only heighten litigation liability. They should be rarely made, and only under extraordinary, reasonable, and fully documented circumstances.

Unjustifiably discriminating on the basis of race, age, gender, disability, or citizenship is expressly prohibited by varying legal authorities. Requiring applicants to disclose this type of information for use in the selection process is risky. By refusing to collect and consider this information, allegations of discrimination are minimized.

Admission policies commonly require applicants to teacher education programs to submit various documents in support of their application. These may include grade point averages, passing scores on standardized tests, letters of recommendation, a written essay, a criminal background check, and an interview. Requiring submission of these artifacts, either collectively or in part, is acceptable.

A diligent review of admission criteria is recommended as the dispositional attributes of applicants are overtly assessed. Are the dispositional qualities and behaviors sought in applicants aligned with predictive indicators of success in the teacher preparation program? Are they aligned with predictive indicators of becoming a quality teacher? Do the rubrics designed to assess the dispositions of applicants allow reviewers to effectively and reliably determine unacceptable or acceptable dispositions of applicants? Withstanding legal scrutiny will largely be determined by the answers to these questions.

Assessing applicants with disabilities, as defined by the American with Disabilities Act (ADA) or Section 504 of the Rehabilitation Act of 1973, often yields confusion about acceptable admission practices. The law is clear. These applicants must be qualified in spite of their disability (*Southeastern Community College v. Davis*, 1979). Furthermore, although necessary accommodations must be offered once admitted, institutions need not lower their admission standards if the criteria represent an essential element of the program (OCR, 2000, 1998).

This concept also applies to dispositional standards. Applicants covered under ADA or Section 504, who fail to meet dispositional criteria their disability, may be justifiably denied admission.

RETENTION

Aspiring teachers, once admitted to a preparation program, must continue their standing by meeting published retention standards. Common criteria may include a minimum grade point average in all coursework completed, minimum grades in particular courses such as the major, and demonstrated acceptable dispositions.

The unambiguous nature of grade point averages and grades (other than an occasional grade appeal) is fairly innocuous. Dispositional standards and the application thereof, on the other hand, lead to potential substantial legal entanglements.

GENERAL CONSIDERATIONS

An all-encompassing statement, such as aspiring teachers will maintain the highest professional and ethical standards, is preferable to a laundry list of acceptable and unacceptable dispositions. Given the enormity of possibilities, no list will address them all. A carefully crafted statement setting forth broad dispositional expectations offers a viable platform to launch dispositional inquiries.

The statement on dispositions should be aligned with the institution's mission and the college's conceptual framework. Additionally, it should be nondiscriminatory and assess relevant dispositional attributes essential to becoming a quality teacher.

As students attending a higher education institution, aspiring teachers are bound by existing institutional codes applied to all students. Illegal activities are expressly prohibited in virtually all institutional codes of conduct. These infractions, depending on the severity, may lead to dismissal. Noncriminal behavior is also addressed in institutional codes of conduct. Aspiring teachers must follow them.

Professional schools may establish and enforce additional standards that exceed institutional behavioral expectations. In the case of teacher education programs, additional dispositions are frequently prescribed. Believing all children can learn, for example, may be a dispositional value required of all aspiring teachers.

But there are many gray areas. How far can teacher educators reach into the lives, attitudes, and behaviors of aspiring teachers enrolled in their programs before constitutionally protected rights are infringed? Teacher educators must determine which dispositionally laden situations merit review and which to ignore because of constitutionally protected rights. This preassessment phase is essential to avoid stomping on constitutional rights. Gathering and analyzing substantive facts is the first step. Deciding whether to launch a formal dispositional inquiry comes second.

CASE LAW

Case law emanating from assessing dispositions in teacher education is relatively limited. A wealth of precedent setting cases arising from dispositional disputes with K-12 teachers over an extended period of time, however, is readily available and offers sound guidance for teacher educators. Generally, aspiring teachers hold the same rights as their practicing colleagues.

Although dress and grooming standards for aspiring teachers are dictated by institutional policy when physically on campus, aspiring teachers completing required field experiences may be subject to different standards. From a policy perspective, since following the dress and grooming standards at the field site is often a condition of acceptance, requiring aspiring teachers to abide by the site's standards is wise. Teacher educators are then within their rights to pursue alleged violations.

According to several federal courts, the Equal Protection Clause of the 14th Amendment protects teachers from adverse actions due solely to their sexual orientation. In the *Jantz v. Muci* (1992) case, the court was clear,

"Homosexual orientation alone does not impair" the ability to perform as a teacher, and therefore, sexual orientation is irrelevant.

Membership in a subversive organization may be abhorrent to personal tastes, but it does not automatically disqualify an aspiring teacher from a preparation program. Joining the organization is a protected right, but participating in its unlawful activities could result in dismissal or other action (*Elfbrandt v. Russel*, 1966).

Teachers, by virtue of the 1st Amendment to the Constitution, have a right to freedom of expression when the communication pertains to a matter of public concern (*Connick v. Myers*, 1983). Aspiring teachers who question the quality of their program, for example, are protected. Expressing grievances of a personal nature through a public forum and speech resulting in a material disruption to the educational process are not protected rights.

Slanderous or libelous expressions of aspiring teachers may be considered dispositionally inappropriate, and possibly illegal, depending on the circumstances. Although these cases are legally difficult to prove in a court proceeding, an institutional review of dispositions is less formal.

Although academic freedom is a deeply held value within the educational community, the right is limited. Curricula, topics, discussions, and materials must be relevant to the subject matter being taught (*Fowler v. Board of Education of Lincoln County, Kentucky*, 1987) and appropriate for the developmental level of the learners. Strictly interpreted, educators are employed to teach the approved curriculum and not espouse their personal views or beliefs where unrelated to their subject.

Disciplining students in schools sometimes leads to dispositional scrutiny. Treating students unfairly, unreasonably, or in a discriminatory manner may reveal insights into deeply held beliefs. All questionable practices should be vigorously pursued.

Aspiring teachers assume risk when meeting their students outside of school in nonschool sponsored activities (*Board of Trustees of Compton Junior College District v. Stubblefield*, 1971; *Hamm v. Poplar Bluff R-1 School District*, 1997; *Yang v. Special Charter School District No. 150*, 1973). A dispositional review may be necessary depending on the nature and scope of the interaction.

Aspiring teachers convicted of a felony are usually dismissed from a teacher education program. (In many states, felons are ineligible to become professionally licensed.) Misdemeanor convictions, on the other hand, are generally exempt from dispositional considerations unless the specifics relate to a matter of unprofessional conduct or moral turpitude.

The previous illustrative examples offer a pathway to understanding acceptable parameters. Legal counsel should be contacted as the need arises.

STUDENTS WITH DISABILITIES

Aspiring teachers who officially report a disability according to prescribed procedures and meet ADA or Section 504 guidelines are not automatically excused from meeting dispositional standards. The Office of Civil Rights (OCR) affirmed this concept in two separate rulings. In one, OCR upheld an institution's refusal to readmit a student with an emotional disability (OCR, 1995), and in the other ruling, upheld the dismissal of a medical student with a bipolar disorder (OCR, 2000). Due to the complexity of these cases, questions of dispositional concerns should be handled specially through a competent legal review and assessment.

RECOMMENDATION FOR LICENSURE

Aspiring teachers who successfully complete all academic, dispositional, and institutional requirements are eligible to receive a recommendation for licensure from their institution. Withholding this institutional recommendation because of unpaid library fines, or other punitive nuisance reasons, is not advised because some courts may construe the recommendation as a property right due the student.

Most states honor the institutional recommendation and grant a professional teaching license to an eligible applicant, while other states impose additional requirements, such as a passing score on state mandated standardized tests.

DUE PROCESS

Due process is a disposition. It is an unwavering commitment to basic fairness. It also guarantees procedural protections for aspiring teachers facing potential adverse decisions. Pragmatically, it establishes minimal safeguards. These include the right to receive a formal and timely notice of the concern, an opportunity to present their side of the story, the right to an impartial review based on factual evidence, and timely notification of the rendered decision.

Institutions modeling dispositional excellence will also provide students an opportunity to be represented by counsel, an opportunity to call witnesses, an opportunity to question accusers, and the right to appeal. Teacher education programs may adopt due process procedures already established by their institutions for the general population of students or they may create their own. Slight revisions to existing institutional processes to accommodate unique professional requirements are common. In all cases, they must be published and widely disseminated.

Academic decisions appropriately made within due process guidelines are rarely overturned. In fact, according to the U.S. Supreme Court, when judges review the substance of genuinely academic decisions, courts refrain from overturning these decisions unless they substantially depart from accepted academic norms. Due process, when meticulously applied, solidifies academic decisions.

Teacher educators have the right to assess the dispositions of aspiring teachers and subsequently take reasonable action based on the findings. This should no longer be questioned. Institutions have this right, and more importantly, the responsibility. Two cases specifically affirm this conclusion. In *Hennessy v. City of Melrose* (1999), an aspiring teacher was dismissed from a preparation program based on the inability to abide by dispositional standards. Specifically, Mr. Hennessy's "unusually forceful espousal, at inappropriate times, of religiously oriented views on subjects such as homosexuality and abortion" raised dispositional concerns. Furthermore, four documented incidents occurring in his student teaching raised serious concerns about his commitment "to respect diversity among school children," a dispositional criterion formally adopted by the preparation program. The court upheld his dismissal.

In the other case, *Banks v. Dominican College* (1995), faculty documented improper conduct and believed the aspiring teacher lacked the temperament and skills to teach children. After displaying numerous incidents of unprofessional conduct, acrimonious disputes with others, and emotional problems, she was dismissed from the teacher education program. The court upheld the institution's decision to dismiss the student in this case also.

In 2003, Ginsberg and Whaley (2003) surveyed colleges of education to determine the extent to which dispositions were infused into their preparation programs. Seventy-six percent considered aspiring teachers' dispositions in their admission and retention decisions. This proliferation is encouraging. The trend will hopefully continue.

Assessing the dispositions of aspiring teachers is noble. Yet, we must not lose sight of the purpose. Are graduates of dispositionally enriched preparation programs better qualified? And in the end, do they ultimately improve the quality of our schools?

REFERENCES

Banks v. Dominican College, 42 Cal. Rpter. 2d 110 (Cal. Ct. App. 1995).
Board of Trustees of Compton Junior College District v. Stubblefield, 94 Cal. Rptr. 318 (Cal. Ct. App. 1971).

Council of Chief State School Officers. (1992). *Model standards for beginning teacher licensing, assessment and development: A resource for state dialogue.* Washington, DC.

Connick v. Myers, 461 U.S. 138 (1983).

Elfbrandt v. Russel 384 U.S. 11, 17 (1966).

Fowler v. Bd. of Education of Lincoln County, Ky., 819 F.2d 657 (6th Cir. 1987), cert. denied, 484 U.S. 986 (1987).

Ginsberg, R., & Whaley, D. (2003). Admission and retention policies in teacher preparation programs: Legal and practical issues. *Teacher Educator, 38*(3), 169-189.

Hamm v. Poplar Bluff R-1 School District, 955 S.W.2d 27 (Mo. App. S.D. 1997).

Hennessy v. City of Melrose, 194 F. 3d 237 (1999).

Jantz v. Muci, 976 F.2d 623 (10th Cir. 1992).

National Council for Accreditation of Teacher Education (NCATE). (2002). *Professional standards for the accreditation of schools, colleges, and departments of education.* Washington, DC: Author.

Office of Civil Rights (OCR). (1995). Applicant not qualified for teaching program. *Disability Compliance for Higher Education, 1*(4). Abstract retrieved September 30, 2004 from LexisNexis database.

Office of Civil Rights (OCR). (1998). Dismissal of law student did not violate ADA, Section 504. *Disability Compliance for Higher Education, 4*(4). Abstract retrieved September 30, 2004 from LexisNexis database.

Office of Civil Rights (OCR). (2000). Medical school properly denied request for academic adjustment. *Disability Compliance Bulletin, 17*(3). Abstract retrieved September 30, 2004 from LexisNexis database.

Southeastern Community College v. Davis, 442 U.S. 397 (1979).

Yang v. Special Charter School District No. 150, Peoria county, 296 N.E.2d 74 (Ill.1973).

13

Teacher Education and the Benedictine Tradition

Patricia Parrish and Denise Skarbek

The National Council for Accreditation of Teacher Educators (2000) and the National Board for Professional Standards (2004) served as an impetus for teacher education programs to identify dispositions of effective teachers. This meant teacher educators were faced with the challenge to identify, define, and measure dispositions. Steps taken to meet this challenge varied; however, most teacher educators were forced to either accept or rethink their existing conceptual framework. In the midst of institutional reform, changes in state expectations, and the desire to demonstrate the value added in teacher education, the faculty of Saint Leo University's department of education engaged in curricular reform.

In 1998, Saint Leo University formed a committee to review their mission statement and decide what core values would guide their work as an institution. Six core values from the Benedictine tradition were selected (see Table 13.1). Once these values were selected, operationally defined, and infused in general education courses, the faculty in the university's department of education began the task of infusing the values in elementary education courses. This work was done as courses underwent significant revisions based on changes in state standards. The decision was made to give the six core values equal weight with standards when developing course objectives, activities, and assessments. The infusion of these values within the teacher education curriculum represents one possible approach for the infusion of dispositions.

This chapter will explore Saint Leo University's core values as teacher dispositions. Each value will be explored in light of its contribution to the development of teacher candidates and in light of how the implementation of the value in the K–12 classroom will improve teacher practice. Additionally,

Table 13.1.   Saint Leo University's Core Benedictine Values

Benedictine Core Value	Definition
Responsible stewardship	Foster a spirit of service to employ our resources to university and community development.
Excellence	Ensure that students develop their character, learn the skills, and assimilate the knowledge essential to become morally responsible leaders.
Personal development	Develop every person's mind, spirit, and body for balanced life.
Community	Foster a spirit of belonging, unity, and interdependence based on mutual trust and respect to create socially responsible environments that challenge all of us to listen, to learn, to change, and to serve.
Respect	Value all individuals' unique talents, respect their dignity, and strive to foster their commitment to excellence in our work.
Integrity	Pledge to be honest, just, and consistent in word and deed.

a beginning plan for assessing the infusion of these dispositional values will be outlined.

DESCRIBING THE VALUES

Current legislation, like the No Child Left Behind Act (2001), challenges teachers to help students meet high standards, regardless of the students' educational and social backgrounds. In order to achieve this level of success with all students, teacher candidates can employ the first of Saint Leo University's dispositional values, *responsible stewardship.* The teacher who practices responsible stewardship is able to use his or her natural, financial, and spiritual resources to improve educational outcomes for students. An important aspect of this disposition is the ability to recognize and enhance individual talents in students. The teacher candidate interested in this type of classroom interaction must allow students to produce knowledge through their unique construction of meaning, encourage students to engage in inquiry focused on the construction of meaning, and permit students to focus their work on projects and inquires that allow success and interest beyond the school setting (Newman & Wehlage, 1993). The challenge of responsible stewardship is to allow students to explore their world in a meaningful way, rather than creating a focus on standards in isolation.

This suggests that teacher candidates can demonstrate the concept of responsible stewardship from simple to complex levels. For example, this can be as simple as not wasting paper or as complex as helping each student develop his or her natural gifts to the fullest extent possible. In order for this to happen, teacher educators must be ever vigilant in helping their students develop their talents, and in supporting them as they explore how these talents can benefit the children they will serve. College classrooms and programs need to foster a sense of belonging and of valuing individual talents within the classroom. This can be done through modeling cooperative learning and active learning in the college classroom. This type of active learning can be used to develop teacher candidate strengths, particularly those of leadership, facilitation, organization, and collaboration.

Within the K–12 classroom, teachers and teacher candidates can foster responsible stewardship in students by allowing students to contribute to the classroom through the completion of assigned jobs and through peer tutors. Students can be given responsibility for maintaining personal and common space in the classroom, thus developing a sense of community. Additionally, students can practice responsible stewardship at the school level through the development of school gardens and other projects that allow students to work together across classrooms.

The value of *excellence* supports NCATE's (2000) model of an ideal teacher candidate, that is, one who has the skills, knowledge, and dispositions characteristic of an effective teacher. These three values—knowledge, skills, and dispositions—are considered connected, interwoven. This means that the values cannot be taught in isolation. The success of this is strongly influenced by the faculty's ability to make a conscientious commitment to the mission, vision, and goals of Saint Leo University.

In attempting to accomplish this, Saint Leo University invited teachers from the community to attend a 2-day workshop called Celebrating Partnerships in June 2003. The primary focus of this workshop was to provide an overview of how the six core values were being infused into the university's courses and the connection between care and the six core values. In addition, service learning was defined and discussed as a possible way to demonstrate and model an understanding of the six core values. This workshop helped teachers identify what they are currently doing in their classrooms that reflects excellence in teaching, which is meeting the academic and spiritual needs of students (e.g., providing training in social skills, building self-esteem, and promoting respect for self/others) as well as identify new ways to promote excellence in teaching (such as service learning).

In the K–12 setting, teachers can demonstrate the core value of excellence by having knowledge of the content area they are teaching. Moreover, teachers need to understand how to incorporate multiple intelligence into their lessons. For additional information on multiple intelligence the reader is referred to Howard Gardner's (1993) work

Providing in-service workshops such as the Celebrating Partnerships workshop is also an example of promoting the core value of *personal development,* which emphasizes the need for effective teachers to continuously seek ways to develop their mind, spirit, and body for having a well-rounded and balanced life. In addition to providing in-service workshops, Saint Leo University promotes personal development for teacher candidates through reflections.

Webster's (1988) defined reflection as the "fixing of the mind on some subject; serious thought; contemplation . . . a turning or bending back on itself" (p. 1128). For teacher candidates, this translates into them being able to reflect on the complexities of teaching and learning. According to van Manen (1977) reflection manifests itself on three levels: technical, practical, and critical. Saint Leo University promotes reflection at all three levels. At the technical level, teacher candidates focus primarily on methodological problems and theory development applied in a given situation. This level of reflection is considered fundamental. At the practical level, the reflective teacher candidate considers his or her underlying assumptions for strategies used and the consequences of these actions. This means that at this level of reflection the teacher candidate attempts to connect theory to practice. Teacher candidates at Saint Leo University are required to complete three semesters of practica prior to their full-time final internship placement. During each practicum, teacher candidates are expected to engage in higher levels of planning and responsibility for classroom instruction. After preparing and teaching lessons, teacher candidates are expected to reflect on what worked, what could be improved, and how this information can positively impact future performance. In other words, teacher candidates examine their educational situations in context and question the practices based on pedagogical knowledge, skills, and dispositions. On the third level, or critical reflective level, teacher candidates consider moral and ethical issues in their actions. Teachers focus on the broader context of curriculum in relation to equality, social justice, and the ethic of care. Consideration of knowledge and social justice is explored through teacher educator and teacher candidate dialogue. This is demonstrated in several ways at Saint Leo University. For example, teacher candidates use reflective dialogue after student teaching experience. This helps them determine "why" the situation was successful or unsuccessful. Through reflective dialogue, teacher candidates can develop new patterns of knowledge, skills, and dispositions; that is, how can their attitudes or beliefs about a situation change to help improve student's learning?

Not only should teacher candidates critically reflect, but children in the K–12 setting should be encouraged to reflect on their learning. Teachers at the K–12 level can achieve this by having children journal what they are learning and what they need to learn. In addition, peer reflective dialogue can also increase their personal development.

Reflection assumes that a teacher will collaboratively and individually take responsibility for decisions made in the classroom. Reflective teacher candidates, therefore, care about ways to improve their teaching practices as well as those of others. A reflective teacher's goal is to maintain caring within him- or herself as well as with those with whom he or she comes in contact (Noddings, 1984). To do this requires a sense of the spirit of community. *Community* is one of the six core values for Saint Leo University. It supports the development of communities within communities, which are based on respect and trust for all. Service learning is one way Saint Leo University accomplishes this.

Service learning has been identified as a teaching method that combines service to the community and the curriculum (Verducci & Pope, 2001). This teaching technique can occur at various levels for example, K–12, higher education, and community-based organizations. The service that is provided needs to be identified as a "genuine community need" that is determined by a needs assessment. Perhaps, the most important element of service learning is the teacher's ability to understand the connection between meeting the goals established by the community as well as those identified in the curriculum. Providing the link between community and curriculum creates an atmosphere conducive for teachers to improve their academic skills and apply the newly acquired knowledge to the school and the community. According to Erikson and Santimire (2001), reflection is a key component to service learning. Teachers reflect and analyze their service experience, and teacher candidates are able to learn about and understand the complexities of community issues. Moreover, reflection provides a way to view the community issues in a broader social, political, and economic context. Reflection also serves as way to help promote the link between service in the community and curriculum content. Saint Leo University's workshop helped teachers identify ways they could begin to infuse service learning into their current curricula. Currently, at the university level, teacher candidates can engage in a service learning activity as part of their course requirements during the first semester of their junior year. Other possible service learning options are being explored, such as having teacher candidates complete a 2-week summer program providing tutoring to K–12 students for whom English is a second language or those considered to be living in poverty.

Teachers can also foster a sense of community at the K–12 level through service learning. The most important element to remember is the connection between curriculum and community. It must be meaningful to the community, such as the clean-up projects that have been used by various schools.

The quality of service learning in the community is heavily dependent on respecting individuals. *Respect*, another core value of Saint Leo University, is having an understanding of and valuing individuality. Demographic changes have impacted the need for including respect in teacher preparation programs. The student population is increasingly changing and becoming more diverse. Multicultural education has the potential for creating an environment that addresses this. It is a goal of Saint Leo University to engage teachers in both multicultural education and service learning. For a more detailed reading on multicultural education and service learning the reader is referred to O'Grady (2000).

For K–12 teachers this translates into infusing diversity into their curriculum. Neito (1996) tells us that accepting multicultural education is not simply celebrating Martin Luther King Jr. Day—instead, it is recognizing and accepting all cultures and religions and creating an environment that accepts and respects all.

The last disposition included in Saint Leo University's approach to a values-driven, values-infused education program is *integrity*. Integrity can be viewed as the heart of education, in that it prepares students to participate in democratic citizenship, the hallmark of U.S. education (Salomone, 2000). Integrity was recently described by a K–12 educator in one of Saint Leo's partnership schools as the string that weaves all the other dispositions together. Dewey (1972) states that educators must recognize that there "cannot be two sets of ethical principles . . . one for life in the school, and the other for life outside of school" (p. 54). Integrity challenges teacher candidates to create a curriculum that prepares students for participation in society by creating a school environment that develops and fosters democracy and democratic citizenship.

Within the classroom, teacher candidates can help students through the value of integrity by helping them become advocates for others. Teacher educators and teacher candidates can encourage students to accept the role of responsible citizens by contacting legislators and becoming active in the local community. It is through integrity that students can learn to actively pursue the values they hold.

As teacher educators, we believe that as these values and dispositions develop within our students, they will be better able to engage in caring with their future students. Although the literature is rich with the benefits of a caring environment on K–12 student performance (Collinson, Killeavy, & Stephenson, 1999; Daly, 1985; Kratzer, 1996; Lambert, 1995; Linkous, 1989; Morse, 1994; Noblit, 1993) no strong relationship has yet been established between dispositions and caring. The following section will begin to make such a connection between the core values described above and an ethic of care.

THE ETHIC OF CARE AND VALUES

The ethic of care can be simply defined as relational caring that requires two people to engage in a reciprocal interaction that considers the ways of life, natures, desires, and needs of each (Noddings, 1984; Ruddick, 1989). A basic premise of those who study an ethic of caring in education is that such study may help educators to value caring in much the same way academic achievement is currently valued (Smith & Emigh, personal communication, July 1, 1999).

Several educators have proposed a caring-focused approach to education (Eisner, 1997, 1999; Noblit, 1993; Noddings, 1984, 1992). Within such an approach, attention to student needs and desires has become a central factor (Noddings, 1992). After the formation of caring relationships with teachers over time, students can be more easily encouraged to focus their learning on areas of interest while being encouraged to take risks and attempt difficult tasks by and with a connected teacher (Noddings, 1992). Student achievement would vary more than in current systems as students develop based on different talents and intelligences. Such an approach to schooling would encourage students to pursue their interests because their teachers would be listening to their needs and desires. It would also create the need for a broadened curriculum, rather than a narrow one which forces "all students [to run] down the same track, measured by the same tests, and whose performance is reported out to the third or fourth decimal place" (Eisner, 1997, p. 271). Such an approach to education would help students develop a sense of responsible stewardship, because they would be developing their natural talents and abilities to their fullest potential. Additionally, this type of caring involves excellence and integrity in the teacher because she would be responsible for providing opportunities for students to engage in high-quality activities geared to their individual needs. Students will only be willing to risk engaging in these tasks if they can have trust in the person who is requesting it of them, their teacher who is consistent in word and deed. Such an approach to education would help students with exceptionality, who often feel that others do not believe in their skills and talents.

Teaching has been described as a moral activity in which teachers need to examine the ethical implications of their actions (Rogers & Webb, 1991). This implies that teachers need to go beyond actions to look at the impact of their actions on relationships. Because an ethic of care emphasizes relationships and responsibilities, rather than rules and rights, it can be viewed as a moral activity (Rogers & Webb, 1991). Glasser (1975) identifies two basic needs: the need to love and be loved and the need to feel worthwhile. These two needs are intricately related to care and to the dispositional values of community and personal development in that genuine caring meets the basic need for security and attachment (or loving and being loved) and, beyond that, connects people to a "self-perpetuating cycle of 'natural' and ethical caring" (Rogers & Webb, 1991, p. 176). This cycle promotes self-worth in those who participate in it, thus fulfilling Glasser's second basic need, the need to feel worthwhile. The connection between people can only be achieved within a community that focuses on belonging, unity, and interdependence; a community that is possible through the development of this disposition. Such a community will help students to develop a sense of self-worth through personal development and the sense of balance that is inherent within personal development.

Though caring has been relatively ignored as part of the teaching equation for children, Morse (1994) identifies it as "the experience desperately needed, especially by troubled children and those at risk" (p. 132). One possible reason to view care as essential to the development, education, and healing of students with exceptionality, and to the optimal development of all students, might be that care moves a person from the idea of merely not hurting another to the possibility of responding actively to self and others in order to sustain a connection (Gilligan, 1982). This sustained connection becomes the basis of a caring relationship, one that can help youth learn to respect others. Such a sense of connection can be fostered by teachers who are interested in helping students see a commonality with classmates who come from diverse backgrounds. The active responding that is central to caring helps form the foundation for a community based on mutual respect; a community that strives for excellence in ethical interaction between its members and that welcomes others to become responsible stewards within a collective environment. This type of collectivity, based on respect and a sense of helping, is common in the Hispanic culture from which more and more of our students come (Rothstein-Fisch, Greenfield, & Trumbull, 1999).

When guided by an ethic of care, teachers make decisions about their students based on the students' needs and expected responses (Noddings, 1991). Such decisions can only occur when teachers and students enter into dialogue over time, thus providing support for the idea of teachers and students staying together for several years (Noddings, 1991). Such long-term relationships give students and teachers time to develop caring, to gain necessary skills in dialogue, and for students to become care givers, as caring is modeled by the teacher (Noddings, 1991). We believe such classroom communities can only be achieved by teachers with a keen sense of relationship-building. By helping teachers to develop dispositions based upon the core values from the Benedictine tradition, the faculty at Saint Leo University believes that its graduates will have a positive impact on the educational and emotional development of children.

ASSESSING THE VALUES: A LOOK TO THE FUTURE

In order to evaluate the effectiveness of a values-driven, values-infused curriculum, such as the one offered at Saint Leo University, the faculty recognizes the need to assess the development of dispositions in its teacher candidates and to plan for long-term assessment of teacher performance.

As stated above, the dispositional values of excellence, respect, community, personal development, responsible stewardship, and integrity were infused in the undergraduate teacher education program at the same time courses were revised to meet new state standards and expectations. After course changes were piloted for a year and improvements made based upon experiences with teaching the new curriculum, faculty began developing rubrics for use in evaluating required assessments within each course. Special attention was given to developing criteria in each assessment that would evaluate the teacher candidates' mastery of the values. Additionally, students complete a pretest related to the values and their application when they enter the teacher preparation unit in the first semester of their junior years. When approaching the end of the final internship, teacher candidates have an opportunity to complete a posttest on the values. Although performance on this pre-post test is not currently used in determining a student's successful completion of the teacher education program, it is hoped that it will inform the continuous program improvement efforts of the faculty.

REFERENCES

Collinson, V., Killeavy, M., & Stephenson, H. J. (1999). Exemplary teachers: Practicing an ethic of care in England, Ireland, and the United States. *Journal for a Just and Caring Education, 5*(4), 349–360

Daly, P. M. (1985). Lessons from 10 years of teacher improvement reform. *Educational Leadership, 52*(5), 26–32.

Dewey, J. (1972). Ethical principles underlying education. In J. A. Boydston (Ed.), *The early works, 1882–1898* (Vol. 5, pp. 54–83). Cardondale: Southern Illinois University Press (original work published 1897).

Eisner, E. W. (1997). The new frontier in qualitative research methodology. *Qualitative Inquiry, 3*(3), 259–273.

Eisner, E. W. (1999, January). *School reform.* Presentation at the University of South Florida, Tampa, FL.

Erickson, J. A., & Santimire, T. (2001). Pscological bases of effective service-learning. In J. B. Anderson, K. J. Swick, & J. Yff (Eds.), *Service-learning in teacher education: Enhancing the growth of new teachers, their students, and communities* (pp. 19–38). Washington, DC: ASCD.

Gardner, H. (1993). *Multiple intelligences. The theory into practice.* New York: Basic Books.

Gilligan, C. (1982). *In a different voice: Psychological theory and women's development.* Cambridge, MA: Harvard University Press.

Glasser, W. (1975). *Reality therapy: A new approach to psychiatry.* New York: Harper & Row.

Kratzer, C. C. (1996, April). *Beyond "effective schools research": Cultivating a caring community in an urban school.* Paper presented at the annual meeting of the American Educational Research Association, New York. (ERIC Document Reproduction Services No. ED 397 211)

Lambert, N. S. (1995). *Perspectives of successful teachers reputed as caring: Explanations for connection in the classroom.* Unpublished doctoral dissertation, University of South Florida, Tampa.

Linkous, V. D. (1989). *Patterns of caring: A study of the perceptions of teachers and students.* Doctoral dissertation, Virginia Polytechnic Institute and State University. *Dissertation Abstracts International, 50,* 07A, p. 1920.

Morse, W. C. (1994). The role of caring in teaching children with behavior problems. *Contemporary Education, 65*(3), 132–136.

National Board for Professional Teaching Standards (2004). Standards and national board certification. Retrieved May 15, 2004, from http://www.nbpts.org/standards/stds.cfm

National Council for Accreditation of Teacher Education. (2000). *Professional standards for the accreditation of schools, colleges, and departments of education.* Washington, D.C.: Author.

Neito, S. (1996). *Affirming diversity: The sociopolitical context of multicultural education* (2nd ed.). White Plains, NY: Longman.

Newman, D., & Wehlage, G. (1993). Five standards of authentic assessment. *Educational Leadership, 50*(7), 8–21.

No Child Left Behind Act of 2001, Public Law 107-110 (January 8, 2002).

Noblit, G. W. (1993). Power and caring. *American Educational Research Journal, 30*(1), 23–38.

Noddings, N. (1984). *Caring: A feminine approach to ethics and moral education.* Berkeley, CA: University of California Press.

Noddings, N. (1991). Stories in dialogue: Caring and interpersonal reasoning. In C. Witherall & N. Noddings (Eds.), *Stories lives tell: Narratives and dialogue in education* (pp. 157–170). New York: Teachers College Press.

Noddings, N. (1992). *The challenge to care in schools: An alternate approach to education.* New York: Teachers College Press.

O'Grady, C. R. (2000). *Integrating service learning and multicultural education in colleges and universities.* Mahwah, NJ: Erlbaum.

Rogers, D., & Webb, J. (1991). The ethic of caring in teacher education. *Journal of Teacher Education, 42*(3), 173–181.

Rothstein-Fisch, C., Greenfield, P. M., & Trumbull, E. (1999). Bridging cultures with classroom strategies. *Educational Leadership, 56*(7), 64–67.

Ruddick, S. (1989). *Maternal thinking.* Boston: Beacon Press.

Salomone, R. C. (2000). *Visions of schooling: Conscience, community, and common education.* New Haven, CT: Yale University Press.

Smith, R. L., & Emigh, L. (personal communication, July 1, 1999). *A model for defining the construct of caring in teacher education* [online].

van Manen, M. (1977). Linking ways of knowing with ways of being practical. *Curriculum Inquiry, 6*(3), 205–208.

Verducci, S., & Pope, D. (2001). Rationales for integrating service-learning in teacher education. In J. B. Anderson, K. J. Swick, & J. Yff (Eds.), *Service-learning in teacher education: Enhancing the growth of new teachers, their students, and communities* (pp. 2-18). Washington, DC: ASCD

Webster's new world dictionary: Third college edition. (1988). New York: Webster's New World.

14

Dispositions as Habits of Body, Mind, and Spirit: Quaker and Native American Perspectives

Marsha Heck and Deborah Roose

> The most important responsibility of teachers is to help children grow to be a human being; having much knowledge is not important. To think for oneself, to learn independently, to treat others kindly and fairly, to work with friends, to encourage others, to say what one thinks, and to act as one thinks: these are the things which are important. And, of course, a strong, healthy body is also important. In other words, a child needs help in developing all aspects of her personality and her life as a human being. These things cannot be taught from textbooks. (Tezuka, 1995, p. 45)

This chapter will examine dispositions in the context of the Quaker tradition at Guilford College in Greensboro, North Carolina, and the Native American[1] learning tradition passed on to Paula Underwood by her ancestors. Each tradition is committed to the growth and development of the individual as a human being in a community.

We suggest that dispositions might be seen as who a person is being, rather than what one does or what one knows. The focus is on how people do what they do, for example, how they listen and the relationship they have with knowledge, not simply that they listen or investigate new ideas. This chapter does not provide a checklist approach to dispositions, although it may provide a theoretical framework for creating one. Rather, we consider dispositional themes, groupings that might be described as "clusters of dispositions," which are demonstrated through one's interactions with others.

We will use Underwood's descriptions of body, mind, and spirit as a paradigmatic approach for integrating multiple dimensions of human experience, acknowledging that there are others. We do not mean "spirit" in a traditionally religious sense, but rather in terms of one's relatedness to others, as described by Underwood. Current educational standards typically frame instructional goals and assessment criteria with terms such as knowledge, dispositions, attitudes, or beliefs, and skills or performances. Underwood's (1994) metaphor of braided understanding can be seen as a model for considering the relationship of knowledge, dispositions, and skills. Her three learning stories braid "Body (the way we live on the Earth), Mind (the way we identify and process information), and Spirit (our awareness of our relatedness to each of our brothers, each of our sisters, to Earth, and to the Universe)" (p. 17). What one knows is defined by what Underwood calls "mind"; who one is being dispositionally can be seen as "spirit" according to her definition, which in turn informs what Underwood might call "body"— one's skills, the way one performs, or "what one does."

Underwood (1994) braids these three dimensions of human experience and explains that each strand "alone may easily ravel, two may be twisted to offer more possibilities and will still ravel, but three "fixed firmly at each end—bound by memory and laced with curiosity—such braids . . . truly last" (p. 17)! So too, we contribute to this volume the conviction that teacher education must firmly fix the strands of content knowledge, dispositions, and performances, thereby strengthening each strand to support graduates who are lifelong learners inclined to draw on the foundation of their preparation programs even as they seek out new and emerging ideas in their own diverse teaching and learning communities.

Although some see this three-part paradigm as recent, nearly 50 years ago Alexander Bloom and his colleagues (1956) delineated three taxonomies that parallel recent trends toward standardizing content, dispositions, and performances, correspondingly: cognitive, affective, and psychomotor. Underwood traces her stories back thousands of years, and her ideas resonate with diverse educators and other scholars. In fact, the reader will see that in comparison to the traditions included in this chapter, credentialing bodies have joined the conversation about teacher dispositions comparatively late in the discussion.

UNDERSTANDING AND DEVELOPING DISPOSITIONS

The art of creating understanding is like weaving a fabric from the many threads of silence, timing, inflection, intent, and other non-verbal cues. It requires a delicate balance between assertiveness and receptivity. Listening is at the core. (Hwoschinsky, 2001, p. 13)

Before looking more closely at both traditions, we will briefly outline a structure for the development of dispositions, define dispositions for the purpose of this chapter, and explain our use of the terms "habits of body, mind, and spirit" to establish a lens that creates a listening for the connections we propose between these traditions. Unique to our chapter is the concept of "clusters" of dispositions. Our discussion does not address discrete dispositions, but rather encompasses multiple dispositions according to what we are calling "dispositional themes." For example, being responsive to diverse others might be seen as a dispositional theme that requires dispositions such as openness, flexibility, honesty, curiosity, and respect, among others. The traditions we discuss share similar processes for developing dispositions and value comparable dispositional themes to support learning with diverse others.

Underwood's (2000a) Four Step Path provides a model for the process of developing dispositions in both undergraduate and graduate students: (1) Be who you are—enhance accurate self-awareness; (2) Be where you are—accept your circumstance, walk past denial; (3) Look around—take in as much information as you can; (4) Decide and Do—and using all of the above, make clear decisions. Not a linear path, this is "a Spiral of continuance" (p. 111). It is this Spiral Path we all walk; A circle, surely, but a sequential path also, and therefore a spiral.

Dispositions in both traditions, as we discuss herein, can be seen to fit this structure. Each begins with who the educator is in the context of the respective tradition. Quaker educator Parker Palmer (1998) writes about the need for teachers to connect their teaching with who they are, and Quaker tradition in general honors the "Inner Teacher." Underwood's (2000b) tradition "places great importance on being who you are" because "being who you are and learning are deeply interconnected" (p. 51).

Addressing the second step on Underwood's path, each of these traditions values diversity and community—where they are. In Underwood's Native American learning stories, when each voice is heard, the community and the individual are impacted. Quakers talk about being present.

In Underwood's third step, looking around carefully at one's community, valuing others, and listening to what is said by each individual occurs. Looking at and listening to other points of view is not only encouraged but honored in both traditions. The Education Studies Program at Guilford College emphasizes their Quaker commitment to living and learning in such a community. Underwood's "Who Speaks for Wolf" (2002) stresses the value of hearing all voices. Her stories affirm that there is much to be considered in decision making and that the community is defined by their decisions—they "become a people who . . ." is the term she uses in "Who Speaks for Wolf" Quaker process honors the truth that emerges through individual seeking and consensual decision making.

In the fourth step, decide and do, the results of this process for developing dispositions is evidenced by actions. The actions of Quaker and Native American educators are a result of who they are being in community with others. Caring decisions and actions can be expected when one values being and learning with others in the ways described above. For example, it can be argued that all teachers listen—it is something they do. A teacher following the four-step path in the Quaker or Native American models we discuss herein will employ a particular quality of listening that can be fittingly described as Compassionate Listening, according to Carol Hwoschinsky's (2001) definition. Hwoschinsky explains that Compassionate Listening means empathizing with and caring for another human being and creating "a safe container for people to be free to express themselves" (p. 3).

In sum, Underwood's four-step path might be seen as a common structure to guide educators in considering dispositional themes from the congruent perspectives of these two traditions. The four-step path structures our discussion of dispositions:

1. Be who you are—enhance self-awareness of the relationship of one's own faith tradition and the teacher within.
2. Be where you are—move past the denial or ignorance of diversity in one's teaching and learning community. Respect, seek out, and nurture diversity.
3. Look around—look, listen, and be present to others in the community and the emergent truth as it reveals itself through conversation in any given time or place.
4. Decide and do—Then, building on the first three steps of ways of being and learning, make compassionate decisions and caring actions.

The reflective teacher does not stop there. He or she spirals back to the first step on this path, which Underwood described as both sequential and circular.

The dispositions that we address through the Quaker and Native American traditions in the discussion that follows are bigger than cultural or religious beliefs. The Education Studies Program at Guilford College describes the goals they have for their students as "habits of mind," many of which are dispositional in nature and which can be seen to collectively represent dispositional themes. Our chapter title expands on Guilford's terminology, adding habits of body and spirit with a focus on awareness of one's relatedness to self, others, and the universe, again, considering human experience as braiding mind, spirit, and body, or knowing, being, and doing.

HABITS OF BODY, MIND, AND
SPIRIT WITHIN THE TWO TRADITIONS

In this section we provide a brief overview of the habits that are honored by these traditions before we discuss each perspective in more depth in following sections. Members of the Religious Society of Friends (Quakers) ponder spiritual questions, individually and as a group. Quakers are known as seekers, an important distinction when discussing dispositions because a seeker by definition is open to new possibilities rather than fixed on one inflexible truth. Quakers also try to resolve differences through consensus in a spirit of love, remembering that everyone has the Light of God within. In this process the individual and the community are transformed. The concept of individuals and groups growing together through the community-building process is also evident in Underwood's Native American learning stories.

Paula Underwood's learning stories, cultural narratives passed on to her by her father,[2] preserve five generations of the family's oral tradition and an ancient learning structure. The Ancient Wisdom created, nurtured, and sustained a diverse community that considered learning sacred and honored each individual perspective. Decisions were made collaboratively, after hearing all voices in the interests of each and all. Underwood Spencer (1990) brings to this chapter the sacredness of learning in community. She says we are all "given a vast and beautiful stage on which to enter and exit, so that we may learn about the variety of possible scripts—and all the men and women are more than merely players. They are Learners! And Learning . . . is so valuable . . . that it is therefore sacred" (p. 22).

Introducing *Soka Education: A Buddhist Vision for Teachers, Students, and Parents* by Daisaku Ikeda (2001), Victor Kazanjian illustrates themes we emphasize in both Quaker and Underwood's traditions in his discussion of a "transformational process of education." Kazanjian references Palmer's deeply ethical education "that would help students develop the capacity for connectedness that is at the heart of an ethical life," and Ikeda's view of learning as "the fundamental force that builds society and shapes an age" (p. vi). Ikeda's view corresponds to a central foundation of Underwood's learning stories, which are grounded in a tradition that considers learning sacred; they provide an account of how one's relatedness to the community furthers the learning of each and of all. Each of these traditions emphasizes a particular vision of education grounded in the origins and history of the respective faith and cultural tenets. Each considers the process of learning and the development of dispositions at least as valuable as the content learned.

As "seekers," the purpose of a Quaker life might be seen as learning. Underwood Spencer (1990) says of her tradition that "our purpose here is Learning" (p. 22). Educators in each practice, grounded in the respective roots of their traditions, can be seen to reflect three dispositional themes: (1) appreciation of human diversity and a dynamic relationship of the individual and community, (2) a commitment to looking at and listening carefully to others and the multiple perspectives that exist in a diverse community, and (3) caring about others not only in theory but also in practice through daily decisions and actions.

In the following sections, we propose that both Quaker and Underwood's Native American views of education are grounded in the roots of their own traditions and can be seen to share habits and patterns such as those as described by longtime Quaker college educator Paul Lacey (2001). In his article "Spirituality in Action: Ethos and Ethic" in *Friends Journal*, Lacey writes about the idea of ethos, the Greek word for "habit," and how an educational institution's "ethos is the single most powerful and pervasive influence on what can be taught and learned there" (p. 10). For example, the strong Quaker ethos at Guilford College permeated the creation of the Guilford Education Studies Program and influenced both the faculty members' and students' development of "habits of mind" that support their own and others learning. Lacey uses George Kuh's (as cited in Lacey, 2001) definition of institutional ethos "an institution-specific pattern of values and principles that involves a sense of belonging and helps people distinguish between appropriate and inappropriate behavior" (p. 10). People within the two traditions in this chapter understand the complexity and power of those institutional patterns of values and principles and spend time cultivating and honoring them.

DEFINING HABITS OF BODY, MIND AND SPIRIT

The concept or text of *Habits of the Heart* of Bellah, Madsen, Sullivan, Swidler, and Tipton (1996) may come to mind for some readers. It explains that Toqueville defined mores loosely as "habits of the heart"; "notions, opinions, and ideas that shape mental habits; and the sum of moral and intellectual dispositions of men in society" (p. 37). This definition further supports our use of the term "habits" of body, mind, and spirit.

Guilford's idea of "habits of mind" grew out of the faculty's own understanding that by building on the Quaker traditions, their ways of teaching and learning would be profoundly influenced. The language used in 1991, when creating the program objectives, focused on verbs that showed learning, teaching, and living certain ways (respect, value, respond) rather than using terms such as "demonstrating" or "understanding," the language of the times regarding state and national standards. Although the term "habits of mind" was not used specifically until 1994, from the beginning of the creation of the program, the faculty members understood that they were working to help students' develop a way of being that informed a way of working in the world rather than disseminating specific technical skills or knowledge and explanations of ideas, facts, and attitudes. They wanted students to take a stance in relationship to learning, curriculum, diversity, and to know why they were taking such a stance. The goal was to have these ways of thinking and being become habits—the default, automatic way of looking at the world and learners and learning. To have the program objectives become habits of mind, students must practice again and again. They need to make the ideas, skills, and attitudes their own, so they need time to challenge, adapt, construct, apply, and question them.

Therefore, the program needed to be about student learning, not faculty imparting information. And it needed to focus on the students' whole understanding. Students needed to read about, try out, create, and experience new ways of approaching the unknown, the confusing, the difficult, and the unfamiliar, and they also needed to watch the faculty wrestle with these ways of being. Thus, the program needed to be interactive and learner-centered based on the premise that one cannot separate the way one interacts with the world from the way one teaches.

QUAKERS: GUILFORD'S MODEL OF QUAKER EDUCATION

> A bell ringing in an empty sky: all things are at the center. All things are exquisite. What hopefully emerges from such disassembling of the clangor are those archaic sounds and resonances that were not of our own assembly in the first place. What hopefully emerges out from under the exhaustion is a deep love and compassion for all things. (Jardine, 1998, p. 100)

The focus of the Guilford College program is on the college students, not the curriculum or rules and regulations. For example, the faculty members use the students' interests and needs to guide curriculum development and practice; the tutorials help students find their own voices through writing, talking and self assessment.

Vito Perrone in *A Letter to Teachers* (1991) encourages educators, when they think about their own schools, to have powerful and important purposes leading their thinking: "we need always to reach back to first things, to guiding purposes, to our richest, most generative conceptions of education and work toward them" (p. 11). In reaching back to its guiding purposes, Guilford College found that its spiritual roots provided and continue to provide a rich climate for creative exploration and invention in program development. Those roots also give strength and depth to the curriculum and daily practice and influence the types of goals the program has for its prospective teachers.

History and General Description of the
Guilford Education Studies Program

The Religious Society of Friends, commonly known as Quakers, founded Guilford College in Greensboro, North Carolina, in 1837. It is a private, 4-year, undergraduate, coeducational college of the liberal arts and sciences.

Quakerism influences the college's mission, curriculum, and daily life. Education is viewed as "transformative," "where the institution and its members model values, behaviors, and attitudes that develop critical thinkers and social change agents based on the Quaker principles of integrity, peace, equality, and simplicity in a strong, inclusive learning community" (Guilford College, 2002–2004). Even in the college's governance, Quaker beliefs are visible—in faculty meetings all have responsibility to speak and listen in the hope that a "deeper, higher unity . . . can be discovered through discussion and silence" (Keiser, 1991).

The college has been engaged in the education of teachers since its beginning. In 1986, the college decided to look again at its teacher education program. A committee of faculty from all different areas of the college was established and its task was to create a new education program respectful of the goals and standards of the rest of Guilford's academic program and congruent with Quaker beliefs.

These Quaker traditions strongly affected the process of creation of the new program. The committee met weekly for a year, sharing ideas, imagining new ways of helping students become teachers, and looking at the task from as many angles as possible. The proposal was then brought to a monthly faculty meeting for business, and *all* faculty members in the college were willing for the new program to go forward, as discerned through a sense of the meeting (often referred to as consensus).

The first class of graduates of the new program was in spring of 1994. Students had a double major, including Education Studies, and did an extensive cross-cultural education internship before student teaching (usually in conjunction with one of Guilford's study abroad programs). There were at that time usually 25 to 35 elementary or secondary Education Studies graduates a year.

Quaker Faith and Practice Connections with the Education Studies Program

At the heart of Quakerism is the belief that each person has "that of the spirit," "a piece of the Light," "that of God" within her or him. If there is a part of the Divine, an "*Inward Light*," in everyone, then each child, each learner, each person needs to be honored and respected. The Society of Friends is not a dogmatic faith tradition, so this belief and its manifestations are not doctrinaire but take many forms. This "Inward Light" is also believed to be an "Inward Teacher," a source of leading that comes from deep within. Thus, each person needs to learn to listen to her- or himself and be open to *emergent truth*: new ways of thinking, new insights into a person or into oneself, new ideas for action, new possibilities, combinations, and connection. *Living and learning in community* where people listen to one another in that same open manner and search together for truths and actions to emerge, in shared silence and candid open talk is another dimension of the Quaker tradition. These three tenets are at the core of the mission of Guilford College and the creation and continuation of the Guilford teacher education program.

In the 1600s, George Fox, the English founder of Quakerism, counseled to educate both girls and boys "in things civil and useful." This practical application of faith has manifested itself in Quakers being actively involved in, for example, opposing war and slavery, a heritage that also influenced the Education Studies Program's goal—to help develop sound, holistic thinker/teachers who are capable of and committed to constructive action in society. In the late 1980s, the Education Studies faculty at Guilford developed a set of working themes that were the vehicles used by the faculty to translate the moral and spiritual beliefs from abstraction or personal spiritual/intellectual experience and knowledge into living, working practice. These themes (see Table 14.1) in turn, influenced the development of the program objectives.

Education Studies Program Objectives

The Education Studies Program helps preservice teachers in their development as educational leaders who:

- Respect the individual characteristics and needs of learners,
- Build community and the sense of mutual responsibility,

Table 14.1. Guilford College Education Studies Department's Working Themes

Self and Community	Liberal Approach to Knowledge	Social/Cultural/Ecological Context
A learner is a discoverer.		
The teacher begins where the student is in his or her cognitive, cultural, emotional, physical, and spiritual life.	Without reflection and articulation, meaningful learning cannot happen.	All knowledge has its context; all learning is in context.
We learn in community, interchanging teaching and learning roles.	Knowledge is integrative in nature. We make connections beyond the boundaries of separate content areas.	Just as a person is of value, so a culture is. The many cultures of humankind require understanding and respect.
Learning is deepened by wonder at the mystery of being.	Learning is continuous over a lifetime. Everyone has a next step to take.	The ecology of human society and the ecology of the natural world must be studied in their local and global contexts.

- Value and balance both the liberating powers of knowledge and cultural structures and bodies of knowledge,
- Develop in themselves and in students the values and the skills necessary for reflection, evaluation, and communication,
- Respond to spiritual dimensions of learning and living,
- Discover, rediscover, interpret, and create knowledge,
- Value dimensions of knowledge that are ambiguous, paradoxical, and symbolic,
- Learn throughout life, enlightened but not confined by developmental perspectives,
- Seek insight into many cultures, discovering common ground and appreciating difference,
- And understand themselves as world citizens with not only local and national but also global responsibilities.

The most influential Quaker beliefs—the "Inward Light" and its accompanying "Inner Teacher," openness to emergent truth, and the importance of a community of seekers—and the working theme or themes that the faculty use to translate these beliefs into guidelines for action manifest themselves in the expectations, content, methods, and relationships in the Education Studies Program. Although the language of dispositions was not present during the creation of the program, the idea of developing certain "habits of mind," or for the purpose of this discussion, dispositional themes such as respect for diverse others and careful listening, permeated the program. Key working themes of the Education Studies Program—community, taking the next step in the learning process, valuing individual and culture, and ecology—are also echoed in Underwood's "Native American Learning Way." The collective dispositions honored and promoted by each tradition readily cluster into themes. Quakers are often called "seekers," a term that encompasses a way of being that engages multiple dispositions such as openness to new ideas, flexibility, curiosity, and so forth. Such dispositional themes will be apparent in the following account of Underwood's "Native American Learning Way."

PAULA UNDERWOOD'S NATIVE AMERICAN LEARNING WAY®

Paula Underwood, M.A. is the Developer and Director of The Learning Way® Center (TLC), whose nationwide award-winning program is used in education, corporate learning, and health services. TLC is based on Paula's lifelong training in an ancient Native American (Iroquois) methodology for learning, organization and health. Her first book, "Who Speaks for Wolf," won the Thomas Jefferson Cup Award for quality writing for young people, has since been declared an Environmental Classic, and has been called "The best book I know of on Systems Thinking!" The educational program based on her work has been declared "Exemplary" by the U.S. Department of Education.

Although this concise biography of Paula Underwood provides the reader a description of her credentials, it does not evidence the important contributions she makes to the structure and content of this chapter. Underwood defined spirit as an awareness of our relatedness to others and to the environment. Hers might be seen as a sociopolitical perspective of spirit that promotes relationships with students as whole human beings who are members of a social and political community. For example, Noddings's (1995) question, "When should moral principles outweigh the demands of Friendship?" (p. 367) is manifest in Underwood's 1994 text "Many Circles, Many Paths."

Underwood's Learning Stories

Underwood's tradition considers learning sacred; all voices and purposes are equally important to the whole, and each one is enabled to "develop the skills necessary to use Life Experience effectively" (2002, p. 11). The Learning Stories (Underwood, 2002) preserve five generations of her family's oral tradition in which learning was sacred and each individual perspective was honored. The stories are designed to "engender questions, not to answer them—to raise issues not to resolve them. They are an invitation to contemplation" (Underwood, 1994, p. 33).

"Who Speaks for Wolf" reminds us that sometimes wisdom "comes only after great foolishness" (Underwood, 2002, p. 39). "Winter White and Summer Gold" explores equity in relationships. In the graduate Classroom Management class at Indiana University South Bend, teachers read "Many Circles, Many Paths" and consider Patient Watcher's anguished struggle to promote cooperation; by putting themselves in his position, they make connections to conflicts with and among students.

One aspect basic to Underwood's teaching and learning paradigm and her view of community is "The Rule of Six" (Underwood, 1994, pp. 31–32). By comparison, positivism, the belief that one right way, one right answer, one truth can be identified, might be seen as a "rule of one." "The Rule of Six" asks that one "devise at least six plausible explanations, each one of which indeed explains the phenomenon. There are probably sixty, but if you devise six this will sensitize you to how many there may yet be and prevent you from focusing in on the first thing that 'sounds right' as The Truth." The process will "keep you from being rigid in your thinking," considered to be extraordinarily counterproductive in her culture (Underwood, 1994, p. 32).

Underwood adds, "we may hold alternate views—and these alternate views may yet augment one another," which is not a disagreement, "as there is no Rights answer—and therefore no Wrong one" (2000b, Chapter 11, p. 9).

The process of determining at least six plausible explanations for any given phenomenon and identifying their probabilities provides content, develops dispositions, and exemplifies skills needed by effective teachers. Underwood explains, "It may seem counter-intuitive, but the process of consensus actually begins by exploring individuality. . . . we are a species of individuals who have a great need to be who we are and to cooperate with each other. . . . Individuality and Community are deeply interconnected" (2000b, Chapter 11, p. 3). The "Rule of Six" provides a means to connect. This idea of connection is not just valued in Underwood's and Quaker tradition, but can be found in other faith traditions. The dispositional theme of connecting with others includes any number of discrete dispositions as illustrated by SGI Buddhist President Daisaku Ikeda. His words are cited by Kazanjian (2001, p. vii) of the foreword to Ikeda's text *Soka Education*:

> The wisdom to perceive the interconnectedness of all life and living. The courage not to fear or deny difference; but to respect and strive to understand people of different cultures and to grow from encounters with them. The compassion to maintain an imaginative empathy that reaches beyond one's immediate surroundings and extends to those suffering in distant places.

There are many apparent connections between Quaker and Underwood's tradition in addition to a sense of spiritual connectedness, such as an emphasis on individual and community development through dialogue, connection to the environment, and the concept of centering. Cajete (1994) explains that the "centering place is a preparation for the holistic journey of learning based on the understanding of one's own creative spirit and capacity . . . 'that place that Indian people talk about', that place of self-knowing and empowerment that forms the foundation for transformative process of learning and creation" (p. 197). For Underwood and her father, learning typically happened when they were gathered around Central Fire. Quakers speak of "centering" or "centering down" when they clear their minds at the beginning of silent worship, to help them settle down and be receptive to the spiritual.

Known for honoring relationships with one another and with the earth, the traditions of Indigenous peoples are also reflected in Quaker values. Underwood's (2000a) research identified "four understandings that seem to be ubiquitous in Native American thinking. . . . Everything is Real. Everything is Alive. Everything is Connected. Everything is Related" (p. xv). Consistent in most Native American thinking, she explains, is the reality of dreams and memories, the fact that there is no inanimate world, as all things contain energy, and the kinship of life through the "Great Web of Life" that connects all living things because "we are all star stuff" (p. xv).

DISPOSITIONAL THEMES BETWEEN THE TWO TRADITIONS

> To "listen" another's soul into a condition of disclosure and discovery may be almost the greatest service that any human being ever performs for another. (Steere, 1986, p. 86)

Educators in these Quaker and Native American traditions can be seen, through their "being," to practice, reflect on, and model for their students the dispositional themes explored above. Such educators are being: (1) authentic by honoring the teacher within—being aware of who they are in the context of their historical traditions, (2) present to and nurturing the diversity of the community in which they live and learn—where they are, (3) aware, attentive, and open to new and even challenging information—looking around and listening carefully to individuals and the emergent truth in the community, and (4) being caring and compassionate in their decisions and actions.

Both traditions addressed in this chapter can be seen to promote community as described by hooks (2000): "remember that spiritual practice helps us overcome the feeling of isolation, which "uncovers the radiant, joyful heart within each of us and manifests this radiance to the world" (p. 83). All people need to be in touch with the needs of their spirits. Quaker educator Parker Palmer (1993) clarifies:

> The connections made by good teachers are held not in their methods but in their hearts—meaning heart in its ancient sense, as the place where intellect and emotion and spirit and will converge in the human self. The heart is asked to hold more than it is able so that teacher and students and subject can be woven into the fabric of community that learning, and living, require. (Palmer, 1993, p. 11)

Martin Buber (1970) explains that spirit "is not in the I but between I and You. It is not like the blood that circulates in you but like the air in which you breathe. . . .It is solely by virtue of his power to relate that man is able to live in spirit" (p. 89). Palmer (1993) considers education to be a spiritual journey that requires individual introspection as well as community relationships and offers alternatives to conventional classrooms in which "the teacher is active and the students are passive" (p. 35). He discusses the role of the teacher in enabling the possibility of such a classroom in his text "To Teach Is to Create a Space" (pp. 69–87). Rather than teachers giving students fixed and known truths, in Palmer's classroom teacher and students are actively open to and searching for new learning, new connections, and new relationships. Similarly, Underwood's tradition "encourages clearing an inner space in which learning can occur" in "preparation for listening" (1994, p. 41) because, she continues, "learning is the responsibility of the listener. Enabling an enhanced learning environment is the responsibility of the speaker" (p. 45). These views of affective and spiritual aspects of education, and the role of listening within them, reveal dispositions of openness to and a relationship with knowing and doing that may be seen to contrast traditional views of knowledge, teaching, and learning.

Both of these traditions not only honor but encourage multiple perspectives and will not rest until all voices are heard. The community is defined by not only the content of these diverse views but also the process of hearing and responding to them. Underwood's Learning Story "Who Speaks for Wolf" poetically emphasizes the need for all voices in a community to be heard—both that one should speak even if his or her opinion differs and that one should listen to each and all perspectives to see the whole. One preservice teacher connected lessons from "Wolf" to her Interstate New Teacher Assessment and Support Consortium (INTASC) dispositional strengths and areas for growth:

> The hardest disposition that I encounter is being able to share my opinion with peers. (I have had too many bad experiences from the many schools that I attended. I learned to shut down, rather than be put down.) I have improved in this class. The set up of this class has allowed me to know people better. Therefore, I feel more comfortable participating. "Who Speaks for Wolf?" taught me how imperative everyone's opinion really is. In a few classes (earlier), I tried to share to keep things positive and hopefully help clarify the student's perspective. For example, I really wish the process of learning were the focus of more classes. This class has taught me to be a better listener. There is a lot more to learn if your ear is tuned to it. Whether with classmates or the material, every class is richer if reflected upon afterwards. In addition to all of this, I appreciate professors that treat students as adults. After graduation it will be our responsibility to get things done, without reminders or pampering.

Listening is a key action common to both traditions, in particular Compassionate Listening, which can be seen as a collection of actions, a way of being, that calls on a cluster of distinct dispositions. Explains Hwoschinsky (2001), "When listeners focus on creating a safe environment, on compassion, empathy, and love, the field is determined by those intentions" (p. xvi). How one manages conflict also demonstrates decisions and actions that are informed by the kind of being, looking, and listening described in this chapter. Hwoschinsky continues to explain that it is "difficult to listen to the opinions of others when in disagreement. It requires impartiality, at least for the moment. We must put our own opinions and judgments aside and pay attention to the human being in whose presence we sit. We are stretching our ability to be present and to include pain without making it our own" (p. 3).

Indeed, after graduation, the process of developing the dispositions teacher educators have emphasized, living into dispositional themes such as active listening, becomes the responsibility of the new graduates. Ideally, in their teacher education programs these individuals have developed lifelong habits of body, mind, and spirit.

RECOMMENDATIONS FOR TEACHER EDUCATION PROGRAMS

> The teacher faces a situation complex as only life can be—filled with doubts, conflicts, humor, pain, frustration, bleakness and beauty, pathos and love, anger and laughter. He needs to be able to live and work with inconsistencies, opposites, and fluctuations. His task is to scrutinize this mass of people, feelings, things, and ideas; to foresee what it can become. He has to transform the everything into a valued something before it becomes a wasted nothing. (Huebner, as cited in Hillis, 1999, p. 2)

We began our discussion with Underwood's "Four-Step Path," and as it does, so too do we spiral and continue the path.

1. Be who you are—be aware of your relationship to your roots and honor the teacher within. Perrone (1991) speaks of needing "larger purposes" in education and is concerned that educators are preoccupied more with "technical than moral and intellectual directions," thinking mostly about "simply getting through the days and weeks" (p. 1). Focus on developing dispositions definitely moves students away from dwelling on technical minutia and toward "larger purposes." Clearly, if dispositions are about nothing else, they are about who each individual is being in relationship to others—to students, peers, and teachers. Surely if teacher education programs want to support students' development and expression of professional dispositions, the educational traditions in this chapter would agree that the place to begin is with not only who the students are but who we are and what each brings with him or her to the teaching and learning community.

2. Be where you are—move past denial or ignorance and value the experience of living and learning in your diverse community. Respect, seek out, and nurture diversity. If there is a place in teacher education for each student to be who he or she is, by definition diversity will occur. The question remains—how do we assess understanding that grows and continues? This chapter might be used to support the practice of assessing student's relatedness to others in the context of dispositional themes, identifying within those individual dispositions that are strengths or which if developed would make a difference for the student. We must not allow standards to standardize the complex humanity of our teaching and learning communities. Where we are must be as much about the needs and desires of individual human beings in our community as about the standards that direct our efforts. Standards, and their corresponding dispositions, must be used to support the diversity of our learning communities, not to sterilize or neutralize it. By comparison, we as educators must be present to the voices of not only accrediting bodies but also the students for whom we seek certification and our colleagues. Hwoschinsky (2001) defines presence as:

> . . . a balanced state of awareness where attention is focused on the present moment. . . . It is a dynamic state in which awareness is expanded to include one's inner state and outer fields of awareness. When listening compassionately, coming to a state of Presence allows one to have focused awareness on all that is in the present moment—within and without. (p. 83)

The accreditation processes at Guilford College seemed to separate faculty members from their interests, beliefs, and visions—who they were (and subsequently who their students were)—and focused them on policy writing, following or defining procedures, developing frameworks, and documenting all aspects of the program to satisfy groups far removed from the day-to-day realities of teacher education in Greensboro, North Carolina. For some teacher educators, state and national accreditation processes diverted their personal and professional energies away from their passion for helping students become good beginning teachers and dampened their zeal for program review, improvement, or innovation.

3. Look around—and listen. Be a compassionate listener, honor all information both seen and heard, and the truth that emerges. Many of today's teacher educators, initially trained to emphasize knowledge and performances, are now more aware of the value of dispositional strengths such as reflection and relatedness. Community—ranging from small group to the university as a learning community and ultimately our global community—has been emphasized in each tradition. Dougherty (1995) identifies the value of group listening and how it moves us further on the four-step path to who we are:

> . . . there is a collective wisdom available for each person. Whereas in one-to-one direction there is a single other person to lend vision to the directee, a group affords the possibility of many faces of truth being uncovered in a given situation. Persons are challenged to take the words of others into the place of Mystery where they can claim what is real for them. (p 36)

Some may jokingly describe dispositions as mysterious, yet the traditions in this chapter can be seen to value this place of Mystery from which they develop. Returning to Underwood's notion of braided understanding, knowledge and performances would unravel without the third strand of dispositions. With the three braided firmly together, a safety rope is available for educators who would venture in to the place of mystery and claim what is real for them.

4. Decide and Do—from this way of being and learning with others make compassionate decisions and demonstrate caring behaviors. Each choice we make as teacher educators, who we are and what we do out of who we are being, sets an example for our students. The traditions in this chapter would suggest if one is to teach and assess dispositions, one must continue his or her own growth and reflection in this realm, and in turn include the mysterious, the unknown, the becoming—the emergent truths and values—discussed above. Traditionally any mention of the spiritual in education is likely to elicit apprehension. Recently, directives to teach and assess individual students' dispositions have also caused many teacher educators to be both personally and professionally apprehensive. Again, the traditions in this chapter would propose that this is when true learning begins. Similarly, while teachers who reflect on and demonstrate dispositions such as care and flexibility in fact model the same for their students, this fact is for us a positive outcome of a spiritual commitment or discipline rather than the objective of our efforts.

As Underwood (2000a) explains, true learning "cannot come from mere memorization. It comes instead from that sudden spark of apprehension that lights the Fire of continued and growing understanding" (p. xvii). As teacher educators, we are those responsible for tending that fire. We would do well to embrace the tension of our lingering unfamiliarity and discomfort with dispositions, and embrace the incendiary possibilities of our apprehensions for ourselves, our students, and the future.

NOTES

1. In this chapter we use the terms Native American and Indigenous and are guided by the words of Haynes and Chavez, guest editors of Action in Teacher Education's special issue on "Indigenous Perspectives of Teacher Education." They introduce the issue with these words: "Naming ourselves is an ontological imperative. We ask the readership to be ever cognizant of how Native peoples name and represent themselves. Representational terms will include Native American, American Indian, Indian, Native, Native peoples, Aboriginal peoples, and Indigenous Peoples. Notwithstanding, we are, as well, cognizant that these same terms have misnamed, misrepresented, and misrecognized this diverse group of Peoples creating unequal power relations. . . . Please note however, most Native peoples will use their specific tribal group name rather than the collective representations mentioned above" (p. 2).

2. The foreword to Underwood's *Three Strands in the Braid: A Guide for Enablers of Learning* (1994) explains that Underwood "accepted the task of becoming the next Keeper of the Old Things for this tradition as it has been handed down in her family" from her father Perry Leonard Underwood (p. 9). In 1800, Tsilikomah, Underwood's grandfather's grandmother, was the first in her family to accept this responsibility in an Oneida community.

REFERENCES

Bellah , R. N., Madsen, R., Sullivan, W. M., Swidler, A., & Tipton, S. M (1996). *Habits of the heart* (2nd ed.). Berkeley and Los Angeles: University of California Press.

Bloom, B. S., Englehart, M. B., Furst, E. J., Hill, W. H., & Krathwohl, D. R., (1956). *Taxonomy of educational objectives; the classification of educational goals, by a committee of college and university examiners.* New York: Longman.

Buber, M. (1970). *I and thou* (W. Kaufmann, Trans.). New York: Charles Scribner's Sons.

Cajete, G. A. (1994). *Look to the mountain: An ecology of indigenous education.* Skyland, NC: Kivaki Press.

Dougherty, R. M. (1995). *Group spiritual direction: Community for discernment.* Mahwah, NJ: Paulist Press.

Guilford College. (2002–2004). Retrieved from Guilford College website http://www.guilford.edu/catalog/index.cfm?ID=120000050

Haynes, J., & Chavez, R. C. (2002, Summer). Guest editors' introduction to "Indigenous perspectives of teacher education: beyond perceived borders" Creating, nurturing and extending a needed conversation for an inclusive cultural citizenship. *Action in Teacher Education: The Journal of the Association of Teacher Educators,* 25(2).

Hillis, V. (Ed.) (1999). *The lure of the transcendent: Collected essays of Dwayne E. Huebner.* Mahwah, NJ: Lawrence Erlbaum.

hooks, b. (2000). *All about love: New visions.* New York: HarperCollins.

Hwoschinsky, C. (2001). *Listening with the heart: A guide for compassionate listening* (3rd ed.). Indianola, WA: Compassionate Listening Project.

Jardine, D. (1998). *To dwell with a boundless heart: Essays in curriculum theory, hermeneutics, and the ecological imagination.* New York: Peter Lang.

Ikeda, D. (2001). *Soka education: A Buddhist vision for teachers, students, and parents.* Santa Monica: Middleway Press.

Kazajian, V. (2001). Introduction. In D. Ikeda, *Soka education: A Buddhist vision for teachers, students, and parents* (pp. 1–34). Santa Monica: Middleway Press.

Keiser, E. (1991, September 11). Minutes of the opening faculty meeting. Friends Historical Collection, Hege Library, Greensboro, NC.

Lacey, P. A. (2001, January). Spirituality in action: Ethos and ethic. *Friends Journal,* 1, 10–12.

Noddings, N. (1995). A morally defensible mission for schools in the 21st century. *Phi Delta Kappan,* 76(5), 365–368.

Palmer, P. J. (1993). *To know as we are known: Education as a spiritual journey.* San Francisco: HarperCollins.

Palmer, P. J. (1998). *The courage to teach: Exploring the inner landscape of a teacher's life*. San Francisco: Jossey-Bass.

Perrone, V. (1991). *A letter to teacher: Reflections on schooling and the art of teaching*. San Francisco: Jossey-Bass.

Spencer, P. U. (1990, Autumn). In celebration of a life well-lived. *Noetic Sciences Review, 22–23*, 20.

Steere, D. V. (1986). *Gleanings: A random harvest, selected writings*. Nashville, TN: Upper Room Books.

Steere, D. (1986). On listening to another. In *Gleanings: A random harvest* (p. 86). Nashville: Upper Room.

Tezuka, I. (1995). *School with forest and meadow* (K. Hori, Trans.). San Francisco: Caddo Gap Press.

Underwood, P. (1994). *Three strands in the braid: A guide for enablers of learning*. San Anselmo, CA: A Tribe of Two Press.

Underwood, P. (2000a). *The great hoop of life*. Vol. 1: *A traditional medicine wheel for enabling learning and for gathering wisdom*. San Anselmo, CA: A Tribe of Two Press.

Underwood, P. (2000b). *Wisdom in the workplace: From chaos to community*. J. Weyer, Ed. Manuscript proposal draft.

Underwood, P. (2002). *Three Native American learning stories with information about the nature of a learning story*. Bayfield, CO: A Tribe of Two Press.

Welch, S. D. (1985). *Communities of resistance and solidarity: a feminist theology of liberation*. Maryknoll, NY: Orbis Books.

15

Dispositions and Teacher Beliefs: A Heuristic to Inform Efforts Toward Improving Educational Outcomes

R. Lee Smith, Tanice Y. Knopp,
Denise Skarbek, and Stephen Rushton

In recent times, there have been numerous calls for improving teacher preparation (Holmes Group, 1986; National Commission on Excellence in Education, 1983; National Commission on Teaching and America's Future, 1996). The book *A Nation at Risk: The Imperative of Educational Reform* (National Commission on Excellence in Education, 1983) claimed that the situation in public education had deteriorated and used the phrase "rising tide of mediocrity" to quickly capture the U.S. public's belief regarding public education. In 1996, in hopes of rectifying these continued and growing concerns, the National Commission on Teaching and America's Future made a number of recommendations including (a) raising the standards for students entering teacher preparation programs as well as for teachers currently in the workforce, (b) reinventing teacher preparation and professional development, and (c) placing qualified teachers in every classroom. Underlying the commission's recommendations is the premise that teacher educators need to recruit, prepare, and support effective teachers.

The recruitment, selection, and retention of highly effective teachers is essential and perhaps more pressing than ever, given critical shortages in some areas in specific areas of education and the numbers of professionals who choose not to remain in the teaching profession (Boe, Bobbitt, Cook, Barkanic, & Maislin, 1998; Boe, Cook, Bobbitt, & Terhanaian, 1998). Many contemporary education professionals believe that our ability to select the most effective teachers for our children is compromised by a shrinking pool of credentialed teachers who will work in our schools, thus necessitating alternative certification and licensure approaches and perhaps creating an environment in which people without effective dispositions to teach children are entering teacher preparation programs and, subsequently, are employed in schools. This open audition approach to selection of teacher education participants and in teacher hiring practices should alert the field to the need for improving the selection processes in university as well as in alternative or nontraditional approaches to entry into the teaching profession. In order to do so, the profession must thoroughly understand the constructs related to dispositions and their underlying beliefs.

Also, it is important to examine the dispositions of candidates for teacher preparation programs because states' public education systems have an inherent moral obligation to society, in general, and to our children, in specific, to ensure that very competent people enter teacher education, complete the programs, enter the teaching field, and stay. To do that, we must be able to determine, with a high probability of success, dispositions and beliefs that are necessary for teachers to be well suited to meet the diverse needs of students in today's educational systems and settings and that are sustainable in a changing educational environment. Activities that more thoroughly examine the beliefs and dispositions of candidates for teacher preparation programs, teachers under consideration for initial employment, and veteran master teachers can enhance our states' educational systems by: (a) improving methods for selecting candidates applying to university and college teacher education program, and, subsequently, better education and preparation of those potential teachers; (b) improving selection of candidates for alternative certification programs; (c) improving methods for selecting teachers in the school-based hiring process; and (d) improving retention of effective teachers, all of which have direct bearing on the quality of education.

In order to enter into the task of identifying, teaching, and evaluating dispositions in teachers with more clarity, education professionals must have an increased and better understanding of the construct of dispositions and their underlying belief structures. In this chapter, we propose a heuristic to classify the studies and encourage more intensive and directed research of teachers' beliefs and dispositions. We begin by clarifying our definitions of dispositions and beliefs for our proposed heuristic. We next discuss examples of past and current methods of study that infer teacher beliefs and dispositions, and then we propose a heuristic for a more intense and holistic study of teacher beliefs and dispositions and discuss the benefits of such study. We close with a recapitulation of the reasons and possible implications that may be relevant to the further study of teacher beliefs and dispositions.

DEFINING DISPOSITIONS

In our long-term quest to identify teachers who have effective dispositions, we, as education teacher educators and researchers, often employ various terms to identify just what is it that makes a teacher effective. However, we complicate the discourse and the application of research findings by sometimes interchanging a variety of terms including *attitudes, beliefs, traits, judgments, characteristics, values,* and *attributes.* Therefore, before presenting our proposal, we first clarify our use of the terms *beliefs* and *dispositions* in order to better define the parameters of our proposal and exclude other factors that may be related to identification, selection, and retention of teachers.

Now that professional education entities have formally identified dispositions, along with knowledge and skills, as one of the three areas of measure of teacher effectiveness, definitions of dispositions abound in the teacher efficacy literature. Perhaps, the most common definition is that from the National Council for the Accreditation of Teacher Education (NCATE). NCATE's definition employs the terms *values, commitments,* and *ethics* to define dispositions and specifies that "beliefs and attitudes" guide dispositions (see Appendix A). Similarly, Taylor and Wasicsko (2000) posit that "dispositions are often defined as the personal qualities or characteristics that are possessed by individuals, including attitudes, beliefs, interests, appreciations, values, and modes of adjustment" (p. 2). The Department of Education at the University of Minnesota–Duluth (2003) defines dispositions to include "temperament, character, personality, nature, demeanor" (p. 10). Unfortunately, these definitions and similar others do little to clarify the term.

To clarify their definition, Katz and Raths (1985) provided the following contrasts with *skills, habits, traits,* and *attitudes*—other terms often used either interchangeably with or in the definition of dispositions. Katz and Raths differentiate between a *skill* as a mastered ability, which one either possesses or not and that may or may not be used frequently, as opposed to a disposition, which "refers to the relative frequency with which an action is manifested in a context" (p. 302). Katz and Raths propose *habits* as "acts that are neither intentional nor consequent to reflection," while dispositions are "a pattern of acts that were intentional on the part of a teacher in a particular context and at particular times" and consider "dispositions as 'habits of mind'—not as mindless habits" (p. 302). Although the term *trait* "suggests a pattern of behaviors over time rather than a cause for behavior," similar to the term dispositions, Katz and Raths differentiate between the two by clarifying that traits are more so used to describe some aspect of a person's character; dispositions describe actions and frequency. In addressing the term *attitudes,* these researchers found that the term is typically used as defined by Rokeach (1968) as "a relatively enduring organization of beliefs around an object or situation predisposing one to respond in some preferential manner" (p. 112), as opposed to Katz and Raths' definition of dispositions as a "summary of actions observed" (p. 302). The term *disposition,* then, is a way to operationalize behaviors that rise from a particular belief.

DEFINITION OF TEACHER BELIEFS

Katz and Raths (1985) use the term *dispositions* to indicate a descriptive construct rather than an explanatory construct. We feel that the working definition of dispositions proposed by Katz and Raths to be most effective in clarifying the dispositions discourse. However, given the focus on disposition related to teacher preparation programs, the discourse also must include attention to the learning of and, in some students, the changing of dispositions. That is, if those involved in the preparation, identification, and evaluation of effective teachers believe that dispositional behavior can be *learned* and *changed*, we assert that those involved in these efforts must look beyond the *what* and look also at the *why* of effective teaching. We therefore submit that the study of teacher dispositions relative to identifying effective teaching cannot be conducted productively without also addressing teacher beliefs. Again, we turn to Katz and Raths to provide clarity to the discourse regarding beliefs that may underlie dispositions. Katz identifies beliefs as "predispositions" (Katz & Raths, 1985; Raths, 2001) as the *why* or the explanatory construct of dispositions.

The complexity of beliefs as related to teacher behaviors has been studied extensively. Current education researchers substantiate significant implications of the role, function, and power of teacher beliefs for teacher education. Based on an exhaustive investigation as to the meaning and nature of beliefs structures to clarify a complex construct, Pajares (1992) maintained that teacher beliefs influence their judgments and ultimately affect their classroom practices so much so that understanding those beliefs structures is essential to improving classroom practice. Given the effect of teacher beliefs on their classroom practice, Pajares verified a number of assumptions that can, and should, be made when studying teacher beliefs: (a) new phenomena are filtered through existing beliefs, which screen, redefine, or distort information processing; (b) the longer beliefs are held, the more resistant they become to change; and (c) rarely are beliefs changed in adults, so much so that some adults will continue to hold beliefs based on incorrect information regardless of the provision of correct information. To those hesitant to recognize the need to focus on teacher beliefs in education research and training, Pajares argued:

> When [beliefs] are clearly conceptualized, when their key assumptions are examined, when precise meanings are consistently understood and adhered to, and when specific belief constructs are properly assessed and investigated, beliefs can be . . . the single most important construct in educational research. (p. 329)

Although education researchers have recognized the role and importance of dispositions in teacher education, the recent NCATE and Interstate

New Teacher Assessment and Support Consortium (INTASC) focus on dispositions in the same frameworks as knowledge and skills may promote a tendency to simplify a complex, sophisticated, and perplexing concept. In practice, we find almost casual talk of promoting, influencing, or developing effective teacher dispositions. Although the focus and acknowledgment of the power and influence of teachers' dispositions on their effectiveness is necessary, the lumping together of such a complex concept with the concepts of teaching *knowledge* and *skills* could possibly lead to an oversimplification of a critical key to defining an effective teacher. Inadvertently, educators may have created a lack of clarity when studying the *why* of teacher actions by using multiple and various terms such as *attitudes*, *traits*, and *characteristics*. If we move forward with a common understanding and definition of *dispositions*, we may be able to work more effectively and efficiently toward, as Pajares (1993) recommends, *cleaning up a messy construct*.

PAST AND CURRENT METHODS FOR STUDY OF BELIEFS AND TRAITS

Researchers have identified and studied teacher beliefs and traits utilizing a variety of methodologies—teacher interviews, checklists and rating scales of teacher traits and behaviors, psychological tests and instruments, analysis of student outcomes related to teacher characteristics, observation, trait and attribute measures, ethnography and interpretive narrative, and self-report and self-study. To fully explore, explain, and provide examples of these methods would take more space than this chapter allows. In the following section, we briefly present several examples of the more common approaches that have been used to study of teacher dispositions and beliefs.

Checklists and Informal Devices

Identification of teacher traits and behaviors is important in both the selection process for teacher education programs and the evaluation of teachers currently employed in the field. Instruments used for these purposes may include specific items reflecting the observation of a behavior or items that reflect an administrator's or supervisor's rating of a class of teacher behaviors, such as those in behavior management. One example of this method is the Teacher Behavior Rating Scale (Randhawa & Pavelich, 1997). This instrument was initially produced to measure the teaching behaviors and characteristics of interns. The scale's 16 items included those intended to measure, through a Likert scale, such characteristics as *enthusiasm for teaching, initiative, confidence,* and *rapport with students*.

Psychological Tests and Instruments

Few, if any, psychological tests are used in screening applicants for their initial training in teacher education programs or, later, in the case of hiring for specific teaching jobs. However, research is being conducted, using the Myers-Briggs Type Indicator (MBTI), on the personality types of preservice teachers once they have entered teacher education programs. An example of this research is presented by Grindler and Stratton (1990), who used the MBTI and determined that of the 101 preservice teachers in elementary education at Georgia Southern College, three of the 16 types were overly represented as compared to a national survey of 804 elementary teachers. Also, Sprague (1997) studied personality type using the MBTI matching and student teaching evaluations. She found that a consistent and positive relationship exist ($r > .25$) between similarity of MBTI classifications and evaluation score.

Interviews

Interviews are used widely in teacher hiring practices and in university selection processes. Laman and Reeves (1983) sent surveys to 147 teacher education programs across the United States in order to determine which methods were employed to select future candidates. An overwhelming 95% of those institutions that responded stated that the use of the grade point average along with a formal application was the primary source of selection. As discussed earlier, screening candidates through an interview process is gaining more ground (Benner, George, & Cagle, 1987; Jacobowitz, 1994).

There are indicators that during the interview processes principals examine dispositional properties. Although GPA is the single most important criteria used by teacher education institutions in determining acceptance into programs, most principals find this the least important in defining quality teachers (O'Hair, 1989; Place & Drake, 1994). Place and Drake's (1994) study demonstrated that principals primarily look for "enthusiasm," "good communication skills," and "interviews evaluations" when hiring new teachers. Similarly, Marcum (as cited in O'Hair, 1989) surveyed both 150 personnel directors and 161 principals in Texas and again found the single most important trait they looked for in hiring is "enthusiasm." This study also stated that both the principals and the personnel directors ranked IQ, GPA, and having a master's degree the lowest on a list of 28 teacher qualities.

A recognized selection method for training of urban teachers that employs interview methodology is the structured Urban Teacher Selection Interview (Haberman, 1993). This interview is used to assist in the selection of candidates for participation in alternative teacher education programs designed to improve the probability that program graduates will be excellent teachers of children from urban settings. Using this method, interviewers examined the following seven dimensions of effective teachers (Haberman, 1995): (a) persistence, (b) protection of learners and learning, (c) application of generalization, (d) approach to at-risk students, (e) professional versus personal orientation to teachers, (f) burnout, and (g) fallibility. Haberman (1995) asserts that this interview process will facilitate the selection of teachers who operate satisfactorily 90% to 92% of the time, and when combined with observations, over 95% of the time.

Analysis of Student Outcomes Related to Teacher Characteristics

Historically, educational researchers have examined the relationship between treatments such as curricular programs, instruction, and student outcomes, as measured by student achievement, through aptitude-treatment interaction methodology (Corno, 1998; Speece, 1990). In a similar way, some researchers have gone beyond the more traditional aptitude-treatment interaction studies that link specific programs to specific student accomplishments and attempted to determine relationships between the effects of teacher's beliefs and attitudes and student achievement. For instance, Harvey and others (1967), in a study of belief systems in teachers, found that the belief systems affect classroom atmosphere and subsequently affects the academic performance of students in positive ways. Squires (1980) concluded that a teacher's belief that each child can succeed is correlated with student achievement.

Other types of studies have focused on dispositions and beliefs. The types of studies that we have used as examples are not comprehensive. Richardson (1996) mentions additional qualitative techniques. The use of dispositions in state assessment and criteria has also been studied (Salzman, Denner, & Harris, 2002). Others have addressed the study of dispositions through ethnographic approaches, self-report and reflection, and studies of teacher beliefs.

A PROPOSED HEURISTIC FOR THE STUDY OF BELIEFS AND TRAITS

We believe that a more careful and in-depth study of teacher dispositions and their underlying beliefs is critical if we are to improve in identifying, teaching, and evaluating effective dispositions in teacher selection, preparation, and retention efforts. Given the present demands for identifying dispositions, along with knowledge and skills, relative to effective teaching, increased research into teacher beliefs and dispositions clearly is warranted. As such, the study of dispositions, beliefs, and traits may benefit from a heuristic that provides a classification system for inquiry and investigation.

A heuristic is a method of investigation that helps to discover or interpret phenomena. In a classic philosophical sense, a heuristic is intended to interpret ideas that are not demonstrable in time and space—ideas such as empathy, caring, love, hate, or freedom. A heuristic for the study of dispositions may help educators research, interpret, and apply the construct of dispositions and the related complexity of teacher beliefs and beliefs change for the purposes of identifying, education, and retaining effective teachers.

As evidenced above, the education literature is replete with studies related to teacher beliefs and traits. The heuristic that we propose (see Figure 15.1) to describe research related to dispositions has the ability to integrate past, current, and future studies. We believe that dispositions and beliefs and traits should be studied using a variety of scientific research methodologies in a variety of philosophical traditions and with both groups of people and with individuals. Our belief is reflected in the structure. Our first premise is that the research on dispositions should be conducted through multiple methods of inquiry with a variety of methodologies. Our second premise is that the research should also involve the study of individual teachers or cases and with groups of teachers. Because of the complexity of factors, including the variety of contexts, beliefs, and attitudes that affect teachers' dispositions, the research and inquiry into this construct should be multifaceted. The center box of the heuristic illustrates the idea that research for teacher dispositions and beliefs interacts with other concepts in education and society, areas such as academic achievement, quality of life, participation and selection related to teacher education, teacher employment and retention, and the application of content knowledge. The outer and inner arrows of the heuristic illustrate the interactive nature between and among the targeted concepts of study, the subjects of study, and the methods of study.

For the purposes of discussion, we have termed the different methods positivistic methods and interpretive methods. We realize this is a very simplistic dichotomy and recognize the contemporary professional debate surrounding scientific inquiry and epistemology in education. We believe that teaching is a relational enterprise between both teachers and children as groups and teachers and a child as individuals. As such, teaching and learning are both social and individual endeavors, and it is important to study beliefs and traits that may occur in the context of those interactions.

The heuristic is intended to study, explain, or classify research of dispositions. By utilizing the heuristic, educators may be able to conceptually place specific research within the framework and to ascertain the state of our knowledge. There are other crucial and important aspects of dispositions for which the heuristic is not applicable. For example, the heuristic may be in-

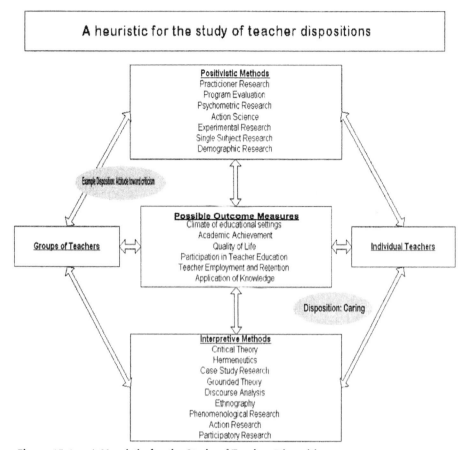

Figure 15.1.   A Heuristic for the Study of Teacher Dispositions

adequate to address concepts regarding ethical use of dispositional knowledge, although critical theory may contribute to this application.

Why Future Study of Teacher Beliefs and Dispositions?

In educational practice today, there is a renewed effort to identify the most effective instructional paradigms based on student outcomes as defined by state standards, and this effort has been coupled with a call for quality teachers (U.S. Department of Education, 2002). As stated earlier, this call for improving teacher quality has been present since the early 1980s. As stated throughout this book, national accreditation bodies, such as NCATE, and state departments of educations, as evidenced through INTASC, have included dispositions as factors in the quality preparation of teachers. The recognition of certain dispositions as desirable characteristics in our nation's teachers should give impetus to educational researchers to approach inquiry into teacher dispositions with similar fervor as the acquisition of skills leading to achievement outcomes in content areas. By better defining dispositions, beliefs associated with dispositions, and the behaviors and skills needed by teachers to reflect dispositional states, the quality of educational outcomes will improve.

We should also study dispositions to reflect the changing society in the United States. Okrah and Domina, in Chapter 4 of this book, iterate the types of cultural beliefs, and subsequent dispositions, that may be necessary for teachers to effectively educate all of our children. Immigration from Central America, Asia, and Africa now rivals in size the great immigrations of the 19th and 20th centuries, profoundly affecting U.S. classrooms. Teachers must be prepared for the fact that about 35% of pupils in classrooms today are non-White, a percentage predicted to grow substantially in the next decade (National Center for Educational Statistics, 1996). To be effective, teachers need to acquire the background knowledge and skills necessary for addressing cultural diversity in their classrooms and to be aware of any stereotypes they bring to the situation (Kea & Utley, 1998; Peterson, Cross, Johnson, & Howell, 2000). Additionally, Grossman (1995) documents many of the issues that children from families in poverty, children from families who are immigrants, and children from families that are from non-European backgrounds may encounter. The new generation of teachers must be able to effectively address students from diverse cultures in America's schools. Many of the contextual issues of being an immigrant, of coming from an impoverished background, or of being from a non-European culture are important in the interpersonal exchanges between teachers and children and a teacher and a child. The importance of the interpersonal nature of teaching and the effects of these exchanges also should lead to increased attention and future study of dispositions.

In addition to the identification and preparation of qualified teachers prior to entry into the teaching force, the study of dispositions may impact the retention of qualified and effective teachers and maintenance of a qualified teaching force. Boe and his colleagues have noted that many who teach and who are prepared to teach never enter the education profession or leave after a short time (Boe, Bobbitt et al., 1998; Boe, Cook et al., 1998). Methods used to identify dispositions and beliefs to inform selection of teacher education candidates, to hire beginning teachers, and to teach dispositions may also be utilized to study the characteristics and increase the retention of veteran or master teachers.

Conclusion

In closing, we believe that identifying teacher dispositions and beliefs is a multifaceted and complex endeavor. However, we believe that increased discourse, dialogue, and inquiry into dispositions will result in an overall improvement of teacher education and the field of education in general. In proposing increased attention to the study of beliefs and traits, we are not discounting the importance of content knowledge and skill development in the teaching profession. We believe that the study of dispositions should be seen as a necessary initiative in the improvement of the teaching force. In a manner and with the attention given the research into the acquisition of content knowledge, as defined by standards, dispositions should be studied.

REFERENCES

Boe, E., Bobbitt, S. A., Cook, L. H. Barkanic, G., & Maislin, G. (1998a). *Sources of supply of teachers for eight cognate areas: National trends and predictors*. Data Analysis Report No. 1998-DAR2. Philadelphia: Pennsylvania University Center for Research and Evaluation in Social Policy.

Boe, E., Cook, L. H., Bobbitt, S. A., & Terhanaian, G. (1998). The shortage of fully certified teachers in special and general education. *Teacher Education and Special Education, 21,* 1–21.

Benner, S., George, T., & Cagle, L. (1987). Admissions boards: The contribution of professional judgment to the admission process. *Journal of Teacher Education, 38,* 5–11.

Corno, L. (1988). More lessons from aptitude-treatment interaction theory. *Educational Psychologist, 23,* 353–356.

Grindler, M. C., & Stratton, B. D. (1990). Type indicator and its relationship to teaching and learning styles. *Action In Teacher Education, 11*(1), 31–34.

Grossman, H. (1995). *Special education in a diverse society*. Needham Heights: Allyn & Bacon.

Haberman, M. (1993). Selecting star teachers for children and youth in poverty. *Phi Delta Kappan, 76,* 777–782.

Haberman, M. (1995). Predicting the success of urban teachers (the Milwaukee trials). *Action in Teacher Education, 15,* 1–5.

Harvey, O. J. & Others. (1967). *Teacher's beliefs, classroom atmosphere, and student behavior: Final Report*. Boulder, CO: University of Colorado. (ERIC Document Reproduction Center No. ED018249)

Holmes Group. (1986). *Tomorrow's teachers*. East Lansing, MI: Author.

Jacobowitz, T. (1994). Admission to teacher education programs: Goodlad's sixth postulate. *Journal of Teacher Education, 45,* 46–52.

Katz, L. G., & Raths, J. D. (1985). Dispositions as goals for teacher education. *Teaching and Teacher Education, 1,* 301–307.

Kea, C. D. & Utley, C. A. (1998). To teach me is to know me. *Journal of Special Education, 32,* 44–47.

Laman, A. E., & Reeves, D. E. (1983). Admissions to teacher education programs: The status of trends. *Journal of Teacher Education, 34,* 2–4.

National Center for the Education Statistics. (1996). *Issue brief: What criteria are used in considering teacher applicants?* Document NCES96-844. Washington, DC: Department of Education.

222   *R. Lee Smith et al.*

National Commission on Excellence in Education. (1983). *A nation at risk: The imperative of educational reform. A report to the secretary of education.* Washington, DC: U.S. Government Printing Office.

National Commission on Teaching and America's Future. (1996). *What matters most: Teaching for America's future.* New York: Author.

O'Hair, M. (1989). Teacher employment interview: A neglected reality. *Action in Teacher Education, 11,* 53–56.

Pajares, F. (1992). Teachers' beliefs and educational research: Cleaning up a messy construct. *Review of Educational Research, 62,* 307–332.

Peterson, K. M., Cross, L. F., Johnson E. J., & Howell, G. L. (2000). Diversity education for preservice teachers: Strategies and attitude outcomes. *Action in Teacher Education, 22,* 22–38.

Place, W. A., & Drake, T. (1994). The priorities of elementary and secondary principals for the criteria used in the teacher selection process. *Journal of School Leadership, 4,* 87–93.

Randhawa, B. S., & Pavelich, B. (1997). Evidence of validity for the teacher behavior rating scale. *Psychological Reports, 81,* 451–462.

Raths, J. (2001). Teachers' beliefs and teaching beliefs. *Journal on the Development, Care, and Education of Young Children, 3*(1), 1–10.

Richardson, V. (1996). The role of attitudes and beliefs in learning to teach. In J. Sikula (Ed.), *Handbook on research in teacher education* (2nd ed., pp. 102–119). New York: Macmillan.

Rokeach, M. (1968). *Beliefs, attitudes, and values.* San Francisco: Jossey-Bass.

Salzman, S., Denner, P. R., & Harris, L. B. (2002, February). *Teacher outcomes measures: Special study survey.* Paper presented at annual meeting of American Association of Colleges for Teacher Education, New York. (ERIC Document Reproduction Center No. ED465791)

Speece, D. (1990). Aptitude-treatment interactions: Bad rap or bad idea? *Journal of Special Education, 90,* 139–149.

Sprague, M. (1997). Personality type matching and student teaching evaluation. *Contemporary Education, 69,* 54–57.

Squires, D. (1980). *Characteristics of effective schools: The importance of school processes.* Washington, DC: National Institute of Education, Department of Health, Education, and Welfare. (ERIC Document Reproduction Center No. ED197486)

Taylor, R. L., & Wasicsko, M. M. (2000). *The dispositions to teach.* Retrieved June 14, 2004, from www.education.eku.edu/Dean/TheDispositonstoTeach.pdf

University of Minnesota-Duluth, Department of Education. (2002). *Candidate dispositions for undergraduate programs.* Retrieved May 1, 2004, from www.d.umn.edu/edu/ncate/standards/standard1/candidate_dispositions9_9.html

U.S. Department of Education. (2002). *No child left behind: A desktop reference.* Washington, DC: Department of Education: Office of Elementary and Secondary Education. Retrieved June 14, 2003, from http://www.ed.gov/nclb/landing.jhtml?src=pb

Appendix A

Definition of Dispositions by the National Council for Accreditation of Teacher Education (NCATE)

Dispositions. The values, commitments, and professional ethics that influence behaviors toward students, families, colleagues, and communities and affect student learning, motivation, and development as well as the educator's own professional growth. Dispositions are guided by beliefs and attitudes related to values such as caring, fairness, honesty, responsibility, and social justice. For example, they might include a belief that all students can learn, a vision of high and challenging standards, or a commitment to a safe and supportive learning environment.

Source: National Council for Accreditation of Teacher Education (NCATE). (2002). *Professional standards: Accreditation of schools, colleges, and departments of education.* Retrieved June 9, 2004, from http://www.ncate.org/2000/unit_stnds_2002.pdf.

Appendix B

Standards and Related Dispositions for Beginning Teacher Licensing from the Interstate New Teacher Assessment and Support Consortium (INTASC)

INTASC Principle 1: The teacher understands the central concepts, tools of inquiry, and structures of the discipline(s) he or she teaches and can create learning experiences that make these aspects of subject matter meaningful for students.

Related Dispositions

- The teacher realizes that subject matter knowledge is not a fixed body of facts but is complex and ever-evolving. S/he seeks to keep abreast of new ideas and understandings in the field.
- The teacher appreciates multiple perspectives and conveys to learners how knowledge is developed from the vantage point of the knower.
- The teacher has enthusiasm for the discipline(s) s/he teaches and sees connections to everyday life.
- The teacher is committed to continuous learning and engages in professional discourse about subject matter knowledge and children's learning of the discipline.

INTASC Principle 2: The teacher understands how children learn and develop, and can provide learning opportunities that support their intellectual, social, and personal development.

Related Dispositions

- The teacher appreciates individual variation within each area of development, shows respect for the diverse talents of all learners, and is committed to help them develop self-confidence and competence.

- The teacher is disposed to use students' strengths as a basis for growth, and their errors as an opportunity for learning.

INTASC Principle 3: The teacher understands how students differ in their approaches to learning and creates instructional opportunities that are adapted to diverse learners.

Related Dispositions

- The teacher believes that all children can learn at high levels and persists in helping all children achieve success.
- The teacher appreciates and values human diversity, shows respect for students' varied talents and perspectives, and is committed to the pursuit of "individually configured excellence."
- The teacher respects students as individuals with differing personal and family backgrounds and various skills, talents, and interests.
- The teacher is sensitive to community and cultural norms.
- The teacher makes students feel valued for their potential as people, and helps them learn to value each other.

INTASC Principle 4: The teacher understands and uses a variety of instructional strategies to encourage students' development of critical thinking, problem solving, and performance skills.

Related Dispositions

- The teacher values the development of students' critical thinking, independent problem solving, and performance capabilities.
- The teacher values flexibility and reciprocity in the teaching process as necessary for adapting instruction to student responses, ideas, and needs.

INTASC Principle 5: The teacher uses an understanding of individual and group motivation and behavior to create a learning environment that encourages positive social interaction, active engagement in learning, and self-motivation.

Related Dispositions

- The teacher takes responsibility for establishing a positive climate in the classroom and participates in maintaining such a climate in the school as whole.

- The teacher understands how participation supports commitment, and is committed to the expression and use of democratic values in the classroom.
- The teacher values the role of students in promoting each other's learning and recognizes the importance of peer relationships in establishing a climate of learning.
- The teacher recognizes the value of intrinsic motivation to students' life-long growth and learning.
- The teacher is committed to the continuous development of individual students' abilities and considers how different motivational strategies are likely to encourage this development for each student.

INTASC Principle 6: The teacher uses knowledge of effective verbal, nonverbal, and media communication techniques to foster active inquiry, collaboration, and supportive interaction in the classroom.

Related Dispositions

- The teacher recognizes the power of language for fostering self-expression, identity development, and learning.
- The teacher values many ways in which people seek to communicate and encourages many modes of communication in the classroom.
- The teacher is a thoughtful and responsive listener.
- The teacher appreciates the cultural dimensions of communication, responds appropriately, and seeks to foster culturally sensitive communication by and among all students in the class.

INTASC Principle 7: The teacher plans instruction based upon knowledge of subject matter, students, the community, and curriculum goals.

Related Dispositions

- The teacher values both long-term and short-term planning.
- The teacher believes that plans must always be open to adjustment and revision based on student needs and changing circumstances.
- The teacher values planning as a collegial activity.

INTASC Principle 8: The teacher understands and uses formal and informal assessment strategies to evaluate and ensure the continuous intellectual, social, and physical development of the learner.

Related Dispositions

- The teacher values ongoing assessment as essential to the instructional process and recognizes that many different assessment strategies, accurately and systematically used, are necessary for monitoring and promoting student learning.
- The teacher is committed to using assessment to identify student strengths and promote student growth rather than to deny students access to learning opportunities.

INTASC Principle 9: The teacher is a reflective practitioner who continually evaluates the effects of his/her choices and actions on others (students, parents, and other professionals in the learning community) and who actively seeks out opportunities to grow professionally.

Related Dispositions

- The teacher values critical thinking and self-directed learning as habits of mind.
- The teacher is committed to reflection, assessment, and learning as an ongoing process.
- The teacher is willing to give and receive help.
- The teacher is committed to seeking out, developing, and continually refining practices that address the individual needs of students.
- The teacher recognizes his or her professional responsibility for engaging in and supporting appropriate professional practices for self and colleagues.

INTASC Principle 10: The teacher fosters relationships with school colleagues, parents, and agencies in the larger community to support students' learning and well-being.

Related Dispositions

- The teacher values and appreciates the importance of all aspects of a child's experience.
- The teacher is concerned about all aspects of a child's well-being (cognitive, emotional, social, and physical), and is alert to signs of difficulties.
- The teacher is willing to consult with other adults regarding the education and well-being of his or her students.
- The teacher respects the privacy of students and confidentiality of information.

- The teacher is willing to work with other professionals to improve the overall learning environment for students.

Source: Interstate New Teacher Assessment and Support Consortium (INTASC). (1992). *Model standards for beginning teacher licensing, assessment and development: A resource for state dialogue.* Retrieved June 9, 2004, from http://www.ccsso.org/content/pdfs/corestrd.pdf.

Interstate New Teacher Assessment and Support Consortium is a program of the Council of Chief State School Officers, One Massachusetts Avenue, NW, Suite 700, Washington, DC 20001-1431, 202/336-7048.

Index

About the Contributors

Karen B. Clark received her Ph.D. from Penn State University. Prior to completing her degree, she was a classroom special education teacher for almost 10 years in New York State. Most of her work was with elementary students identified as having learning disabilities, emotional disabilities, and mild mental disabilities. She teaches both undergraduate and graduate courses in the special education program, and enjoys working with IUSB students at all levels. She is a consulting editor for the journal *Behavioral Disorders*, published by the Council for Children with Behavior Disorders. Her current research interests involve an examination of professional dispositions critical to being an effective educator. Dr. Clark is currently the assistant dean at Indiana University South Bend.

Meryl Domina is lecturer in Alternative/At-risk Education at Indiana University at South Bend. She is currently working on her Ph.D. at the University of Illinois at Chicago, in curriculum and instruction. She has extensive experience with the alternative schools in Chicago and northern Indiana that serve students who are unable to be successful in traditional schools. She holds a Master's Degree from Northwestern University in the arts of teaching and from the University of Illinois at Chicago in educational leadership and administration. Ms. Domina is also a parent, an artist, and has served as creativity specialist in a private school in Chicago.

Constance Dueschle has worked in public schools as a school nurse and a student assistance counselor for 9 years. She has consulted with the Indiana Department of Education for 13 years, and has been at IUSB as an assistant professor in counseling and human services for 6 years. Her focus on dispositional attitudes and behaviors is reflected in her research on supervision of school counselors and mentoring.

Lynda Emigh, M.A., is a teacher in Sarasota County, Florida. She is a National Board certified teacher and has had extensive experience as a teacher in elementary and special education classrooms. Mrs. Emigh has an interest in the affective attributes of teachers and how they affect children in schools.

David Freitas is currently dean of the School of Education and professor of education at Indiana University South Bend. He has also served as an elected city school board member, State Department of Education official in Massachusetts, an appointed member of the Illinois Teacher Certification Board, University Teaching Fellow, and a public school teacher and administrator. He is a frequent speaker at international and national professional conferences. His doctoral and master's degrees were earned at Boston University in educational leadership, and his undergraduate degree was earned at the Boston Conservatory of Music. Various organizations, including Phi Delta Kappa, Pi Kappa Lambda, Pi Lambda Theta, and Phi Alpha Theta, have recognized his accomplishments through induction into their professional honor societies.

Marsha Heck is an associate professor of education at Indiana University South Bend. She is committed to the transformation of individuals and communities through their full self-expression. Her work addresses cultural understanding, the arts, and the wholeness of human experience in education.

Daniel T. Holm has been in the field of education for 28 years. During his tenure, he has been an elementary school teacher, a teacher at a California Youth Authority facility, a grade-six teacher in England, and a university professor. As a university professor, he teaches reading and language arts methods courses, children's literature, psycholinguistics, and diagnostic reading. Dr. Holm's research interests center on the importance of story in reading development and in understanding the art of teaching.

James R. Hurst is a faculty member of the Counseling and Human Services Program at Indiana University South Bend and interim director of the Campus Counseling Center. Dr. Hurst is a licensed clinical psychologist, and he teaches graduate counseling courses in counseling theory, ethics, psychopathology, and group counseling. His research interests include professional identity issues, youth violence and alcohol use, and the scholarship of teaching.

Tanice Y. Knopp is an assistant professor at the University of South Florida in the Department of Special Education. Before joining the faculty at USF, she worked extensively in the Florida public school system and as a program specialist for the Florida Department of Education. Dr. Knopp conducts research in the areas of teachers' beliefs and dispositions, teaming models that empower school-based educators to meet the complex learning needs of students with disabilities, collaborative partnerships, and program evaluation. Dr. Knopp has been active as a principal and coinvestigator in $1 million funded grants, and engaged in developing and facilitating formal collaborative partnerships among school districts and the university.

Judith Oates Lewandowski earned her Ph.D. in educational technology from Purdue University. Prior to joining the faculty of IUSB, Judith served as a high school educator, professional development specialist, and K–12 outreach coordinator for Purdue University. Her research and pedagogical interests include technology integration, issues of privacy and security, and the development of authentic assessment within technology integration courses.

Gwynn Mettetal is a professor of educational psychology at Indiana University South Bend. She received her Ph.D. in developmental psychology from the University of Illinois in 1982, and has been teaching the dispositions course at IUSB since 1991. She is the author of numerous articles on classroom action research and her website (http://mypage.iusb.edu/~gmetteta) is a frequently cited resource for teacher-researchers.

Kwadwo Okrah is director of the Center for Global Education and assistant professor of education at Indiana University South Bend. Educated in Ghana and the United States, Dr. Okrah earned his B.A. degree in religious studies and linguistics with a concurrent diploma in education from the University of Cape Coast, Ghana. He entered the Ohio University, earning an M.A. in international affairs and a Ph.D. in social studies education (curriculum and instruction). He is the author of numerous books and articles on African culture and educational issues including: *The Wisdom Knot: Toward an African Philosophy of Education, African Indigenous Knowledge and Science; Ghana Arts & Culture for Home and Classroom, Toward Global Conflict Resolution; Language, Education and Culture; Academic Colonization and Africa's Underdevelopment;* and *Teachers as Transformative Intellectuals: Globalizing the Curriculum and Strategies for Classroom Instructions.*

Patricia Parrish is an assistant professor of education and the assistant director of graduate studies in education at Saint Leo University, where she teaches coursework in exceptional student education and educational leadership. Her research interests include caring in the student-teacher relationship and values-infused education. She has published and presented at national and international conferences on the topics of caring and the education of those with cognitive disabilities.

Deborah Roose is professor of education and chairperson of the education department at Albion College in Michigan. She was previously chairperson of the Education Studies Department at Guilford College, a Quaker institution in Greensboro, North Carolina. She helped create the present teacher education program at Guilford, which is grounded in its Quaker roots, and is helping to develop a new teacher education program at Albion. Her interests and research focus on reform in teacher education and how liberal arts colleges can add to that conversation.

Hilda Rosselli is the dean of the College of Education at Western Oregon University, where she also is a professor in special education. She received her Ph.D. in special education and served as a faculty member in both secondary and special education at the University of South Florida. During her 19 years at USF, she served as the director of the Education Honors Program, both assistant and associate dean for teacher education, principal investigator on over $1.5 million in grants, and helped raise another $1.5 million in corporate gifts. Her research continues to focus on teacher preparation, professional development schools, and gifted education.

Stephen Rushton is an associate professor in the Department of Elementary Childhood Education at the University of South Florida at Sarasota. He supervises student teachers and teaches courses in research, elementary education methods and the writing process. His research interests are teacher effectiveness, personality types using the Myers-Briggs, and brain-based teaching.

Sara Sage is an associate professor of secondary education at Indiana University South Bend. A former special educator and research and professional development coordinator, she received her Ph.D. in curriculum, instruction, and professional development from the Ohio State University in 1995. She is coauthor of *Problems as Possibilities: Problem-Based Learning for K–16 Education*. Sage's teaching and research interests include problem-based learning, psychological type and learning, constructivist theory and practice, differentiated instruction, and qualitative research.

E. Marcia Sheridan is a professor of education at Indiana University South Bend. She has taught at the university level in both China and Malaysia. Dr. Sheridan has a long-standing interest in the area of critical thinking. Her scholarly interests also include authentic assessment, professional dispositions, and teacher education. She teaches in the areas of middle/school secondary content reading and social foundations

Denise Skarbek is currently an assistant professor and program coordinator in special education at Indiana University South Bend. Her publications and research interests include youth violence, special education, and teacher education, particularly in the areas of action research and safe schools.

R. Lee Smith has published in the area of teacher education and special education. Dr. Smith's current research interests are in the area of affective traits of teachers, and in particular, a caring disposition. He has worked as a teacher and administrator in public school special education. R. Lee Smith is currently an associate professor in special education and the associate dean in the School of Education at Indiana University South Bend.

Ella Taylor, Ph.D., is an associate research professor in teaching research at Western Oregon University. Currently, she coordinates research and data analysis with the National Technical Assistance Center for Children and Youth Who are Deaf-Blind (NTAC), is the project director for the NCLB Oregon University/School Partnership grant, is the lead evaluator for the Oregon Department of Education Advanced Placement grant, and participates in the evaluation of a number of other grants. Her background includes prior grants management and evaluation (Florida Virtual Varying Exceptionalities Grant, Florida Accountability in Gifted Education, Florida FutureThink, and several Florida Governor's Summer Program grants), graduate program coordination, graduate and undergraduate course development and delivery, and research within teacher education, gifted education, and the social sciences. In her previous position at the University of South Florida, Dr. Taylor coordinated two online master's degree programs and taught courses in special education, gifted education, and statistics. Dr. Taylor received her doctorate in curriculum and instruction from the University of South Florida.

Linda J. Young is director of student teaching and a member of the associate faculty in the School of Education at Indiana University South Bend (IUSB). Her teaching experiences have included courses on the integration of technology in the classroom, education, and social foundations. Ms. Young also supervises student teachers. Her research interests include teacher education, technology in education, Native American issues, and portrayals of Columbus in textbooks.

Diane C. Youngs, M.S.Ed., is a lecturer in elementary education and coordinator of field experiences for the School of Education at Indiana University South Bend. She teaches upper-level methods courses in developmental literacy and diagnostic reading. She also supervises students in field experience placements. Prior to joining the IUSB faculty in 1998, she taught students with disabilities at the elementary level in public schools for 19 years.

A NOTE OF APPRECIATION

The editors wish to acknowledge Miriam Altman and Leslie Stockdale for their contributions in researching materials for several chapter authors. Ms. Stockdale currently is a doctoral student at The Ohio State University. Mrs. Altman is currently a teacher of preschool children with special needs in Gainesville, Florida.